D0025234

11/22
STRAND PRICE
$ 5.00 EACH

The
Winnowing Fan

BEYOND CRITICISM

Taking advantage of new opportunities offered by digital technology and new insights from contemporary creative practice that take us from abstract theory back to literature itself, *Beyond Criticism* explores radical new forms that literary criticism might take in the twenty-first century.

http://thebee.buzz

Series Editors:

Katharine Craik (Oxford Brookes University, UK), Simon Palfrey (University of Oxford, UK), Joanna Picciotto (University of California, Berkeley, USA), John Schad (University of Lancaster, UK), Lilliana Loofbourow (University of California Berkeley, USA).

Published Titles:

Macbeth, Macbeth, Ewan Fernie and Simon Palfrey
Ceaseless Music: Sounding Wordsworth's The Prelude, Steven Matthews

Forthcoming Titles:

Blank Mount, Judith Goldman
Character as Form, Aaron Kunin
Desire: A Memoir, Jonathan Dollimore
Just Play: Theatre as Social Justice, David Ruiter
Orpheus and Eurydice: A Graphic-Poetic Exploration, Tom de Freston with Kiran Millwood Hargrave

The Winnowing Fan

Verse-Essays in Creative Criticism

Christopher Norris

Bloomsbury Academic
An imprint of Bloomsbury Publishing Plc

B L O O M S B U R Y
LONDON · OXFORD · NEW YORK · NEW DELHI · SYDNEY

Bloomsbury Academic

An imprint of Bloomsbury Publishing Plc

50 Bedford Square	1385 Broadway
London	New York
WC1B 3DP	NY 10018
UK	USA

www.bloomsbury.com

BLOOMSBURY and the Diana logo are trademarks of Bloomsbury Publishing Plc

First published 2017

© Christopher Norris, 2017

Christopher Norris has asserted his right under the Copyright, Designs and Patents Act, 1988, to be identified as Author of this work.

All rights reserved. No part of this publication may be reproduced or transmitted in any form or by any means, electronic or mechanical, including photocopying, recording, or any information storage or retrieval system, without prior permission in writing from the publishers.

No responsibility for loss caused to any individual or organization acting on or refraining from action as a result of the material in this publication can be accepted by Bloomsbury or the author.

British Library Cataloguing-in-Publication Data
A catalogue record for this book is available from the British Library.

ISBN: HB: 978-1-4742-3632-4
ePDF: 978-1-4742-3634-8
ePub: 978-1-4742-3633-1

Library of Congress Cataloging-in-Publication Data
A catalog record for this book is available from the Library of Congress.

Series: Beyond Criticism

Cover design: Alice Marwick

Typeset by Deanta Global Publishing Services, Chennai, India
Printed and bound in Great Britain

To find out more about our authors and books visit www.bloomsbury.com. Here you will find extracts, author interviews, details of forthcoming events and the option to sign up for our newsletters.

For Valerie

CONTENTS

FOREWORD: POETRY, THEORY AND 'CREATIVE CRITICISM'

I

If it didn't sound pompous as well as offering too many hostages to critical fortune, I would say that these pieces are mainly intended to launch a revival of that nowadays neglected literary form, the philosophical verse-essay. That I say it nevertheless, albeit under cover of a paltry subterfuge, is due to my long-held belief that such a revival is well worth attempting not only as regards that particular *genre* but also, more generally, by coming out against the anti-argumentative (even anti-intellectual) bias of much recent poetry. No doubt some will think it absurd to advance any such proposal despite all the manifold shifts of social, intellectual and literary culture since the eighteenth-century heyday of the form. I hope that both elements – the positive claim and the qualifying doubt – get an adequate airing in the poems, since the claim will surely be rejected if they don't find room for the doubt, and the doubt will have nothing of substance to query if they don't make a plausible job of pressing the claim. There are multiple factors that tend to make this a hazardous enterprise but which also, like the recent growth of interest in hybrid forms like 'creative criticism', bear witness to a sense among contemporary writers that the hazards are worth confronting. Then it may be possible to rethink and re-imagine the philosophical verse-essay in a way that takes on board some of the strictly unignorable developments (German philosophical idealism and literary Romanticism chief among them) that have occurred during the past two centuries.

This is why I conceived the project as seeking not so much to annul or dissolve the boundary between poetry and prose – an aim that my chosen verse forms very plainly disavow – as to raise various questions concerning the relationship between poetry, criticism, literary theory and philosophy of literature. Hence this extended introductory essay, which might otherwise seem out of place or suspiciously like special pleading. Needless to say I am very far from being first in the field. During the early 1970s, Geoffrey Hartman wrote a piece – 'The Interpreter: a self-analysis' – where he went in for some decidedly *outré* (at least by common standards of academic discourse) reflections on the literary critic's role and predicament.[1] Long before that Matthew Arnold had expressed himself in very different terms, though with some of the same insecurities in view. Arnold famously treated himself as a belated Romantic, a poet born after his time, fortunate enough to inherit something of that first fine rapture but able to do so only at a distance – a temporal, cultural and emotional remove – that allowed nothing more than fitful and oblique recollections of it.[2] Hartman confessed a chronic inferiority complex vis-à-vis creative writers but also, in very partial compensation, a superiority complex vis-à-vis most other literary critics or interpreters, especially those brought up on something like Arnold's perverse ordinance of ritual self-abasement before the altar of literary creativity. Quite simply, why shouldn't critics – if so inclined and gifted – deploy the full range of figural and other poetic or fictive-narrative devices by way of talking about other, so-called 'primary' texts that don't necessarily surpass their own in point of linguistic or stylistic inventiveness?

Hartman presented all this very much as a liberationist plea and a cultural call to arms on behalf of a self-consciously American (US) breakaway movement in literary theory/criticism aimed at dislodging the oppressive hegemony of Anglophone or Anglophile models and precedents. Only thus could it escape that disabling Arnoldian sense of 'living in the secondary', or the fate of always (as the 'old' New Critics firmly decreed) acknowledging its due subservience to those features of literary texts (metaphor, ambiguity, paradox, irony and so forth) deemed to constitute their special or distinctive character. Above all it was T. S. Eliot whom Hartman took as the most influential exponent of a cultural politics that placed this veto on critical creativity at the service of a much larger agenda – monarchist in politics, Anglo-Catholic in religion, classicist (or anti-Romantic) in literature – directly opposed to everything envisaged in Hartman's critical-creative manifesto.[3] If Arnold had pitched the claims far too low, as concerned both his own poetry and what he deemed the strictly ancillary or gatekeeper 'function of criticism' in a post-poetic age, then Eliot had taken that line of argument and pushed it in the opposite direction. He echoed the devaluation of criticism – the insistence that it not indulge jumped-up notions of its own creative remit – but deployed this in order to promote his poetry and its likewise ultra-classicist take on matters such as tradition, poetic impersonality or the doctrinal errors of humanism and Romanticism.[4] By such means Eliot contrived to assert not only his claim to critical authority as the scourge of heterodox beliefs but also his pre-eminence as the single most authentic (since studiously self-effacing) voice of modernist poetry.

Hartman wasn't alone among US literary critics and theorists of that period in challenging the way criticism had over-readily accustomed itself to a modest, glad-to-be-of-service role. His colleagues at Yale, Harold Bloom and J. Hillis Miller, launched more or less simultaneous campaigns to assert larger freedoms of style, register and speculative scope for a criticism newly and exuberantly aware of its freedom from those old constraints.[5] This went along with a distinct sense that there were deep cultural, historical and political issues in the background including – most explicitly in Bloom's case – an intense dislike of the conservative and Anglo-Catholic tone that characterized Eliot's prose writings, not to mention his occasional downright anti-Semitic remarks. Indeed it may be that Bloom's singular critical, stylistic and intellectual trajectory was launched at least in part by his revolt against this once-common British habit of deploying a certain exaggerated politesse in order to pass off various strains of social, religious and ethnic prejudice. At any rate nothing could be further from the Eliotic doctrine of poetic impersonality and the classicizing canon of poetry that went along with it. Moreover, nothing could more defiantly flout Eliot's discreetly modulated protocols of style and address – 'like a rolled umbrella in limbo', as Hugh Kenner once described them – than the Bloomian conception of literary history as one long series of life-or-death struggles by 'strong' poets to throw off the influence of their great dead precursors and wrest a vital margin of creative freedom by successively absorbing, overcoming and radically transmuting that influence.[6]

This 'anxiety of influence' was one that clearly extended to the psyche and hermeneutic practice of the 'strong' literary critic, or to any interpreter (like Bloom) who refused to rest content with the strictly subaltern role prescribed by Arnold, Eliot and their acolytes.[7] The critic, like the poet, faced a stark choice of alternatives with its model in Freud's ironically named 'family romance'. For the poet it was a question of either confronting the great precursor in an all-out war of liberation from the dead hand of Eliot's 'tradition' or else settling for the humble role of a lifelong 'ephebe', apprentice or imitator. For the critic it came down to the choice between reading poems *via* the six Bloomian 'revisionary ratios' – reading them in a powerfully original, transformative or creative way – and just producing further minor variations on a received (most often academic) theme. This was emphatically a Romanticism-centred view of literary history, again defined very much in programmatic opposition to Eliot. It saw the English Romantic poets as having found their truest, that is, most strenuously 'antithetical' successors in a culture – that of late-nineteenth- and twentieth-century

America – mercifully untouched by the creative inanition and stifling civility of their British counterparts. From its great revisionary achievements, as in Wallace Stevens, it was no large distance (so the implication ran) to those of Bloom himself, an interpreter with the courage, creativity and critical acumen to devise the theory and come up with the sorts of strong (mis) reading required to continue that legacy. Thus Bloom provides something like a large-scale practical vindication of Hartman's more personal and anecdotal plea for liberation from the psychologically, culturally and institutionally deep-laid inferiority complex that had so far prevented literary criticism from asserting its creative prerogative.

The Yale 'moment' in criticism and literary theory between (roughly) 1975 and 1990 witnessed probably the single most determined, resourceful and concerted effort in Western cultural history to place those disciplines on a creative footing fully equal to that of poetry or 'literature' in general. This claim was soon given further stylistic and performative support, as well as theoretical warrant, by the writings and regular presence at Yale of Jacques Derrida whose early texts were taken up – very often in a somewhat selective, partial, 'literary' way – by those in revolt against the restrictive protocols of the 'old' New Criticism and on the lookout for new sources of inspiration.[8] What Derrida supplied, to their way of thinking, was a mode of philosophically informed creative criticism or a discourse undecidably suspended between philosophy, literature and criticism which implicitly claimed on its own behalf all those cherished prerogatives that the Yale critics wished to wrest free from the guardians of academic orthodoxy. Actually Hartman rather blew the gaff on this fine ecumenical vision when in *Saving the Text*, his freewheeling commentary on Derrida, he disarmingly confessed that so far as he was concerned all those heavyweight philosophical names like Kant, Hegel, Nietzsche, Husserl, Heidegger et al. were scattered through his writing mainly just in order to stir up the placid waters of literary academe.[9] That they – like so many of Derrida's primary source texts – were all of German nationality was an added bonus since, Hartman remarked, a lot of the anti-philosophical bias among Anglo-American literary critics was really a matter of 'fee-fo-fumming against Hermann the German'. So it was not so much the detailed deconstructive engagement with these thinkers that Hartman admired in Derrida's work but rather its – and their – strategic value as a counter to prevailing ideas about the scope and proper limits of literary criticism.

It doesn't take much historical acumen to detect here another reason for the eagerness of these dissenting voices within US literary academe to align themselves with continental currents of thought and, more specifically, with Derrida. His interpretative practice must have struck them as embodying just the kind of challenge to all things British, not least the cultural politics implied by that long-lived 'Arnoldian concordat' around the virtues of a civilized, low-key, strictly subaltern critical function. Indeed Hartman's writing often evokes something very like a new call to arms in the cause of a US–French revolutionary alliance against the political, intellectual and cultural decadence of perfidious Albion. This goes along, in Hartman as in Bloom, with a strong revaluation of the English Romantic poets, as against Eliot's frequently disparaging remarks and the routine disparagement of them common among the 'old' New Critics. It is designed to make the point – with reference to German idealism and its aftermath – that a certain variety of inventive, creative or speculative criticism is able to provide the most advantageous meeting point between poetry and philosophy. This suggests in turn that Eliot was right by his own conservative-classicist lights since the effects of any such heterodox conjunction between the expressive–creative and the conceptual–speculative are apt to reach well beyond the borders of all three disciplines.

However I have not – you'll perhaps be relieved to hear – rehearsed this episode from recent literary-critical history by way of precedent, pretext or model for the poems that follow. These are indeed exercises in the critical-creative, hybrid or crossover genre that Hartman and Bloom envisaged but they are otherwise about as different as possible from those critics' ideas of what ought to count as a passable instance of it. They are written in verse, not poetically oriented prose, and moreover in verse of a decidedly formal character as regards its metrical structures and rhyme schemes. They all have topics of a reflective, philosophical or literary-critical character, and they treat them for the most part through a combination of narrative and argumentative discourses that make rather few concessions to received (roughly Romantic–modernist–postmodernist) ideas of what poetry ought to be. If they do tick a couple of boxes on the Hartman/Bloom list of desiderata – albeit in ways that would probably get the ticks scribbled out soon enough – then it is by raising questions that would most likely interest critics and interpreters while doing so in a literary mode which at any rate bears all the markers of creative-poetic intent. They were written with the primary intention of showing not just that it is possible to think, reason, reflect and even theorize in verse but that verse might actually have certain distinct advantages if one wants to do these things in a performative, self-reflexive or more than straightforwardly expository way.

II

By comparing these verse-essays with the practice of eighteenth-century poets like Pope and Dryden I intend only to offer help with generic orientation for readers nonplussed, or maybe affronted, to find such anachronistic means deployed in the service of such 'advanced' theoretical or speculative ends. Besides, the analogy has sharp limits: although the verse forms here are tightly structured and the rhyme schemes regular they never (I hope) fall back into the style of heavily end-stopped and at times overly sententious wisdom that typifies the eighteenth-century style at its complacent worst. That risk is all the greater with a form like terza rima – which

I have adopted for several of the poems here – where the rhymes run on as if endlessly via the link from line two of any given stanza to lines one and three of the next. Yet if the pieces come anywhere close to working as intended, then this has to do with the occasions – I hope not too infrequent – when exigencies of rhyme or metre turn out to produce some novel idea or new turn of argument that would almost certainly not have come to mind without them. Formal requirements, so far from imposing artificial constraints, can at best be a means of extending the poet-thinker's range of conceptual-expressive resources in unexpected, inventive and even revelatory ways. This they do most often through some seemingly random rhyme-induced prompt to explore certain up-to-now unlooked-for semantic possibilities, or some metrical resistance to the 'natural' flow of words that has the (quite literally) thought-provoking effect of a jolt to our normal, linguistically habituated mental processes.

This will all be old hat to anyone acquainted with the work of the Russian Formalists and their hallmark stress on the defamiliarizing impact of verbal art, its ability to make the commonplace strange or to sharpen our everyday jaded perceptions through novel poetic or narrative devices.[10] Similar ideas are to be found in literary critics of a thoroughly diverse character, from Eliot's talk of how poetry involves the creative 'dislocation' of customary sense and F. R. Leavis's praise for the sensuous particularity of poets like Shakespeare, Donne and Keats to the project of a theorist like Paul de Man, striving to define a level of sheer linguistic 'materiality' that would resist all appeals to sensory-perceptual experience, familiar or unfamiliar, as products of 'aesthetic ideology'.[11] What makes them all formalists, even those who programmatically disown that title, is their belief that one chief function of poetic language is to complicate the two sorts of passage – from word to word and from word to world – that are normally accomplished with minimum effort by language users in everyday contexts and with everyday-communicative purposes in mind. This complicating function may be exercised in various ways, among them the Eliot–Leavis-approved mode of sensuous or quasi-physical 'enactment' or the more theory-laden kinds of resistance (including the resistance to that other sort of theory) invoked by de Man.

However literary 'formalism' is a loose and baggy sort of concept that covers some diverse and even decidedly antagonistic modes of thought. The main thrust of avant-garde poetics over the past few decades has been directed towards an idea of literary language that locates the resistance primarily in 'the text', this latter conceived – in poststructuralist fashion – as a site of rival readings or conflicting significations that are best defined in terms applying with equal pertinence to poetry or prose.[12] That is, it tends to neglect matters of a formal (by which I mean primarily metrical, rhythmic, prosodic, grammatical or verse-structural) character so as to engage more intently with the textual and intertextual aspects of poetic discourse. These aspects are more amenable to treatment by those – especially philosopher-critics or theorists bred up on a mixture of post-Kantian idealism with poststructuralist ideas about language – who see it as their chief role to mediate (in Bloom's case, trump or dialectically sublate) the relationship between poetry and theory. Or again, they are apt to exert a powerful appeal among interpreters of a broadly Hegelian mind – Yale School acolytes among them – who work with a historically informed awareness of that same complex and evolving (whether genial or fraught) dialectic. Although these critics do on occasion take note of certain formal-structural-prosodic features, it is usually by way of a brief detour from that other, to them more absorbing and philosophically as well as poetically important business. Moreover it strikes me – no doubt as an interested party – that much of the modern or contemporary poetry approved, promoted, anthologized or encouraged by such criticism can itself fairly be said to suffer from a kindred defect. It often goes beyond the modernist revolt against 'traditional' rhyme and metre – a revolt quite compatible (as in Eliot) with a high degree of formal inventiveness in both respects – to something more like a cultivated disregard for such elements.

The result, in many cases, is a flattening-out of verse rhythms through the lack of any metrical counterpoint. One feels that the poem might just as well have been written in prose since there is nothing – or nothing of a properly poetic, that is, formally constrained but also formally inventive and liberating character – to warrant that generic description. This applies especially to the language poets (or L=A=N=G=U=A=G=E poets, as they like to be known) who emerged as a loosely associated movement in the 1970s and occupied ground that, in principle at least, overlapped to a striking extent with the territory I have been trying to stake out here.[13] These poets, Charles Bernstein and Steve McCaffery among them, are highly self-conscious and theoretically aware about the kinds of effect they wish to achieve in creative practice and the kinds of relationship they seek to establish with various poetic and philosophical precursors. In brief: they reject (what they see as) the prevailing subjectivist or expressivist (i.e. neo-Romantic) ethos of much contemporary poetry; go in wholeheartedly for poststructuralist ideas of *écriture*, the 'revolution of the word' and the limitlessly plural or *scriptible* text; enthusiastically, and for just those reasons, endorse the Barthesian 'death of the author'; likewise approve the poststructuralist idea of literature's sociopolitical function as the undoing of bourgeois ideology by deconstructive, semioclastic or other such textual means; and, again following Barthes, take the naturalization of the signifier/signified dyad as the basic mechanism by which language colludes in our willing submission to the lures of 'common-sense' thinking. Along with these goes the further belief that the signifiers 'poetry' and 'poem' (not to mention 'poet') have for too long served to promote a notion of literary works as affording privileged access to realms of experience beyond reach of prosaic or rational grasp.

The language poets advance this case with a passion clearly born of 1960s political–cultural ferment and transposed, via poststructuralism, to the register of a dissident or radical poetics squarely at odds with the whole bad hegemony of received languages and verse forms. They also – as scarcely needs adding – have a deep (and in some ways healthy) suspicion of the first-person subject whose agonies and ecstasies, along with more humdrum emotions, are the fulcrum of most poetry in the mainstream lyric tradition. I won't deny the appeal that such ideas have exerted, and continue to exert, on my own thinking about poetry and theory. Nobody who reads these pieces with an ear and eye to their formal (narrative as well as verse-poetic) aspects would be likely to take them as straightforwardly expressing my own beliefs or indeed the belief-set of any unified, autonomous or integral first-person self. To that extent I am happy to acknowledge an affinity with what the language poets – or their most influential promoters (usually the same people) – place high on their creative-critical agenda. There is also a genealogical connection in respect of our shared sources in that line of jointly poetic-philosophical writing that goes back through Yale School deconstruction to the Jena Romantics. However, in the case of the language poets, there is something too easily or unresistingly achieved about that two-way reciprocal passage between poetry and theory, or the fluency with which these writers modulate from a (nominal) poetry overtly engaged with issues in criticism and theory to a theoretically angled criticism with claims – not always very strongly borne out – to constitute poetry in itself. The result is very often a hybrid discourse that fails to match either the creative flair of the best literary theory or the subtlety, range and conceptual resources of a poetry that makes best use of verse techniques for its own distinctive purposes.

This can most plausibly be put down to a deficit of just those formal attributes, such as rhyme and metre, that the language poets frequently denounce as at best mere relics of an antiquated verse tradition and at worst a means of inducing compliance with the norms of bourgeois subjectivity. On the contrary, I'd say: it is just those formal attributes that best, most effectively and durably exemplify poetry's power of resistance to ideological conditioning, whether by the sometimes restrictive effects of first-person (e.g. lyric) individualism or – more to the point here – by the subject's proclaimed dissolution into a multitude of intertextual discourses, codes and conventions. Hence the feeling of linguistic inertness in so much language poetry and the impression it gives of endlessly announcing but never remotely achieving that revolution of the bourgeois signifying order first envisaged a full half century ago by the left wing of French structuralist poetics.[14] My opening verse-essay about Mallarmé is relevant here since it reflects on the various sources of a double and co-implicated movement of thought which all these poems set out to question or resist in different ways. It starts from Mallarmé's diagnosis of a 'crisis' afflicting the high culture of nineteenth-century French classicism and goes on to trace the increasing permeability of any generic boundary between poetry and theory, along with the erosion of those formal features that once underwrote (albeit in historically and culturally variable ways) that same distinction.[15] As a matter of 'content' or overt theme these pieces might seem to be doing pretty much what a critic like Hartman wanted, that is, pushing hard for just such a collapse of all the constraints that would keep criticism safely confined to its subliterary service role, and poetry likewise safely fenced off from any too direct or intimate dealing with philosophy, theory or politics. In formal terms, on the other hand, there is much about them that is flat opposed to that basically neo-Romantic set of values and priorities endorsed by large sectors of present-day literary academe. These include the anti-formalist bias mentioned above and, closely allied to that, the prejudice against any poetry that argues a philosophical (let alone a political) case as distinct from deploying symbolist-approved modes of oblique, evocative, highly metaphoric, non-discursive, analogical, nonconsecutive, spatially conceived and hence maximally non-prosaic language.

However what this attitude gives to poetry in terms of expanded creative-imaginative and even, in a certain restricted sense, intellectual horizons it promptly takes away in terms of formal resources and capacity to earn its keep as a discourse of reason and dialogical exchange. The precedents again go a long way back, to the English Romantics at least, although it wasn't until recent times that the idea of radically rejigging the poetry/prose dichotomy was translated from the realm of generalized precept to poetic practice. Thus Wordsworth said that the relevant distinction was that between poetry and science, not poetry and prose, while Shelley – with larger territorial ambitions in view – said that all major thinkers, discoverers, reformers, scientists and other visionary types should properly be accorded the title of poet. Yet neither of them, even Wordsworth in the prosier parts of *Lyrical Ballads*, went so far as to draw the inverse corollary of this and remove even those vestiges of rhyme and metre that remained of the old (now despised) eighteenth-century 'poetic diction'.[16] That was left to the avatars of twentieth-century Modernism and its various, often to begin with academically sponsored but nowadays far more widespread and popular manifestations. Hence, no doubt, the somewhat defensive-aggressive edge of these remarks on the highly unfashionable virtues of a formalist poetic joined with a readiness to exploit what certain verse techniques have to offer by way of argumentative (and not just persuasive or Horatian pill-sugaring) resources.

Anti-formalism has had yet further harmful effects. One has been the regrettable division of labour between literary theorists working in the self-conceived vanguard of movements like poststructuralism or deconstruction and scholar-critics of a more traditional, often philological bent with a primary interest in prosody, metrics, stylistics, structuralist poetics and genre-theory. (To be sure there are those, like Derek Attridge, who refuse that division and pursue both projects with notable success.[17]) Meanwhile a good deal of recent poetry – including, non-coincidentally, some of the work most favoured by university-based critics – continues to make a point, even a chief virtue, of its indifference to such presumptively obsolete or otiose formal concerns. Moreover one gets the impression that a main requirement for any poem appearing in some metropolitan literary journals is that it bear no formal marks of being a poem except those of having an unaligned right-hand margin and, very often, a looser grammatical (as well as thematic and argumentative) structure than one expects of decent prose. It seems to me that this has often gone along with a sizeable and uncompensated loss of those manifold expressive, technical and (not least) philosophical-reflective resources that are there to be had from rhyme and metre. Anti-formalism and pan-textualism can perhaps be seen as flipsides of the same post-Romantic coin, a coupling that I think has a lot to answer for in terms of current poetic and literary-critical practice.

III

Here I would suggest we look to William Empson as the single most impressive example in recent times of a writer whose achievement in poetry, criticism and literary theory evinced a keenly analytical intelligence integrally related to creative-imaginative gifts of the highest order.[18] That Empson's work was so routinely passed over by all but a very few exponents of the *Nouvelle Critique* and its successor movements is itself a fair indication of how great a distance had by then opened up – and continues to exist – between the currency of 'advanced' thinking about poetry and those earlier, more formalist-oriented theories that were still influential on the emergent discourse of late-1960s French structuralism. Indeed one can date the change from just about the time that Julia Kristeva published her essay 'The Ruin of a Poetics', where she argues that old-style literary structuralism, with its strong links back to the Russian formalism of the 1920s, had run aground on technical/ideological quandaries of its own engendering.[19] It should therefore give way, she urged, to a more radical poststructuralist practice of *sémanalyse* with its sights fixed on the Joycean ideal of an infinitized textual plurality of sense far beyond the grasp of any such formal methodology. When I first read Kristeva's essay in 1973, as a novice postgraduate student just catching up with the then much-heralded structuralist 'revolution' in literary theory, it struck me as very exciting and *avant-gardiste* but also extremely confusing, like having recently learnt to use some new word-processing package and the next day finding it rendered obsolete by the latest update. In retrospect I am not at all sure that it represented anything like the purported great leap forward, whether in terms of literary-theoretical insight or – Kristeva's other chief claim – its left-political valence. On the contrary, the most striking example of a really productive alignment between the creative and critical dimensions of literary practice is that of 1920s Russian formalism and its Czech structuralist successor movement.[20] After all, these were ventures that, however briefly, managed to bring together poets, novelists, critics and theorists – sometimes within the same individual – without all the conflicts, anxieties or rivalries that have typified their relations in other, less convivial (e.g. present-day academic) contexts.

This is mainly because the formalist/structuralist emphasis on specifiable features of the literary text – aspects of its form or structure amenable to analysis in fairly objective or at any rate intersubjectively valid terms – was such as to provide a far stronger purchase for assessments and commitments of a progressivist nature. Thus it didn't bank too heavily on notional appeals to the 'infinitely plural' text, or the Joycean 'liberation' of the signifier from its bondage to the bourgeois-acculturated signified, which were always decidedly tenuous as regards their theoretical warrant and – even more – their claims to political radicalism. What's at issue here is the long-running quarrel within Western Marxism between an idealist-influenced though materialist-inflected conception of art premised on a highly theoretical idea of its world-transformative power and a more practical, hands-on, Brechtian idea of art as primarily a matter of technical-productive resources applied to politically emancipatory ends. The Russian Formalists along with some of the earlier, formalistically inclined French structuralists came out on the Brechtian side, whereas poststructuralism and its allied movements tended more towards an idealist conception

of poetry's role vis-à-vis the post-Kantian antinomies of subject
and object or mind and world. That claim is borne out by
reflection on the tight and mutually reinforcing relationship
between formal elements and argumentative or propositional
content in the work of politically engaged poet-thinkers like
Brecht, early Auden, MacNeice, James Fenton, Tony Harrison
and (let's not assume the left has all the best prosodists) Philip
Larkin or A. D. Hope. At any rate these are a few of the reasons
or motivating interests for my choice of some highly wrought
verse forms and rhyme schemes.

Of course it might be said – and at times I incline to this
view myself – that such efforts are beside the point since the
pleasures and rewards of a well-crafted line, stanza, verse
paragraph or poem are sufficient unto the purpose of poetry
and stand in no need of theoretical justification. On the other
hand, my own poems are here offered as verse-essays in the
hybrid genre of creative criticism and may therefore quite
reasonably be expected to evince a high degree of reflective
or theoretical awareness with regard to such issues. Among
contemporary theorists it is undoubtedly Giorgio Agamben
who has gone furthest towards rethinking the relation between
poetry and prose and, prerequisite to that, the precise function
of rhyme, metre and other formal elements. In *The End of the
Poem* and *Poetry and the Idea of Prose*, Agamben puts forward
a radically formalist poetics that would render poetry pretty
much synonymous or coextensive with verse, here conceived
as what results when formal-prosodic constraints cut across
those of syntax or sentence structure. It would therefore make
'free verse' quite simply a contradiction in terms, at least on
any definition that gives 'free' something like its proper sense.[21]
Especially welcome from my point of view as verse practitioner
is Agamben's focus on the crucial role of enjambment, the
running-over of syntactic units such as sentences from one
verse line to the next so that prosody and grammar constantly
diverge or fail to coincide. For Agamben, this is the formal
feature that most decisively distinguishes poetry from prose
and which always confronts an ultimate crisis as the poem

approaches its end and the prospect looms of their finally converging in a moment of staved-off formal-syntactic resolution. Poetry involves 'the opposition of a metrical limit to a syntactical limit, of a prosodic pause to a semantic pause', while prose – in common with (at any rate the majority of) free-verse productions – has absolutely no room for any such occurrence.[22] Thus, 'no definition of verse is perfectly satisfying unless it asserts an identity for poetry against prose through the possibility of enjambment', while moreover 'this sublime hesitation between meaning and sound is the poetic inheritance with which thought must come to terms'.[23]

One notable consequence of Agamben's theory is to challenge the venerable *doxa* that would find a chief source of aesthetic value – or locate the very essence of poetry – in a convergence of sense and sound, content and form, the intelligible and the sensuous, or (as he conceives it) the syntactic and the formal-prosodic. To this extent it chimes well enough with my practice here, since these poems must count as formalist by any standard and deploy a wide range of devices (enjambment conspicuous among them) that clearly meet Agamben's specification. Indeed, as I have said, the frequent use of enjambment is one way that they avoid – or try to avoid – the sort of smugness or dogmatism that some readers nowadays dislike in many instances of eighteenth-century verse. All the same there is more than a hint of dogmatism in Agamben's ultra-formalist view of these matters, that is, his pitching the claims for poetic divergence, disruption, conflict, non-resolution and terminal crisis so starkly against those of convergence, structural integration, unified sensibility or the sound as echo to the sense. One problem with this, so far as I am concerned, is that it pretty much denies the title of poetry to any verse that maintains at least enough alignment between rhyme scheme, metre, syntax and thematic (including discursive or argumentative) content for the reader to follow what's happening and not run up against perpetual blocks and stoppages. No doubt Agamben could turn this objection straight around and say: yes, and that's why what you've written is more or less competent verse rather than poetry in the true (formally disjunctive) sense of the term. However he would then be taking a drastically exclusionist line with regard not just to heavily end-stopped rhyming couplets in the eighteenth-century mode but also to a great many other periods, genres and styles of poetry that fail his somewhat tendentious and overly prescriptive test.

Another problem with Agamben's hypothesis, for me anyway, is that it pushes formalism to a point where – as with the 'old' New Criticism of 1950s US academe – the poem is conceived as autotelic or as somehow belonging to a self-enclosed realm of mutually co-implicated meanings and formal structures that allow of no commerce with anything outside that privileged domain.[24] Hence, famously though controversially, the various New Critical vetoes on any appeal by literary critics to such 'extraneous' matters as authorial intention, biography, psychology, historical background or cultural context. There was always a whiff of hocus-pocus about this since clearly the resultant readings, no matter how close and hermeneutically resourceful, were none the less reliant on importing all sorts of often quite specialized extra-textual knowledge in order to make their interpretative points.[25] The same goes for the New Critics' veto on paraphrase, their idea that since poetry possessed that radically autonomous character – that sharp discontinuity with the world of prosaic or everyday-practical discourse – its meaning must therefore be thought of as evading, exceeding or transcending any possible rendition in some alternative (simplified even if lengthier) verbal form. I have here steadfastly ignored such misplaced doctrinal scruples and supplied whatever might be useful to the reader by way of headnotes, epigraphs, glosses, references and occasional bits of paraphrase. Once again I take comfort from Empson's example in not worrying too much about the supposed bad form, literary and social, of telling readers what to look out for.[26] This went along with his lack of inhibition when it came to using paraphrase along with close rhetorical and formal analysis as another perfectly legitimate approach to the reading of literary texts. Very often it involved multiple attempts to paraphrase the same passage on the principle, as Empson said, that by piling up as many alternative readings as possible, one might come closest to teasing out what made the words so elusively beautiful, memorable or haunting.

This has always seemed to me far more sensible than letting one's responses be artificially narrowed in advance by adherence to some *a priori* creed, whether in the guise of New Critical dogma or Agamben's ingenious formalist theories, well matched though the latter are to certain aspects of my own verse practice. If these poems find readers with something like that Empsonian catholicity of outlook, then any faults they impute will be entirely down to me.

(NB: I have annotated only those words, phrases or passages where a quick Google search failed to turn up an adequate source, definition, translation or explanatory gloss. Any smaller provision might seem a discourtesy to the reader, while any greater might be taken as an insult besides adding unnecessarily to the book's length.)

Notes

1 Geoffrey Hartman, 'The Interpreter: A Self-analysis', *New Literary History*, Vol. 4, No. 2 (Winter 1973), pp. 213–27.

2 Matthew Arnold, 'The Function of Criticism at the Present Time', in *Culture and Anarchy and Other Writings*, ed. Stefan Collini (Cambridge: Cambridge University Press, 1993), pp. 26–52.

3 See also Hartman, *Criticism in the Wilderness: The Study of Literature Today* (New Haven, CT: Yale University Press, 1980) and *Saving the Text: Literature/Derrida/Philosophy* (Baltimore, MD: Johns Hopkins University Press, 1982).

4 See for instance T. S. Eliot, 'Tradition and the Individual Talent', in *Selected Essays*, ed. John Hayward (London: Faber, 1964), pp. 3–11.

5 See especially Harold Bloom, Jacques Derrida, Geoffrey Hartman, Paul de Man, and J. Hillis Miller, *Deconstruction and Criticism* (London: Routledge, 1980).

6 Hugh Kenner, *The Invisible Poet: T.S. Eliot* (London: Methuen, 1965), p. 54.

7 Harold Bloom, *The Anxiety of Influence: A Theory of Poetry* (London: Oxford University Press, 1973).

8 Jacques Derrida, *Of Grammatology*, trans. Gayatri C. Spivak (Baltimore, MD: Johns Hopkins University Press, 1974), *Writing and Difference*, trans. Alan Bass (London: Routledge & Kegan Paul, 1978) and *Dissemination*, trans. Barbara Johnson (London: Athlone Press, 1981).

9 Note 3, above.

10 See for instance Lee T. Lemon and Marion J. Reis (eds), *Russian Formalism: Four Essays* (Lincoln, NE: University of Nebraska Press, 1965).

11 F. R. Leavis, *Revaluation: Tradition and Development in English Poetry* (Harmondsworth: Penguin, 1972); Paul de Man, *The Resistance to Theory* (Minneapolis: University of Minnesota Press, 1986) and *Aesthetic Ideology*, ed. Andrzej Warminski (Minneapolis: University of Minnesota Press, 1996); also Christopher Norris, *Paul de Man and the Critique of Aesthetic Ideology* (New York: Routledge, 1988).

12 For a fairly representative sampling of work in this vein, see Christopher Norris and Richard Machin (eds), *Post-Structuralist Readings of English Poetry* (Cambridge: Cambridge University Press, 1987).

13 See especially Bruce Andrews and Charles Bernstein, *The L=A=N=G=U=A=G=E Book* (Carbondale: Southern Illinois University Press, 1984); also Bernstein, *A Poetics* (Cambridge, MA: Harvard University Press, 1992) and *My Way: Speeches and Poems* (Chicago, IL: Chicago University Press, 1999); Lyn Hejinian, *The Language of Inquiry* (Berkeley, CA: University of California Press, 2000); Steve McCaffery, *North of Intention: Critical Writings 1973-86* (New York: Roof Books, 1986) and *Prior to Meaning: The Protosemantic and Poetics* (Evanston, IL: Northwestern University Press, 2001); Bob Perelman, *The Marginalization of Poetry: Language Writing and Literary History* (Princeton, NJ: Princeton University Press, 1996); Ron Silliman, *The New Sentence* (New York: Roof Books, 1987);

Geoff Ward, *Language Poetry and the American Avant-Garde* (Keele: British Association for American Studies, 1993).

14 See for instance Catherine Belsey, *Critical Practice* (London: Methuen 1980); Julia Kristeva, *The Revolution in Poetic Language* (New York: Columbia University Press, 1984); Robert Young (ed.), *Untying the Text: A Post-structuralist Reader* (London: Routledge & Kegan Paul, 1981).

15 Stéphane Mallarmé, 'Crisis in Poetry', trans. Mary Ann Caws, in *The Norton Anthology of Theory and Criticism*, ed. Vincent Leitch (New York: W. W. Norton, 2010), pp. 841–51.

16 See William Wordsworth, 'Preface', in William Wordsworth and Samuel T. Coleridge *Lyrical Ballads* (London: Routledge, 1991), pp. 286–313; also Percy Bysshe Shelley, 'A Defence of Poetry', in *Shelley's Poetry and Prose*, ed. Donald H. Reiman and Neil Fraistat (New York: W. W. Norton, 2001), pp. 476–90.

17 Derek Attridge, *Poetic Rhythm: An Introduction* (Cambridge: Cambridge University Press, 1995) and *Moving Words: Forms of English Poetry* (London: Oxford University Press, 2013).

18 See notably William Empson, *Seven Types of Ambiguity* (London: Chatto & Windus, 1930), *The Structure of Complex Words* (Chatto and Windus, 1951) and *The Complete Poems*, ed. John Haffenden (London: Allen Lane, 2000); also Christopher Norris and Nigel Mapp (eds), *William Empson: The Critical Achievement* (Cambridge: Cambridge University Press, 1993).

19 Julia Kristeva, 'The Ruin of a Poetics', in *Russian Formalism*, ed. S. Bann and J. Bowit (Edinburgh: Scottish Academic Press, 1973), pp. 102–19.

20 See Note 10 above; also Vilém Fried, *The Prague School of Linguistics and Language Teaching* (Oxford: Oxford University Press, 1972); J. Vachek, *The Linguistic School of Prague* (Bloomington, IN: Indiana University Press, 1966).

21 Giorgio Agamben, *Idea of Prose*, trans. Sam Witsitt and Michael Sullivan (Albany, NY: State University of New York Press, 1995) and *The End of the Poem: Studies in Poetics*, trans. Daniel Heller-Roazen (Stanford, CA: Stanford University Press, 1999).

22 Agamben, *The End of the Poem*, p. 109.

23 Ibid., pp. 39, 41.

24 See especially W. K. Wimsatt, *The Verbal Icon: Studies in the Meaning of Poetry* (Lexington, Kentucky: University of Kentucky Press, 1954).

25 For some cases in point, see Cleanth Brooks, *The Well-Wrought Urn* (New York: Harcourt Brace, 1947).

26 See Empson, *Collected Poems* (Note 18, above).

ACKNOWLEDGEMENTS

I am grateful to all the people who helped this project along by commenting on poems, inviting me to read them at various events, providing opportunities for journal publication, and – nearer home – indulging my frequent bouts of (let's say) creative abstraction. Val Pinheiro put up with having large chunks read out at all hours and was unfailingly generous, wise and supportive. She is also – as it turned out – a really gifted verse reader whose searching rendition made fresh sense of passages I'd come to find elusive or obscure. It was great to have Alison, Clare, Jenny and Dylan always within calling distance, and my comrades in Côr Cochion Caerdydd did their usual marvellous job in keeping my spirits up. John Schad was quick to recommend that my book be among the first volumes in this series and has since then been a great source of help and encouragement. Terence Hawkes, a good friend and colleague over many decades, sent me some really heartening comments about my poetry very shortly before his death in January 2014. I, along with many other early beneficiaries of the theory boom in literary studies, owe Terry a huge amount in terms of friendship, personal loyalty, intellectual stimulus, practical support and the chance to publish in just the right places at just the right time.

I should also like to thank Robin Attfield, David Jonathan Bayot, Peter Boxall, Shelley Campbell, Damian Walford Davies, Andrew Edgar, Ron Goodrich, Ann Heilman, David Hume (b. 1947), Peter Thabit Jones, Kathleen Kerr-Koch, Colin MacCabe, Vesna Main, Ann McCulloch, Kevin Mills, Marianna Papastephanou, Josh Robinson, Joe Sterrett, Rob and Helen Stradling, Manuel Barbeito Varela and Pat Waugh, all of whom helped – in various ways – to bring this project to fruition.

Some of these poems are revised versions of pieces previously published in the print and/or online journals *Double Dialogues, European English Messenger, Innisfree Poetry Journal, Philosophical Pathways, Scintilla, The Seventh Quarry, SubStance, Textual Practice* and *Think*. I am grateful to the editors and publishers concerned for permission to include them here.

Cardiff
March 2016

1

Mallarmé 1: Verse-crisis

This book opens, as indeed it closes, with a verse-essay about Mallarmé and what he perceived as the looming crisis in late nineteenth-century French poetry and poetics. Taking that as its starting point, the poem then pursues a whole series of related topics having to do with intertextuality, the suspension of the referent, the rival claims of Classicism and Romanticism, the influence of symbolist doctrine on later (e.g. post-structuralist) literary theory, the pairing of Mallarmé and Joyce as twin lodestars of the *Nouvelle Critique*, and – a central theme here and elsewhere – the highly ambivalent politics of all such *soi-disant* 'radical' projects to decouple signifier from signified in a utopian free play of liberated sense. These matters are all taken up and discussed in an argumentative way that again has its closest affinities with English eighteenth-century poetic practice, although (as I have said) less constrained by the formal proprieties, especially as regards the convergence of syntactic and metrical or verse structure. The general point is to stick up for the virtues of Empsonian 'argufying' as against a poetics based on the dubious theoretical premises of a Joycean/post-structuralist 'revolution of the sign'.

Mallarmé of course stands in a distinctively French line of literary descent, although one not altogether untouched by the German idealist and English Romantic traditions. Indeed it is the Franco–German confluence of ideas and lineages that finally produces that highly eclectic post-structuralist conception of 'the text' that asserts and celebrates its way of overrunning all formal, generic, disciplinary or work-based specification. In any case my poem is about as remote as could be from Mallarmé's ultra-symbolist practice and prescription. Indeed it would much likelier have served his purpose as diagnostic evidence of what he thought had gone wrong than as a hopeful prognosis of the best way forward from the current impasse. Empson was no great admirer of French Symbolism – in fact he once described it, or its literary-critical offshoot, as 'a technique for insinuating scandal, as at a cats' tea-party' – so the poem's attitude towards its subject is, to say the least, characterized by a certain (I hope) productive ambivalence or tension.

It seemed to him a full-scale *crise de vers*.
　　Not long since a well-turned alexandrine,
Despite all its historic wear and tear,

Could still stamp genius on an end-stopped line.
　　But now the whole contraption seemed to jam
On some root defect in the old design

That made it sound like just a way to cram
　　More words, or sense, or weight, or mere syllabic clout
Into each sagging measure. So iamb

And dactyl badly needed sorting-out
　　Lest the new zealots of *vers libre* took
This as their opportunity to tout

An end to all things in the poet's book
　　That cramped their style. Not in the least his way,
Our crisis-worrier, as the quickest look

At any line of his will soon convey,
　　Though apt to leave his own verse-measures cramped
By some *dérèglement* that Mallarmé

Knew he'd not put to rights till he'd revamped
    Every last notion of poetic form.
Better now turn the page on that tri-amped

Loquacity that once defined the norm,
    Then trust his muse to furnish some idea
That sheltered genius from the gathering storm

Of mere verse-anarchy and so shone clear
    To future times. On this brave view the *crise*
Would surely pass whatever might appear

Proof positive that all their expertise,
    Those hierophants of alexandrine skill,
Could frame no precept that the referees

Of free-verse conduct might not bend at will.
    Too deep-bred in him, that first rule of art
Which said: let noble precedent instil

The discipline it takes to give new heart
    To those old forms and cultivate a blend
Of skills hard-won with genius to impart

An added grace. Let each line have its end,
    Whether between one strophe and the next
Or just so far as genres might extend,

With a fine sense of how the classic text
    Sees off those new barbarians that throng
Its distant borders. Though their clamour vexed

His ear and wrought a discord in the song
    Of those more highly strung or less inclined
To heed the claims of metric right and wrong,

Still you might think the 'crisis', so defined,
    Was something Stéphane Mallarmé should view
As just a transient upset of the kind

That scarcely registered amongst the few
   Possessors of a birthright unimpaired
By anything the *vers-libristes* could do

To queer its pitch. Yet, though our poet shared
   Their faith up to a point, still he divined
A crisis more epochal than they cared

To take on board, those classicists, or find
   A source of growing discord in their own,
No matter how exquisitely refined

Verse-music. Such disturbance was unknown
   To them since lying quite beyond the range
Of high verse etiquette by which the tone

Of formal diction vetoed any change
   Beyond the upper limit set to keep
Its overtones from striking false or strange

On ears long used to wandering half-asleep
   Through graceful modulations. Yet, he thought,
The thing went too far back and ran too deep

For any quick-fix nostrums of the sort
   Applied by Rimbaud or Verlaine in hopes
Of fetching up in some exotic port

As far as could be from the crowded slopes
   Of old Parnassus. Rather it untuned
The music of those tutelary tropes

And classic forms that seemed as if marooned
   On some far island like Philoctetes
With nothing but a suppurating wound

And sense that the malodorous disease
   For which they'd cast him out was the best way
To reinforce what mere good taste decrees.

So much at least the *Zeitgeist* had to say
   About the verse-forms that they'd soon describe,
Those free-verse freaks, as worse than *dépassé*

Since offering a large state-sponsored bribe
   Topped up by notions of the poet's aim
To 'purify the dialect of the tribe',

Or kindred variations on the same
   High theme that made a gross syllabic count
From line to line the mark of lasting fame.

This reckoned genius strictly by amount
   Of metric tacking back and forth required
To press upstream against the ceaseless fount

Of syllables along with the desired
   High-classicist conjunction of a grace
Past reach of art and inspiration fired

By antique muses. So he has to face
   This way and that between the rival suits
Of native genius and what still gives place

To every skill that poetry recruits
   To ride this crisis out. Then he'd redeem
At last the ancient promise that the fruits

Of nature/nurture might transplant the theme
   To a new key that modulates beyond
That false dichotomy and comes to seem

The tonic note to which our souls respond
   Once they've seen through the mimicry of good
Poetic form that waves its magic wand

And lets us into the enchanter's wood
   With no path leading out. Yet there's his point:
That even if by skill or chance he should

At length accomplish that degree of joint
  Perfection where the senses were all soul
And souls all sense, still who should now anoint

Him the arch-*symboliste* who might make whole
  A shattered sphere that seemed to leave no room
For healing ministry? And so the role

Was one this Parsifal thought to assume
  By such self-emptying of voice and style
As left him quite uncertain what or whom

To thank when it turned out, once in a while,
  That on the page his words no longer fell
Back into that strict isometric file

By which the alexandrine worked its spell
  And marshalled even stragglers to comply
With its directive. Now the words strayed well

Beyond his own *parole* to overfly
  La langue until the constellated page
Had more the aspect of a cloudless sky

At night than any verse that could engage
  The eye and ear in metric give-and-take
Whereby its very movement might assuage

Their mutual need. And yet he asks: why make-
  Believe that some neat trick of rhymester's speech
Could do as much to cure that mortal ache

As interstellar distances where each
  New signifier in each cosmic zone
Betokens how a single word can reach

Beyond such mere velleities of tone
  And metric pulse that kept old verse alive,
Like formal greetings on a mobile phone

Or other means by which we still contrive
   To feign communication. Whence his task:
To show how poetry might yet survive

The letting-drop of that archaic mask
   Whose features once took shape in all the modes
Of a poetic diction that would ask

The *hypocrite lecteur* to scan its codes
   With ear half-cocked or eye half-turned aslant.
So might they credit that Horatian odes

And suchlike artefacts grew like a plant
   From the rich culture of some native clime
Which had sole power or wherewithal to grant

That seeming spontaneity of rhyme
   And verse-form that, no matter how remote
From customary usage at the time,

Seemed what the *genius loci* underwrote
   As nature's way with words. This he abjured,
This alexandrine metric got by rote

Yet spliced with speech-like rhythms that ensured,
   At least to ears tuned up on Mont Parnasse,
That its high artifice would be obscured

By letting such demotic notes amass
   A volume not so massive as to bring
The great tradition to a brute impasse,

But just enough to let its accents sing
   A tune that kept those ears on the *qui vive*
And gave *les prolos* just a glimmering

Of such arcana. Yet we might take leave
   To question so complete a stripping-bare
Of every fibre in the subtle weave

That balladeers and *hautes*-Parnassians share,
   Or such a sacrifice of all that went
Into the hard-won synthesis of their

Verse-discipline with scope to reinvent
   Just how the rules apply. Thus they disclose
Speech-nuances that metre would accent

Ineptly if decoupled from what goes
   Most naturally in language of the type
That makes the grade as good colloquial prose,

Or poems where the style's not overripe
   And diction never too far out of touch
With lively talk. Then you may think his gripe,

Though fairly aimed at loosening the clutch
   Of inkhorn classicists, is apt to jar
When hitched to a poetic creed of such

Exorbitance, at least to those whose star
   Shines brightest when it lights a human frame,
Since *de vulgari eloquentia*

Gave voice not only to the poet's claim
   For mother-tongue, but to his sense that she,
His Beatrice, and not some 'shapeless flame'

Was the one guide whose ministry might free
   His restless soul. 'Angels affect us oft',
As Donne remarks in neo-Platonist key,

But more by faces, forms, or accents soft
   Than any of those more ethereal traits
Supposed to bear the Christian soul aloft

Or show how wisdom truly correlates
   With love and beauty only by command
Of disincarnate *logos* which dictates

That flesh be dumb. So should we understand
    Why Dante chose this *terza rima* scheme,
Out of the many forms that came to hand,

As best equipped to bring his cosmic theme
    Back within range of human hopes and fears
Where it belonged. The link-rhyme joined extreme

Soul-hankering with what, to mortal ears,
    Declares how skilfully the poet wrought
A language where the music of the spheres,

Though vibrant still, must note by note consort
    With *musica mundana* or the strains
Of a speech-melody that runs athwart

The metric bar-lines. So the pulse remains,
    A voice-inflected heartbeat that resounds
With everything his poetry contains

Of griefs infernal, suffering beyond bounds,
    Or paradisal joys that else would strike
A chord so dissonant that it confounds

All harmonies of sense and soul alike
    And cracks the spheres. Salvation lies in verse,
That rhyme-led switch of scene or rhythmic hike

By which his *terza rima* lifts the curse
    Of end-stopped lines or myriad souls dead set
For endless weal or woe. What they rehearse,

Those chain-linked tercets, is a way to get
    Clean out of making any such bad choice,
Whether (like Mallarmé's) the one that let

No echoes of the poet's speaking voice
    Disturb the silent zone he opted for,
Or (as with Dante) one that would rejoice

The heart of any grand inquisitor
    Fired up by worshipping the savage muse.
Still, if we read like this, then we ignore

How rhyme and rhythm sound a note that skews
    Our sympathies flat counter to the creed
That held the true believer bound to choose

Against his better self and so accede
    To that harsh doctrine. Yet his every word
Of poetry declares its crying need

Of transmutation by the feelings stirred
    When such inhuman edicts meet the test
Of finding voice in ways that might be heard

As not too out of kilter with our best
    All-human-ways-considered sense of things
And not too soul-upliftingly expressed.

One hopeful sign of that's a line that sings,
    Not necessarily a 'singing line'
In lyric mode, but one that spreads its wings

Enough to lift it just short of cloud nine
    And let us know that here's a verse-form apt
For middling themes, not dismal or divine

As with the *paysage moralisé* mapped
    By Dante's stark cosmology. It's more
Like his tight cross-laced rhymes that still adapt

To rhythmic shifts the purist might deplore,
    Or the arch-symbolist declare *passé*,
And yet which bring to birth that fine rapport

Of sound and sense that led him to essay
    The kindred shift of moral ground whereby
Whole cultures may find out some better way

To order things. Just turn an ear and eye
    To how his every verse-effect redeems,
Even while his doctrine damns, those souls that cry

Aloud for the compassion that he seems
    Officially forbidden to extend
By that least human-kindly of regimes

That he devoutly served. Yet we transcend
    Not orthodoxy but the stubborn will
To break its hold if we endorse the trend,

Post-Mallarmé, that takes the poet's skill
    To lie in figuring how best to trace
A constellation in the words that fill

Disseveral portions of the soundless space
    That terrified Pascal. This should perhaps
Give pause to those who think it a disgrace

That versifiers even now should lapse
    Back into forms where rhyme and metre stand
Prepared to suture all the textual gaps

And substitute assurances of bland
    Voice-music for the salutary shock
That comes when they reject that helping hand

And let the word-stars signify *en bloc*
    Yet at such distances that call-signs pass
Only if synchronised by Einstein's clock

At speed of light. So texts post-structuralists class
    As cutting-edge are mostly those that break
All fond illusions save the looking-glass

In which their own self-image tends to take
    That same remote and abstract form that he,
Its first deviser, made-believe could make

The world anew by textual alchemy
    Or, by some *bouleversement* in the roles
Of signified and signifier, see

An end to those old realist protocols
    That bound the bourgeois sign. Not so, we find,
After much scanning of the sacred scrolls

Marked 'Mallarmé' or 'Joyce', then intertwined
    With much high theorizing in the mode
These world-to-text transducers had in mind,

Thus leaving later theorists to decode
    How best the process might be turned around
And launched upon the post-post-structuralist road

By which a switchback portal might be found
    From text to world. It's Bacon's truth we learn
As travellers through this signscape without sound:

Pitchfork dame nature out, and yet she will return.

Notes

p. 1: *Nouvelle Critique*. Movement in French literary theory during the period (roughly) 1968–85 which witnessed the transition from structuralism to post-structuralism and embraced elements of linguistics, semiology, philosophy, psychoanalysis and political (mainly Marxist) theory.

p. 2: *crise de vers*. 'crisis of verse' or 'crisis in poetry'.

p. 2: *vers libre*. free verse, that is, poetry devoid of any formal rhyme scheme or metrical norm.

p. 2: *dérèglement*. 'derangement', 'deliberate disordering'. The poet Arthur Rimbaud wrote in a letter that the poet can attain visionary power only by attempting 'an immense, protracted, deliberate derangement of all the senses'.

p. 4: *Philoctetes*. Refers to the mythical Greek hero who was banished to an island because of his malodorous wound but was then sought out again by his compatriots when they embarked on the Trojan War and needed the aid of his magic bow. These lines were prompted by memories of reading Edmund Wilson's book *The Wound and the Bow* (1941) which connects that myth to a wide range of nineteenth- and twentieth-century literature.

p. 5: *dépassé*. old-fashioned, dated, outmoded.

p. 5: '*to purify the dialect of the tribe*'. Cites a line from T. S. Eliot's 'Little Gidding', the fourth of his *Four Quartets* (1942).

p. 6: *Parsifal*. Wagner's naïve-saintly hero in the opera of that name. The comparison here has to do with his quest, like Mallarmé's, to bring about redemption through self-sacrifice, as for instance by sacrificing rhyme and metre to the requirements of a symbolist–modernist poetics.

p. 6: *parole* and *langue*. Speech and language or – more specifically – individual speech acts and the total (trans-individual) structure of language at any given time, as distinguished by the early-C20 linguist and founder of structuralism, Ferdinand de Saussure.

p. 7: *hypocrite lecteur*. 'hypocrite reader': T. S. Eliot in *The Waste Land*, himself quoting Baudelaire.

p. 7: *genius loci*. 'spirit of place', a trope or idea widespread among (especially) Romantic poets and critics, one that connotes a whole range of poetic, aesthetic, national, cultural and (sometimes) pantheist or mystical senses.

p. 8: *hautes*-Parnassians. The poets Mallarmé was out to discredit and thus make way for his own poetic revolution; those who deployed a highly mannered, artificially elevated style.

p. 8: *de vulgari eloquentia*. 'On Eloquence in the Vernacular', title of unfinished Latin essay by fourteenth-century Italian poet Dante Alighieri.

p. 8: *Beatrice*. The poet Dante's fictive guide in parts of his *Divine Comedy*. Beatrice takes over this role from Virgil towards the end of *Purgatorio* and resumes it in the last book *Paradiso*.

p. 8: '*shapeless flame*'. '*angels affect us oft*': phrases from John Donne's metaphysical love poem 'Aire and Angels'.

p. 9: *terza rima*. The rhyme scheme used in the present poem and also by Dante in his *Divine Comedy*.

p. 9: *musica mundane*. In medieval/renaissance mystical doctrine, earthly or mortal music as opposed to the spiritual music of the spheres.

p. 10: *paysage moralisé*. Literally 'moralised landscape', as in poetry (e.g. W. H. Auden's 'In Praise of Limestone') that reflects on the geography, topography or physical character of certain regions and relates it to aspects of human experience.

p. 11: Blaise *Pascal*. 'The eternal silence of these infinite spaces terrifies me'.

p. 12: *bouleversement*. Overturning, upending, violent reversal.

2

Symbolon: An essay on rhyme

This poem brings together many of the themes and ideas from other pieces in the present book, as well as reflecting on formal issues such as the choice of certain metrical arrangements and rhyme schemes for certain poetic purposes. It engages with a range of topics in recent literary-critical debate, including the symbol/allegory distinction raised to a high point of speculative interest by Walter Benjamin and Paul de Man, along with discussions in genre-theory, sexual and gender politics, myth criticism, hermeneutics and, of course, formalist or structuralist poetics. Running through it – as through all these poems, I now realize – is a problematic though animating tension between the more discursive type of poetry that finds room for argument or debates of this sort and the symbolist tendency that has exerted such a powerful hold on English verse from Romanticism to Modernism and beyond. The aim with this one, in short, was to show (not merely state) that both could be had without prejudice to either so long as their respective claims to attention didn't push to the point of a full-scale poetic creed with its attendant apparatus of critical dogma. That the latter has for some time been a feature more apparent on the imagist–symbolist than the rational-discursive or Empsonian 'argufying' side is a point that this poem prefers

to play down – compared with others in the book – precisely
for such reasons, call them tactical or tactful.

One half of some big truth is what they tell,
    The poets – one side only of some twin-
Faced spheric *symbolon* whose fractured shell
    Might yet take on an oscillating spin
And so, by hysteresis, work to quell
    Our zeal for that big truth. It may begin
As pure conjecture and so let us dwell
    On flipside options, but then have us pin

Our bets on the front-runner and expel
    To mere oblivion all the might-have-been
Alternatives whose Bayesian quotient fell
    Below the figure reckoned fit to win
The truth-stakes. One technique to break the spell
    Of certitude is that which lies within
The rhymester's gift: to show how words rebel
    Against the rules that stipulate what's kin

To what by strict enforcement of the claim
    To conjugate in ways that make good sense
By spurning rhyme's seductions with the same
    Strict vigilance as springs to the defence
Of all those mine-strewn boundaries that frame
    Our sexual like our verbal couplings. Whence,
One might surmise, the curious taint of shame
    Or odd capacity to give offence

(Think Wittgenstein) in any language-game
    That opts to 'go on holiday', dispense
With ordinary usage, junk the aim
    Of communal accord, and thus commence
On wayward paths. These tempt us, in the name
    Of verbal art, so tightly to condense
The gist or (now think Jakobson) untame
    Rhyme's latent chaosmos at the expense

Of common parlance as to leave small room
   For those proprieties that custom might
Commend to our best selves or law presume
   To lay down in its will to reunite
The cultural with the natural and so groom
   Us up in strict accord with what's deemed right
In love and language. So who pairs with whom,
   And does so legally, is within sight

Of other questions like why critics fume
   So much (or anyway the more uptight
Amongst them) when they hear a rhyme-word loom
   Despite the regnant veto, and take fright
As if it presages some Poe-type doom
   Or catastrophic gender/*genre* blight
Let loose by any effort to exhume
   The noisome corpse of rhyme and so invite

The Usher-style come-uppance that awaits
   Such ventures in a necrophiliac vein
That flout what modern decency mandates.
   And so the word-health warning goes: abstain
From any verse-craft that resuscitates
   Old tricks like rhyme just as you'd best refrain,
So far as sexual rectitude equates
   With formal etiquette, from that old bane

Of kindred-love that kicks in when the mates
   We first select and shared delights we gain
By consanguinity are what the fates
   Then use to plague us, whether through a strain
Of botched gene-replication that dictates
   Worse ills to come, or else more in the vein
Of Oedipal disaster that creates
   Unending woe for lovers too germane.

So with those false accoutrements of rhyme,
   Its critics say, which turn up bang on cue

And then, like some dark portent from a time
   In our or mankind's infancy, accrue
The mythic resonance that lets them chime
   With atavistic needs and twist askew
All sense of reason, custom, and – the prime
   Consideration here – what words can do

To help us poor Eurydices who climb
   Just so far upward, then rejoin the queue
Of lost souls Hades-bound. Our only crime
   Was briefly to forget how well they knew
That old word-music and its power to mime
   The passions with a vividness that drew
Soul-echoes such that only the sublime
   Or the ridiculous – to whit, those two

Chief attributes of every tragic plot
   From Sophocles to Ibsen – can remind
Us why she might have faced around, or what
   Seductive strain of sound and sense combined
By rhyme's primeval agency first got
   Conniving ears to block our more refined
Thought-processes. Best then ensure we're not,
   Through such malign enchantment, left behind

To rue the music in some lovelorn spot,
   While Orphic resonances still unwind
His melody in modes that each allot
   To each rapt listener just the special kind
Of fate that, like Mephisto, on the dot
   Turns up to keep the rendezvous assigned
To all who'd let right reason go to pot
   For vocables melodiously entwined.

Let's grant the anti-rhymesters all they say
   About its artifice, its chronic lack
Of motivation in the normal way
   Of language-usage, sudden shifts of tack,

Gross deviations from our everyday
    Speech-habits, fumbling sculptor's drive to hack
The stuff of language like a lump of clay,
    Wrong-headedness, or Scrabble-player's knack

For turning up *trouvailles* that just betray
    How meagre its reserves or slim the pack
Of trump-cards English rhymesters have to play.
    Then – above all – there's what it does to stack
The ear-enticing bits so high that they
    Make way for primal words that echo back
When sense and logic fail to hold at bay
    The mind-bewitching notion that would track

The source of all authentic truths to some
    Old riddle of the *logos*. This decrees
That any access to them now should come
    By grace of Being's few late legatees,
Those poets (German mostly) who could plumb
    The language-depths where thought might yet reprise
Whatever wisdom surfaced through the hum
    Of idle speech in all its clashing keys

Or struck the finely-tuned sensorium
    Of hermeneuts too *dichterisch* to seize
Stuff on the cheap from some emporium
    Of new-stock language-goods, yet so at ease
In Being's purlieus that their words succumb
    To old-stock bargain lines. Thus, by degrees,
They mimic an *Ursprache* that strikes dumb
    The cautious voice of reason and so frees

Dasein to brood authentically on all
    That's been forgotten, covered, or repressed
From stage to stage throughout the age-long haul
    Of Western metaphysics. One good test
Of poetry's response to Being's call
    (The anti-rhymester holds) is how that quest

For authenticity makes accents fall
    Awry and sense askew at the behest

Of rhyme or suchlike ear-tricks to enthral
    The *logos*-hearkener's mind once dispossessed
Of any means or motive to forestall
    Those etymons that artfully suggest
What riches may reward his earnest trawl
    At language-depths unknown to those who rest
Content with just the vanishingly small
    And scattered fragments of a truth expressed

Entire, if anywhere, then in what seem
    Like random sound-events or Edward Lear-
Type rumblings of an *echt*-Gromboolian scheme
    To dull our minds. So why accept its sheer
Haphazardness as something we should deem
    Prerequisite to crossing the frontier
Twixt sound and sense – the one enduring theme
    Of formalist poetics – or, if we're

More mystically inclined, should so esteem
    As to suppose it mends the broken sphere
Of Plato's *Symbolon*? This might redeem
    Us allegorists from having to steer clear
Of any symbol-saturated dream
    That makes such prosy protocols appear
Just stuck-in-place diversion-signs downstream
    Of a pure source that shines distinct and clear

For all who see beyond the outer bound
    Of custom. Still, the case goes, we should treat
Rhyme, formal artifice, or sense-and-sound
    Concordances as merely tricks to meet
Procrustean rules the style-police have found
    Well-suited to their purpose of discreet
Yet forceful culture-management that's crowned
    With full success once able to complete

Its *Sprachgleichschaltung*. Apt to run aground,
  These thoughts, on counter-thoughts that may defeat
At length the utmost efforts to propound
  A case ear-plugged or proof against the beat
Of rhyme's eurhythmic power to turn around
  The anti-rhymester's every last conceit,
Since it's just when his highest flights are downed
  By language-turbulence that rhyme's retreat

Stops short and moves in step with Orpheus, while
  It sends an up-yours signal to the mode
Of free-verse manners in the middling style
  Now *de rigueur.* So much, then, for the code
Proscribing any trope that might beguile
  Us readers with the alchemy bestowed
On rhyme and meter by those versatile
  Sound-sense artificers who felt they owed

Us and themselves the gift to reconcile
  Prosaic virtues with a craft that showed
How readily their civil muse could smile
  On verse-forms tight as a Pindaric ode.
My point's that rhyme may find its domicile
  Wherever words serve not just to download
Some message that requires a single-file
  Parade of signifiers neatly sewed

To Lacan's serial *points de capiton*
  But, like the symbol's sundered halves, aspire
To hypostatic union and take on
  The lineaments of a body-soul's desire
To leave behind each stage of that foregone
  Life-passage through the Heraclitean fire
And see at last why pure soul-talk's a non-
  Contender. So let's not strive to acquire

Such un-flesh-sullied soulfulness and don
  That would-be angel-state that suits the higher-

Rank company or top-grade echelon
 Where, as in Keats, true lovers never tire
Of yearning since forever called upon
 To yearn in vain as all the fates conspire
In their still-virgin plight. The *symbolon*,
 Recall, was rent in twain then made entire

When the two halves matched up and – as the Greek
 Philosophers and rhetoricians held –
Revealed how love and language at their peak
 Of rapt intensity could mend or meld
The disject fragments of our tongue that seek,
 Each one, its longed-for other half, then weld
The pair into a perfectly unique
 And soul-perfecting sphere whose rondure spelled,

For Plato, our escape from such oblique
 Or skewed communication as compelled
Our restless search. Then kindred souls could speak
 A common tongue, just as those double-shelled
Hermaphroditic spheres rolled cheek-by-cheek
 Where once the errant hemispheres rebelled
In a divinely prompted fit of pique
 Until their plenispheric union quelled

All further strife. One shot at what it meant,
 That pleasing allegory, is how we err
Or misinterpret Plato's true intent
 By taking 'allegory' to be a fair
Since tactful term by which to circumvent
 The awkwardness of having to declare
Expressly what he sought to represent
 By that cleft sphere. The notion just won't square,

So scholars think, with doctrines that he spent
 A large part of his dialogues elsewhere
Defending steadfastly against the bent
 Of just such crazy myths as had this pair

Of crackpot souls first woefully fragment
  Then joyfully conjoin. But just compare
The definitions and you'll soon dissent
  From any *parti pris* that seeks to snare

His image of their union in the sort
  Of allegorically extended tale
That uses temporality to thwart
  Symbolic cravings. Granted, our time-scale
Declines to sync with anything as short
  As that split second when the symbols male
And female fused because it must comport
  With time's exigencies or else derail

The whole shebang since programmed to abort
  Such projects by insisting they should fail
For lack of time enough to play the *fort/*
  Da game of allegory along the trail
Of endless sense-deferral. Yet a thought
  That takes the symbol for its holy grail
Where hemispheres unite is one we ought
  At least not to decree beyond the pale

By reason just of pitching it so high,
  That conjoint claim for language and the grace
Of perfect reciprocity whereby
  Redemption's figured in the face-to-face
Communing known by those whose words defy
  The allegorist's demand. This bids them chase
A sense whose soul-dismantling alibi
  Contrives, Scheherazade-like, to displace

Itself from sign to sign and so comply
  Devoutly with the rule that it keep pace
With time's unyielding passage. Best not try
  To syncopate or skip a beat in case
That jump-cut moment make things go awry,
  Stop all our clocks, and tempt us to embrace

A creed that promises to touch the sky
    But scarcely manages to leave a trace

Of its high claims or the low reasons why
    We fell for them. Still, should we hope to base
Our lives on something finer than the dry-
    Souled allegorists propose, it's no disgrace
If we grant symbolism's gift to tie
    Up swiftly the disseveral shards of space
And time in ways the sceptic may deny
    But only by foreclosing any place

In language, life or love where thought can fly,
    Like Icarus, with verse-forms fit to brace
The wings of birdmen myth-condemned to die
    Yet symbol-destined to redeem their race.

Notes

p. 15: *symbolon*. In Plato's *Symposium*, an image deployed by
Aristophanes to represent (symbolize) the idea of soulmates, or
lovers who – like the wandering halves of a sphere split in two – are
forever in search of their perfectly matching other-selves. For the
ancient Greeks the term also had the wider sense of 'token', 'key',
'watchword' or 'password'. Hence its increasing usage in literary
discourse – first by the sixteenth-century poet Edmund Spenser – to
signify any textual element that promised some interpretative yield
beyond the plain or literal sense of the words.

p. 16: *hysteresis*. The joint determination of a system's future states
by its current state along with the history of its past states.

p. 16: *Bayesian quotient*. After Thomas Bayes: term in probability
theory having to do with evidence, predictive power and (crucially)
changing degrees of belief.

p. 16: Jakobson. The Czech structural linguist Roman Jakobson who
produced some remarkably detailed and intensive readings of poetry
in various languages.

p. 19: 'by grace of Being's few late legatees'. This and following stanzas have to do with Martin Heidegger's depth-ontological ruminations on thinking, poetry and philosophy's epochal 'forgetfulness' of the question of Being.

p. 21: *Sprachgleichschaltung*. Compound coinage meaning 'operation to level differences, or ensure perfect uniformity, in matters of language or speech'. This carries strongly threatening connotations, as of such campaigns waged in Germany during the 1930s and 1940s.

p. 21: 'Lacan's serial *points de capiton*'. Quilting points: metaphor used by French psychoanalyst Jacques Lacan to indicate those moments in discourse when the otherwise perpetual slippage of sense is briefly halted to generate the illusion of punctual, plenary or self-present meaning.

p. 23: *fort/da game*. Reference to Freud's highly speculative account of infantile separation anxiety.

p. 23: 'game of allegory along the trail'. See Paul de Man's classic essay 'The Rhetoric of Temporality' for the most influential recent discussion of symbol, allegory and the temporal dimension of language.

3

Ectopiques

'Ectopiques' has to do with the notion of turn – or tipping point – across various discourses and subject areas. They include poetics (trope), politics (revolution), utopia/dystopia, tragedy (peripeteia), change of heart (or conversion) and the Epicurean/Lucretian 'swerve' (*clinamen*) by which the falling shower of atoms was supposed to introduce an element of chance, and hence (rather questionably) free will and choice, into the otherwise deterministic order of things. The terza rima form is well suited to this topic with its rhyme scheme linking line 2 of each stanza to lines 1 and 3 of the following stanza. This sets up a pattern where the turn is both expected and unpredictable, or where the poet is forced into sundry inventive turns – seekings-out of some perhaps unlikely or *recherché* rhyme word – so as to keep up interest and involvement. More than that: it is through just these kinds of exacting or (as they might seem) highly artificial constraint that traditional, that is, formal verse schemes like this are best suited to poetry of a reflective or philosophical character. They are the kinds most apt to take the poet's and the reader's mind off in directions often strikingly remote from the course of habitual or customary thought. Thus the very need to meet those exigencies of rhyme and metre may sometimes suggestively enact what occurs in the more exploratory-creative modes of philosophical work, or in the way that conceptual rigour combines with inventive thinking to produce some unlooked-for discovery. Alain

Badiou has provided the nearest thing we have to a worked-out account of these breakthrough moments by deploying the set theoretical technique of 'forcing' as a precise formal analogue to what will later be found to have occurred with such breakthrough events in science, politics and the arts.

Among the advantages of tightly disciplined rhyme and metre is their capacity to force exactly that sort of Epicurean swerve in the process of thought that opens up new philosophical as well as poetic possibilities. I believe that those formal structures still have a place in contemporary poetry, and indeed that they are more valid or pertinent than ever at a time when thinking has to confront multiple concurrent crises and dilemmas. In brief, the poem says that this is best, most effectively and least riskily done not by going all out for utopian or omni-transformative solutions but by opting instead for carefully calibrated 'ectopic' departures from the sociopolitical or intellectual norm. The risk, more specifically, is that of flipping over into reactive (dystopian) despair and a resultant conservative backlash, or retreating – as Socrates cautions in the *Phaedo* – to a 'mislogistic' outlook of contempt for reason and all its works. The ectopic or ectopian view of things at least holds out a fair chance of coming up with some workable solution, advance in knowledge, or improvement in the currently prevailing state of things. Moreover, and crucially, it has better resources for coping with disappointment and resisting the dystopian or mislogistic lure. At the 'Tipping-Points' conference in Durham where I first read this piece I had to meet the criticism that it argued for a gradualist, reformist or moderate vision of social change as against anything more radical or hopeful. Rather than adopt the old cop-out line that poetry is not in the business of arguing a case, I answered that the kind of fine-tuned modal (or alternative-possible-world) thinking in question is as radical as can be when interpreted, as here, via points of contact with thinkers like Marx, Brecht, Benjamin, Adorno and Badiou. No doubt this sometimes takes speculative thought to a point where

it might seem to risk losing touch with this-world social
and political realities. But it does so – I would suggest – for
reasons that the poem does a fair amount to justify in terms
of philosophical argument.

Of course, there is absolutely no guarantee that much of
this will come across to the reader. While the stronger forms
of anti-intentionalism in literary theory were always a self-
defeating absurdity, it is just as fallacious and self-deluding to
confuse the multiplicity of actual readers with the ideal reader
implied or projected by every act of authorship. In particular,
there is always the distinct possibility that those sound/sense
trouvailles that provide such a happy sense of creative discovery
for the writer may fail so to strike the reader, or (worse) strike
them as forced in the pejorative and not the Badiouan sense.
All the same I can report – for what it's worth – having been
often caught off guard (though not, as the word count goes to
show, ever quite nonplussed) by some rhyme-induced new turn
of thought. As Derrida reminds us, 'invention' derives from the
Latin verb *invenire*, which originally meant to 'to discover' in
the sense 'to come upon' or (roughly) 'to stumble across in
the course of investigation or enquiry'. Taken along with the
word's modern, more creatively oriented sense, this etymology
catches what the poem tries to convey and perform, that is,
the combination of chance and necessity – or the serendipitous
with the formally constrained – that is the greatest gift of
rhyme to thought. And if we're to think productively about
crises, dilemmas and turning points, then ectopic/ectopian
thinking is our best hope of managing something analogous in
the sociopolitical and ethical spheres.

> They got it wrong who placed it out of sight,
>   Too far off, long ago, or far ahead,
> Or just too other-world to shed much light
>
> On *hic et nunc*. That's why they lost the thread,
>   Those old utopians, and went astray
> So grievously when what we want instead

Is just a slight deflection from the way
    Things currently go on, or how they look
When viewed close up and in the light of day.

The trouble is, those fabulators took
    So far-out a perspective on their own
Bad here-and-now that it became a book

Unreadable by anyone who'd known
    Just so much brute facticity as fell
Within that same capacious border-zone

Beyond which dreams as well as dragons dwell.
    So those brave touters of a world elsewhere
Were apt to find they'd nothing much to tell

Us this-world dwellers save the fact that their
    Fine promises would quickly turn to threats
Once history had done its timely share

To prove (as Auden said, without regrets)
    How nothing came of hopes pitched heaven-high,
Or how utopian reverie begets

Its lethal opposite when facts belie
    Some dearly wished-for way things might have been.
This, I surmise, is just the reason why

Those starry-eyed purveyors of a scene
    Light-years from ours were usually the first
To wax flat-out dystopian, or careen

From bright-side twitter to resentment nursed
    Through years of disenchantment as the bad
Turned worse, then left them to project the worst.

So now the question is: how not to add
    Another voice to the unending plaint
Of hope-denouncers crying 'I've been had!'.

Best then we exercise a due restraint
   And limit our utopias to a range
Of nearby other worlds without the taint

That comes of thinking everything must change
   And then, when things don't work out quite as planned,
Allowing disappointment to estrange

The actual world until that promised land
   Takes on the lurid hues that Breughel chose,
Or paranoia gets the upper hand

And we're in Orwell's world where no one knows
   What 'actual' means. One lesson then stands clear:
That the ectopian is that which goes

Just so far counter to the world that we're,
   Like it or not, at home in as to grant
Us passage back and forth through the frontier

That otherwise would stipulate we can't
   Do border-crossings lest some drastic shift
Of focus leave our vision so aslant

That all our journeyings go far adrift.
   Then we're an easy prey for just those kinds
Of paradox that Orwell thought a gift

To any crazed ideologue who finds
   Their logic-bending power a great device
To still the stirring of rebellious minds.

So if the amply documented price
   Of Morris-type utopias is to draw
This Orwell-type rejoinder, let's think twice

Before embarking on a road that saw
   So many pile-ups in so many dreams,
Or stark reiterations of the law

Which says that books with desert-island themes
    May start like Stevenson but must conclude
Like Golding since those contrary extremes

Are sure to make the *Treasure-Island* mood
    Of *Boy's-Own* moral uplift seem a piece
Of downright moral idiocy when viewed

In light of Piggy's plot-decreed decease
    And the short road that leads from Golding's tale
Of games gone wrong to Orwell's thought-police.

Yet though the signs say all utopias fail
    And by that failure breed some hell on earth,
There's hope a change of angle might avail

To ward off melancholy at the dearth
    Of counter-instances. The only thing
That's half-way likely to redeem the worth

Of that long history whose failures cling
    To our all our lives until despair takes hold
Is to catch our utopias on the wing,

Give over questing for an age of gold,
    Seek small transcendences in everyday
Events, and so repudiate the old

Dystopian wisdom that would have us pay
    No heed to such minutiae but attend
Solely to how high hopes at length give way

To low, dishonest fears that soon descend
    Yet further and endorse the cynic's bet
That all ideals turn putrid in the end.

First lesson, then: on no account to let
    That Orwell diagnosis get a grip
Or that bipolar malady upset

The equipoise that otherwise might tip
    Propitiously, though not toward some great
Tsunami-wave that says, Abandon Ship!,

Leave me to scuttle that old leaky crate
    Your *vita ante acta*, and let this,
Your *vita nuova*, be to navigate

New worlds whose seaways old-world sailors miss
    Because they figure nowhere on the maps
Drawn up when 'u' so quickly changed to 'dys'

In all those –topias that filled the gaps
    In their cartography. More it's a case
Of some small shift or momentary lapse

In our coordinates of time and space
    That gives us the first inkling of a chink
Through which we might just glimpse another place,

One that may vanish at a second blink
    Yet lingers as a sense of zones unmapped
In any atlas since beyond the brink

Of any world where atlases are apt
    To service just those travellers whose need
Is chiefly to avoid becoming trapped

In some new world whose guide-books supersede
    All sources known to them. What others spy,
Though at first darkly, once they've learned to read

The signs is that they've accessed a nearby
    Or not-quite-actual world, yet one that shares
With the old one they left a common sky

And history enough to make it theirs,
    This *autre-monde*, since not so far apart
From *monde quotidienne* that nothing squares

With any landmark noted on their chart,
    Or everything conspires to lock them tight
In fairyland where all dystopias start.

So let's suppose it gets things roughly right,
    The doctrine that plain *actualité*
Is what best helps to curb the errant flight

Of counterfactual reveries when they
    Begin with some utopia like a star
That far outshines the pallid light of day,

But end in a deep night that's just as far
    From solacing us earthly types whose lives
Depend on daylight quotas up to par,

Yet whose good health and sanity survives
    Only if no disaster – no excess
Of solar luminosity – deprives

Our kind of the nocturnal spells that bless
    Their lucid watch so long as daylight lasts
With promise of benign forgetfulness.

Still this diurnal trope is one that casts
    Too long and dark a shadow over all
Those mindscapes where utopia contrasts,

Not *grosso modo* but in sundry small
    And hard-to-notice details, with the sheer
Self-evidence that holds our minds in thrall,

Or this-world actualism that helps steer
    Us clear of fancying there might exist
A world elsewhere, though not so far from here,

In which stand plain to view those landmarks missed
    On our last routine visit. This applies
So generally that to make a list

Of such scene-shifters or anatomise
   The myriad ways they make the world anew
Would simply be utopia in the guise

Of some great tickbox list of 'things to do
   Before we die'. Among the options ticked
Most often are the ones where any clue

As to just how or why their message clicked
   Like that demands that the enquirer go
Some lengthy ways around to contradict

The whole idea that only if we know
   Enough about the X we're looking for –
Its name, place, nature, all things *à propos* –

Can we lay claim to offer any more
   Utopian a perspective on the stuff
Of daily life than might supply a poor

(Since not produced with skill and care enough)
   B-movie script or fourth-rate TV soap.
That's no doubt why utopia gets a rough

Ride when the actualists test its high hope
   Against a crass reality that's straight
From movie land and so restricts the scope

For world-refashioning to a change of state
   Where everything stays pretty much the same
For fear that changes more extreme might rate

As zero-scorers in the current game.
   Else they'd most likely be disqualified
From the word go since their utopian aim

Is so far skewed toward the other side,
   The yonder-world of any here-and-now,
That it lacks means or method to provide

The smallest indication as to how
    The two realities might intersect,
Or the plain prose of everyday allow

The poetry of 'what if?' to inflect
    Its metric with an accent that derails
The rhythmic beat our well-trained ears expect.

Still best not push so far that this entails
    Expiry of the patient through mere lack
Of oxygen, or – if some switch-point fails

To keep our train reliably on track
    Across those gaps – the pile-up that ensues
When hairline faults amass to form a crack,

Or sound and sense decouple and we lose
    All contact with whatever once sustained
Their rhythmic interplay since words refuse,

Like rolling-stock, to keep themselves entrained
    As some wild motion bucks the snaky line.
Thus any promise of new freedoms gained

By *vers-libristes* who wish to redefine
    Verse-forms utopically is apt to prove
Delusive when these factors all combine

To crash their programmes, make them jump the groove,
    And thereby (if unwittingly) reveal
How close the link between those things that move

Our minds by some slight detour from the real
    And gain all the more leverage for not
Essaying some transformative big deal,

And those fine shifts of stress that hit the spot
    More perfectly for never losing touch
With rhythmic subtleties that go to pot

Once turned loose altogether from the clutch
   Of verse-scheme, rhyme and meter. All this means
Is that where poets used them as a crutch

They now fall back on other fixed routines,
   Though such as tend increasingly toward
The private realm since nothing intervenes –

No verbal artifice that might afford
   A crossing-point back into the fresh air
Of public discourse – and the poet's word

Becomes an idiolect that few can share
   Since now confined to such a narrow sphere
Of self-preoccupation. So it's rare

For words like that to penetrate the ear
   Of some responsive reader by a route
That offers fine acoustics once it's clear

Of all those baffle-boards set up to mute
   The rousing accents of a voice provoked
Not by its own (distinctly sub-acute)

Soul-maladies or ego-bruises stroked
   With every nostrum in the soul-quack's kit,
But rather by what's soul-and-body yoked

In any world with contours shaped to fit
   Our non-Cartesian needs. This leaves no room
Either for false utopias that split

Ideal from actual so as then to zoom
   Straight in on those slight defects that preclude
All real (hence non-ideal) bouquets from bloom,

Or so the anti-rhyme-and-meter brood
   Of free-verse fanciers can rate the cause
Of liberty a good to be pursued

By flat-out opposition to the laws
   Laid down by some (they think) restrictive code
Of mere good manners. What should give them pause

Is reckoning with the new-found freedoms owed
   To those slight deviations, lapses, swerves,
And *clinamina* whose event bestowed,

Or so Lucretius thought, the jolt that serves
   To send our thoughts off into worlds unknown
Just where the old familiar coastline curves

Back on itself, and so occludes what's shown
   To anyone whose line of vision takes
This as its point of entry to the zone

Where smallest change is often that which makes
   The biggest difference. So these themes converge,
Utopia and poetics, since the stakes

For both concern the prospects that emerge
   Not from some vast upheaval in the whole
Existing scheme of things, but on the verge

Of possibility where vision's role
   Is more to take a shrewdly cock-eyed squint
Than give the focused watcher full control

Lest his fixed viewpoint disallow the hint
   That there's some angle on the way things stand,
Or *vue de loin*, from which they take a tint

Beyond the range of those routinely scanned
   By users of a colour-chart that shows
Its shades and hues only from near-at-hand.

Switch 'u' to 'ec' is one thing I'd propose
   Since an ectopic turn from this-world fact
To near-world counter-fact may then disclose,

By exercise of epistemic tact,
   The tiny gap between them that subtends
Their angle by a measure so exact

That not a single contour smoothly blends
   From world to world, no landmark blurs or fades,
Yet from each one ectopia extends

By just so far. Though it has lights and shades
   In plenty still their spectrum's so precise
As perfectly to match up with the grades

Of likelihood that, at a pinch, suffice
   To navigate our passage through the shoals
Of actuality while playing dice

Not, like the Ancient Mariner, for souls
   (His and his shipmates') otherwise in hock
To life-in-death, but more to shift the poles

Between which his tale moves and so unlock
   By small adjustment what's consigned to mere
Utopian reverie by all *en bloc*

World-shaking leverage of the homely sphere
   We take for real. So might we best construe
Why Leibniz should regale us with the sheer

Vast plenitude of worlds he simply knew,
   On *a priori* grounds, could leave no gap
Unfilled by possibilia, yet drew

The line at notions too far off the map,
   Like Newton's physics with its space-time frame
So absolute that, should God make a snap

Decision to create the very same
   World just one second later or one inch
To left or right, then this would be a game

With rules so arbitrary as to clinch
　　The case for Leibniz. Let us then relieve
The cosmos of Sir Isaac's chronic pinch

By claiming better warrant to conceive
　　How nothing's absolute since all transpires
At various stitch-points in the spacetime weave

Of relativity. What this requires,
　　To stick with our analogy, is that
We deem 'utopian' only what inspires

Some far-out voyaging from where it's at
　　In our world *hic et nunc*, and don't so deem
Whatever strikes us as a trifle flat

Since its departure's that much less extreme
　　And aimed toward those margins of the good,
The just, the fine, or beautiful which seem

To set their sights on nearby worlds that should
　　Require no parting waves to the locale
Of actuality that long withstood

The old desire that nothing should corral
　　Our *echt*-utopian longings. But it's time
To leave off fashioning a rationale

For turning poet lest you think that I'm
　　Just multiplying reasons of the sort
Most apt to shift attention from the prime

Matter at hand. Let's say ectopias ought
　　To spring from not-quite-nowhere and upgrade
The not-all-bad into what's still far short

Of such high virtues as might be displayed
　　By denizens of some pluperfect state
Past hope or need of change. What's then conveyed

Is less a splendid gesture to negate
    The *nunc stans* at a stroke, and more the kind
Of focal shift by which the average rate

Or normal run of things that once defined
    Reality turns out to have concealed
Perspectives that now strike the eye and mind

As if by miracle. So stands revealed
    Another world just fractionally skewed
From the old axis yet with power to yield

Such a rare gift of insight as renewed
    The ancient covenant between those twin
Though conjoint magisteria imbued

With mind's sure knowledge of a sense akin
    To vision, and with vision as the sense
That only some idea of mortal sin

Bone-deep in us could count a dire offence
    Against soul's purity. Ectopia's just
That border-crossing stage where we commence

The perspectival switch that shows we must
    First off adapt our past to present needs
Of world-refashioning, and then entrust

This fragile construct to a route that leads
    Beyond the checkpoint zone of what compels
All sub-utopian thoughts. So one who reads

The signs may see how this projection spells
    The end of any mindscape so composed
As perfectly to fit whatever gels

With extant notions of a world foreclosed
    By just such fixed parameters as serve
To head off any challenge to hard-nosed

Or hard-line actualists. So thought gains nerve
   By measuring its strength against the lure
Exerted by a strictly bounded curve

Of this-world likelihood, yet must ensure
   That none of its inventions break the mould
So thoroughly that their utopian cure,

Just as for cancer or the common cold,
   Proves in the end a medicine so strong
It kills the patient. This, then, we may hold

The stock descant to every siren-song
   Of worlds transformed, as well as the refrain
Routinely struck up when the dream goes wrong,

Most often in a *schadenfreudlich* vein
   Involving switches to a minor key
And wrong-note harmonies that mark a strain

Of 'See, I told you so!'. Perhaps it's glee
   That all those splendid plans have come to grief
On their first run-through with the ABC

Of spellers who resolve to take a leaf
   From no book save the one that lays down rules
Decreeing any other-world motif

Should pretty much conform to what the schools
   Of head-screwed-on plain commonsense require.
So strict orthographers think none but fools

Would let their deviant letterings conspire
   With other kinds of anarchy that spell
Ruin for all things in the line of fire,

Such as the plans that might have turned out well
   In some quasi-alternate *autre-monde*
Had the utopians' heaven not made hell

Its destination in the great beyond.
    Still let's take comfort from those other modes
Of fictive world-creation that respond

To challenge not by scrambling *all* the codes,
    As the French think Joyce did in *Finnegans Wake*,
But more by travelling light on different roads

And holding Stendhal's mirror up to make
    Quite sure no detail of the passing scene
Go unreflected, or – should mirror break –

That every fragment, shard, or smithereen
    Still capture some perspective on a world,
A monad (after Leibniz), or the bean

In which, said Barthes, the Buddhist saw unfurled
    The limitless potential *mises-en-scène*
Of worlds and narratives that all lay curled

In embryo. The message here, again,
    Is not some cynic counsel to make terms
With what the pundits and the anchor-men

Of brute reality would say confirms
    Their expert diagnosis, even though
Reason itself revolts and conscience squirms

At having to accommodate so low
    Or downright cacotopian a view
Of what reality might have to show

Once hope contrived some slackening of the screw
    That circumstance forced down on it so hard.
Then thought-police had nothing more to do

Than make sure every access-point was barred
    To those ectopic shifts of mind whose threat
Was all the greater since the winning card

Lay close concealed in every well-placed bet
   On outcomes that appreciably improved
The gamesters' chance of happiness. And yet

This wager ran no risk that might have moved
   Their calculation out beyond the realm
Of such apt choice-procedures as behooved

Those whom no wild surmise could overwhelm
   Since, when it came to reckoning the odds,
Their ship of dreams had reason at the helm

And placed no trust in what the fickle gods
   Of future possibility might choose
To actualise, or what the awkward squads

Of dreamscape-planners might elect to use
   In ways flat contrary to what they meant.
Such were the seers and vision-framers whose

Most splendid dream-constructions never went
   So far as to deny themselves the trick
By which a blueprint of their true intent

Arranged things so the master-code would click
   Always and only when the planners' draft
Kept that intent in mind, and else would stick

Well short of where those wreckers aimed to shaft
   The framers' dearest wish. Still let's not slide
Back into that dystopia where 'graft'

Can never mean such work as occupied
   The lives and best endeavours of those graced
With more than common power to set aside

Self-interest, but belongs to some debased
   New usage where the word's semantic stretch
Extends no further than to match the taste

Of grafters whose idea of what will fetch
  Them max returns is one that well befits
A language so corrupt that a brief sketch

On lines historical will show how its
  Once copious reserves of hope have run
Down low. Thus any rescue from the pits

Of word-and-world depravity is one
  Whose likelihood's in truth about as high
As hitting on some means to leave undone

All those past wrongs, or retro-rectify
  The world's accumulated woes though some
Time-cancelling exercise of thought whereby

Those travails *ex post facto* then become
  The signposts marking out another path
That might yet bring deliverance from the slum

Of lives embittered in hope's aftermath.
  Else they'd be left to drag their lifetimes out
Under the shadow of a judge's wrath

Whose dark decree they never think to doubt
  Although its justice, or the ancient sin
Of which they stand accused, their most devout

Soul-searching efforts simply can't begin
  To fathom. Yet it's here, deep in the gloom
Of Kafka's courthouse, that we might yet win

Our first slight intimation that the doom
  Pronounced on us for who knows what small flaw
According to what rule by who knows whom

Is maybe not so worthy of the awe
  With which we (much like Kafka and his tribe
Of earnest exegetes) invest the law.

No doubt its heavy sentence may inscribe
    Our flesh in ways that other grisly tale
Of his narrates so all the details jibe

With every notch-up on the torture-scale
    That marks the point where some dystopic shunt
From metaphor to what it must entail

In literal truth compels us to confront
    The horrors visited by legal force
On those poor body-souls who bear the brunt

Of law's gross corporality. Of course
    This point needs making if you grant the least
Credence or sympathy to cries whose source

Is all the victims of a world policed
    By church and state through centuries of wars
Fought to placate some commissar or priest

Of either regimen. Still there's no cause
    To give up prematurely on the hope
That bids us not augment the loud applause

That tends to greet proposals we should cope
    With this bad situation by the ruse
Of taking up some Kafka-scripted trope

And letting its grim purport disabuse
    Our cynic selves of every bright idea
Whose rainbow hues once promised to suffuse

Our thinking with the confidence that we're
    At any rate still able to discern
Some hopeful glimmer from the far frontier

That comes up close once the ectopic turn
    Brings realists at last to take the point
Of hope's solicitation. So we learn

The lesson offered up by every joint
    Display of how reality both ticks
Us off should we be tempted to anoint

Some current patch-up job or short-term fix
    Our promised land, yet counts us either nuts
Or wicked if we kick against the pricks,

Refuse to tolerate the ifs and buts,
    And so make sure this second time around
For the old farce is when its stage-door shuts

So firmly there's no chance it might be found
    Next season starting up in some cut-price
Location where theatre in the round

Is just the most convenient device
    For keeping everyone (as Foucault taught)
Panoptically surveyed. Thus they'll think twice

Before objecting that they've all been caught,
    Audience and actors, in a playscript penned
By some bad dramaturge whose only thought

Is how to bring this freak-show to an end
    While keeping that bunch well and truly hooked.
Then they'll come back in droves and so extend

His current season to the date he'd booked
    With a theatre-manager whose sole
Concern, like his, was that the audience looked

No further than the sorts of bit-part role
    Their own lives shared not only with the lot
Of walk-on characters but with the whole

Troupe, leads included. For the only plot
    This management approves is one that leaves
No room for thoughts or actions beyond what

A strictly-trained *répétiteur* conceives
    The playwright to have had in mind, or if
There's just no telling, then what he believes

Best suited to avoid a nasty tiff
    With management or critics who adopt
The sort of moral tone that lets them sniff

Out any hints the actor may have dropped
    Of views utopian or so heterodox
That surely this production will have flopped

Within a week. Yet Brecht found ways to fox
    The censors West and East by making his
Utopias so thick-hedged around with blocks

To ready comprehension, like a quiz
    For dialecticians of the yet-to-be,
That they enjoyed a measure of showbiz

Success as well as letting people see
    The very mechanisms that conspired
To hold them back from ever breaking free

Of just those mechanisms. Though what fired
    The zeal of old utopians cannot gain
Much purchase here the spark's not yet expired,

As anyone who's watched Brecht's plays with brain
    Half-way engaged will surely testify,
Since their great strength's the courage to refrain

From *dénouements* too upbeat to apply
    In any world like ours. Instead they seize
On just those moments when things go awry,

Yet do so in a way that guarantees
    The audience will divide not just along
Class lines, or gender lines, or both of these

Plus other boundaries that pass among
   Some fractured collectivity, but more
By finding room for that discordant throng

Of inner voices that all know the score
   Note-perfect as their single line unfolds
And lets them harmonise the frail *rapport*

Of personhood. So the one thing that holds
   Their selves together must be just the cracked
Old carapace that wishful thinking moulds

Into the unity they always lacked,
   That myth of soul's autonomy that Brecht
Laid bare (think *Galileo*, final act)

Through sundry kinds of *Verfremdungseffekt*,
   Though often (think instead *Der Gute Mensch
Von Sezuan*) to make sure we then reflect

On how good deeds in naughty worlds can wrench
   Hope from despair. So there appears that slim
Last chance to dissipate the lingering stench

Of hopes betrayed, or turn around the grim
   Dramatic irony that else dictates
Their constant quashing at the merest whim

Of what old dramatists put down to fate's
   Inexorable workings. Here they show
Up clearly in the sudden switch of states,

From woe to weal or (likelier) weal to woe,
   Produced by agents whose appointed task,
Less grandly, was to keep the status quo

Secure against all slippage of the mask
   Long worn by bourgeois justice lest a glance
Behind it spurred the multitude to ask

How they'd been led this less-than-merry dance,
    And (Brecht would add) why those high-tragic types,
From Sophocles on down, could so entrance

The groundlings as to make them feel that gripes
    Like theirs were downright trivial when weighed
Against a tragic view of things that wipes

Clean out of mind those histories that laid
    On lives destroyed their less-than-tragic mark.
Here stands the record of those hopes betrayed

In detail more than adequate to spark
    The poor to revolution rather than
The rich and poor alike to think how dark

Man's doom or destiny since time began,
    And then (for tragedy requires no less)
Resignedly give up on any plan

For world-renewal. Then their sole redress
    Comes, if at all, not by the casting down
Of class divides but when they acquiesce

In the bestowal of a martyr's crown
    Or tragic victim's willingness to cede
The chance of well-earned activist renown

In poor exchange for what some high-class creed
    Of timeless values or eternal truth
Bids them accept as something that we need

More urgently than (say) a plan for youth
    Employment or for reckoning the lost
Life-chances of the jobless. It's uncouth,

That Brechtian take on tragedy's high cost
    In wasted lives, but maybe it's our best
Or only way to get behind what's glossed

Point-beggingly in all ideas to test
　　The claims of tragic uplift by appeal,
Though purely circular, to what's expressed

Just through those highest forms of art that deal
　　Exclusively in matters far above
The grasp of dwellers in the humdrum real

Or hopeful types who, when push comes to shove,
　　Would rather pin their trust to earthbound plots
Like Brecht's. These show how any claim for love

As world-transformer should join up the dots
　　In such a way that no-one gets to stake
Their truth on some world-picture that allots

To *agape* alone this power to make
　　A real and lasting difference since the drive
Of *eros*, city-builder, cannot slake

The spirit's thirst though mind and body thrive
　　In its salubrious region. That old lie
Is just the one by which the gods connive,

Along with their new converts on the sly,
　　Our this-world actualists, to stop the word
'Utopian' from ever getting by

Or carving out a niche in the preferred
　　Lexis of those self-deputized to watch
For any slightest hint of such absurd

Attempts to ratchet hope another notch
　　Beyond the current norm, and – should the signs
Point that way – do their level best to scotch

The snake by doses of between-the-lines
　　Dystopian irony or warning notes
In which a certain levity combines

With a selection of hope-dashing quotes
    From sundry sources. Thus they plan to stuff
Utopian claptrap straight back down the throats

Of those naïve, obtuse or rash enough
    To mean it straight or sans the *de rigueur*
Scare-quotes intended as a firm rebuff

To hopers whom no danger-signs deter,
    Since they're the ones who take their bearings still
From a true North whose heading they infer

Not by some gyroscope-assisted skill
    In navigation, but by a shrewd mix
Of Bloch's fine *Hoffnungsprinzip* that thought ill

Of nothing in the *Zeitgeist*'s bag of tricks,
    However bargain-basement, if it held
The last least chance of giving us a fix

On some utopia whose glimmer spelled
    Its possibility, with (so you'd think)
Its polar opposite. That's what compelled

Adorno to suspect that any link
    Utopians might discover or construct
Between two such completely out-of-sync

Realities as one the hopers plucked
    From the far distant world of their ideals,
And one (his own) that had those hopers fucked

At every turn, undoubtedly conceals
    The yet more hideous world-to-come that gave
Orwell and Co. their stock-in-trade appeals

To that dark recess deep in Plato's cave
    Where all our fears and lost illusions join
To tell us the deliverance we crave

Is counterfeited in the common coin
   Of every dream gone sour. Yet we should bear
In mind how Teddy saw fit to purloin

From Ernst a striking image here and there
   That wrests some gleam of hope from the debris
Of ruined life and tells us that the pair,

Despite their long estrangement, came to be,
   If not of one mind, then agreed on this:
That while (Adorno's point) the giddy spree

Of hope untouched by dread was sure to miss
   Its mark and leave us helplessly exposed
To Hitler's progeny, still the abyss

Might yet be circumvented if not closed.
   What's more (Bloch's point) the prospect may demand
That, while its fearsome depths should not be glozed,

As once by Trilling's students, with a bland
   Remark like 'Some abyss!', its looming threat
Is better dealt with if we take our stand

In that ectopic margin where there's yet
   A foothold for the realist, but as well
The space for opportunities to get

An angle on the actualist cartel
   That fixes things so no utopian tinge
Of nearby other-worlds can help dispel

Our bad reality, or else unhinge
   The doors of our perception that swing shut
On any world beyond the outer fringe

Of this-world fact. For so it is we cut
   Clean out of our perspective every odd
Small detail that might lift us from the rut

Of habit-dulled perception as we plod
    Along known paths whose vistas strike us mute
With *ennui*, not amazement, since we trod

Them map in hand so often that they suit
    No purpose worthier than a postcard home
With scrawled inscription 'Thought the view was cute,

Wish you were here'. Yet (Bloch would say) just comb
    Through all those shoebox-hoarded cards and then,
Quite possibly, amongst the polychrome

Beach-shots and scatty notes that people pen
    For lack of space, you'll hit on something like
The detail that made someone look again

And snap whatever scene happened to strike
    Their jaded eye. For Barthes, this was the trait,
The *punctum*, that provoked a sudden spike

Of *jouissance* through its power to fascinate
    And pierce the photo-viewer with a sense
Of *déja vu* that simply won't translate

Out of that idiom so that rules of tense,
    Grammatically construed, might say just where
Our memories stop and future dreams commence.

Thus *studium* might infallibly declare
    (As Barthes once thought in old high-structuralist mode)
How photographs, like narratives, all share

Subjection to the self-same master-code
    That it was semiotics' task to break
Once and for all, until his late texts showed

How vain that dream of method in the wake
    Of one especial *punctum*. This provides
A handy instance, for post-structuralists' sake,

Of what new forms that turning of the tides
   From a fixed past to open future might
Conceivably bring forth once thought decides,

With Aristotle's blessing, that the right
   Way to interpret sentences of form
Future-contingent is to deem them quite

Exempt from the determinist's strict norm.
   Then it may yield us just the means required
To sift those few utopias from the swarm

Of other worlds that most should be desired
   By creatures, like ourselves, whose best chance lies
In figuring how to tweak what's not hard-wired

About our lives and worlds, then improvise
   As freely as admits a due concern
For the fine-tuning that alone supplies

A sense of just how far the world might turn
   Toward some orientation more benign,
Or helps us frame perspectives to discern

Its advent. Still the *Umwelt* should incline
   No further from its axis than permits
Trans-world explorers licence to assign

A system of coordinates that fits
   Both worlds, the actual and its nearest-by
Ectopic counterpart that subtly pits

Against it what the keenest may descry,
   Since only by such miniscule degrees
Of deviation can the practised eye

Perceive slight shifts beyond the expertise
   Of strict one-world cartographers whose pet
Projections offered ample scope to squeeze

Out every landmark save those few that met
    Their routine gaze. If this experiment
In rhyme-led reasoning has maybe let

Some light through and redeemed the efforts spent
    On formal artifice, that's because rhyme
Is just the kind of opportune event

In language, as in thought, that makes 'sublime'
    An adjective quite fittingly deployed
For serendipity of verbal chime

As much as for those detours through the void,
    Those chance deflections of the atom shower,
That Epicurus, like his follower Freud,

Took as a perfect image of the power
    By which our intellects may learn to dump
The false persuasions that would have us cower

Before fake deities. The atom's jump
    Then figures, 'metaphorically' perhaps,
But aptly, as an intuition-pump

Which shows that no absurd 'god of the gaps'
    Is needed to explain the endless strife
Of opposites or laying-down of traps

By each for other in the kind of knife-
    Edge lethal dialectic that embroils
The pleasure-principle and what its life-

Denying opposite drags through the toils
    Of that harsh principle by which, Freud claimed,
Libido at the crisis-point recoils

Into a drive that's ultimately aimed
    Toward its own extinction. Still that's just
One view, a grim one, of the doctrine framed

By Epicurus and received on trust
   By stoics as by Freud in sombre mood,
And apt to fire the anchorite's disgust

At all things merely bodily and lewd.
   Whence the inventions put around by those,
Like Jerome, in whose tale Lucretius brewed

An aphrodisiac that induced the throes
   Of death, not sensual transport, and so brought
His life (quoth Jerome) to a fitting close.

What got the pious brethren overwrought
   About Lucretius' hexametric spin
On the same lessons Epicurus taught

Was not, perhaps, so much the fear that sin
   Might prove too tempting once we learned to do
Without thoughts of an afterlife wherein

Accounts were settled, but their sense that through
   Its rendering in verse that doctrine took
A form that let the chance events accrue –

The errant tropes or turns that cocked a snook
   At plain-prose virtue – and so found a way
To grab the reader's interest, or a hook

(Like those Lucretian atoms) lest it stray
   Beyond the finely calibrated zone
Of randomness that regulates the play

Of chance within strict limits. These alone
   Permit the atom-swerves to intertwine
And so define a switch-point from the known

To whatsoever dawns beneath the sign
   Of hazard, chance, contingency, event,
Turn, trope, *trouvaille*, or that which makes a line

Of verse ring true as if by accident.
    For – Jakobson's my witness – nothing but
Cosmic coincidence or heaven-sent

Alliterative chance explained the glut
    Of complex verbal patterning that's found
In any line or chunk you care to cut

Out for analysis of how the sound
    Is echo to the sense. That's why (his phrase
For it) the poetry of grammar's bound

To strike the keen-eared linguist who essays
    The task of saying what it is about
Some haunting passage that at length repays

The time and effort that it took to scout
    Each level of poetic artifice
And then, lest anyone profess to doubt

The evidence, show how we're prone to miss
    Some crucial point or nuance of the sense
If we leave out of our analysis

Those phonematic levels that condense
    The structural resources of *la langue*
Into a preternaturally intense

Act of *parole*. This rises into song
    Each time that verbal discourse undergoes
A switch of focus from what moves along

In linear-horizontal style, like prose,
    To what occurs when (Jakobson's idea)
The axis shifts and then we juxtapose,

So to speak vertically, whatever we're
    Well practised at selecting from the class
Of contrasts or resemblances that here

Require the language-faculty to pass
   Beyond those more prosaic sorts of tie
That have us mostly view things through a glass

Darkly. Ectopia's sign-posted by
   That same poetic function which decrees
(Here Jakobson again) that we apply

Its axis-shifting principle to tease
   Out through analysis what makes the grade
Not just in poetry designed to please

Fastidious tastes, but in the sort that made
   Such a big hit of slogans, nonsense-rhymes,
Catch-phrases, jingles, and tricks of the trade

Such as (his favourite) 'I like Ike' at times
   When hucksters try to get the folk on board
With a well-crafted sound-bite that so primes

The listener's subconscious that he's floored,
   Once it wears off, to get a fix on what
The hell it was that struck that errant chord

Of rhyme against all reason. Still it's not
   Good form for me at this point, having penned
Three-hundred-odd rhymed stanzas on the trot,

To bring my poem to a pyrrhic end
   By now declaring rhyme the kind of freak
Linguistic happening that should offend

Our rational selves or count as just a weak
   Capitulation to the rhymester's spell
Worked up into a full-scale verse technique

That poets use, but demagogues as well,
   Along with advertisers, since they know
How easily these sound-effects compel

The drowsy mind to just go with the flow
　　Of sound-suggestion like the nonsense-verse
Of Lewis Carroll, Edward Lear and Co.

Maybe they wanted us to ask: what's worse,
　　A bit of suchlike rhyme-led stuff that makes
No big deal of the poet's ancient curse,

The arbitrary sign, or that which takes
　　It bitterly to heart and so aspires,
Like Tennyson, to capture all the aches

Of love and loss as if performed by choirs
　　In a verse-music of such perfect pitch
That between signifieds and signifiers

No bar remains. The secret's in that switch
　　From chance to choice, or (*pace* Mallarmé)
From some odd string of vocables that hitch

Up purely through a random *coup de dés*
　　To what turns out the true *don de poème*,
Though not by pushing hazard all the way,

But more by seeing how the ills that stem
　　From over-estimation of the mind's
Possession of a sure-fire stratagem

For conquering chance are nothing to the kinds
　　Induced by over-emphasis on all
That makes us slaves of circumstance or binds

Our lives to how the throw of dice might fall.
　　That's why Mallarmé thought the only means
Of giving creativity some small

Though crucial edge on verse-forms like machines
　　(Hence the great *crise de vers*) was to decide
That free-will wasn't worth a hill of beans

Since the pure hazard-concept, if applied
    With quasi-mathematical finesse,
Would more than compensate the wounded pride

Of inkhorn classicists who liked to stress
    How far this was from living up to their
High creed. So they refused to acquiesce

In the idea that poetry might share
    With chance the possibility that each
Sheer master-stroke of genius or rare

Thrice-welcome turn of happenstance should teach
    No more than how the self-same root's contained
In 'happiness' and happen'. So we reach

A simple truth without the sorts of strained
    Folk-etymology that claim to plumb
Truths more authentic through a wisdom gained

By dwelling on those etymons that come
    Back to remembrance only when we cast
Aside the whole accumulated sum

Of errors in the light of which our past
    And present stand accused under the sign
Of *Seinsvergessenheit*. No theme so vast

(Nor, for that matter, subtext so malign)
    As Heidegger's is ours in making out
This case: that nothing says we can't combine

An edge of optimism with the doubt
    Implanted by those multiple defeats
That gave dystopia its current clout,

And take our stand where age-old failure meets
    The turning-point toward a world where chance
Reveals the hold'em hand where it competes

With mere necessity and looks askance
    At any bid, like his, to make it seem
Ananke's closest kin and so enhance

Its hope-defeating power. That's why the theme
    Ectopian had better set its sights
On some point short of the far-distant gleam

Where *echt*-utopia shines out from the heights
    Above wanhope's abyss. Yet it's just when
The darkness falls that hope's eclipse invites

At first a sombre reckoning, but then
    The will to find a stance less crisis-prone
That might acknowledge how the tongues of men,

However harsh or disparate in tone,
    Should find in this old Babel a fresh source
Of hope renewed and not in some unknown

To us since purebred speech that would enforce
    Full-scale *Apartheid* of the language-tribes
By constantly reminding them how coarse

Were pandemonian tones. This then prescribes
    A flat conviction that all plans to build
A new world-language-tower where the mixed vibes

Might form one perfectly harmonious guild
    Must bite the dust since what these hopers bring
To it by expert draughtsmanship or skilled

Construction does no more than press the sting
    Of failure home. And so the message reads
That no world-betterment can ever spring

From Shangri Las beyond our selfish needs
    For *Lebensraum* in language as in land,
In which case any shrewd contractor heeds

The parable and lets the tower he'd planned
 Stay safely locked inside the planner's brain
Or on their sketch-pad, while he takes in hand

Only such groundhog projects as maintain
 A discreet profile tucked in well below
The circumjacent skyline. Still my main

Idea at every turn has been to show
 How often it's utopia's *après-coup*,
The tower destroyed, which then affords us no

Hope-raising trope for how we might make do
 With a slight switch of focal length that lacks
The radiance of a fine utopian view

Yet yields up suddenly, between the cracks
 In actuality, what grants our eye
A view ectopic, slant, or parallax

Of a new world beneath the common sky.

Notes

p. 30: 'as Auden said, without regrets'. Alludes to W. H. Auden's great poem 'Spain': 'history to the defeated/May say alas but cannot help or pardon'. This was one of the passages that led to Auden's later disliking and disowning the poem on moral grounds, most likely prompted in part by George Orwell's caustic remarks.

p. 31: 'Morris-type utopias'. Reference to William Morris's *News from Nowhere* (1890).

p. 32: alludes to R. L. Stevenson's *Treasure Island* and William Golding's *Lord of the Flies*.

p. 33: *autre-monde*, *monde quotidienne*: other-world, everyday world.

p. 34: *grosso modo*: roughly, approximately.

p. 36: *vers-libristes*. Exponents of free verse.

p. 37: bouquets from bloom. Alludes to line by French symbolist poet Stéphane Mallarmé who evokes the 'ideal flower, absent from all bouquets'.

p. 38: *clinamina*. Refers to those occasional random swerves in the falling path of atoms that Epicurus – and after him the poet Lucretius – deemed to be the only loci of freedom in an otherwise wholly deterministic and materialist conception of the cosmos.

p. 39: Gottfried Wilhelm *Leibniz* (1646–1716). Early deviser of a multiverse metaphysics that anticipated modern logicians – as well as certain quantum theorists – by conceptualizing the modal notions of necessity and possibility through his talk of possible worlds that coexisted with – but were inaccessible from – our actual world.

p. 43: 'as the French think Joyce did'. Allusion to the curious habit among French post-structuralists and other late twentieth-century avant-garde literary theorists of regarding James Joyce's *Finnegans Wake* as the ultimate 'revolutionary' text. This had to do with its supposed power to subvert or undermine the dominant (bourgeois) codes of realist narrative and representation.

p. 46: 'no doubt its heavy sentence may inscribe'. Refers to Franz Kafka's gruesome story 'In the Penal Colony'.

p. 49: *Verfremdungsaffekt*. 'Alienation-effect', 'effect of making-strange', 'defamiliarising impact'. Term used by German Marxist dramatist Bertolt Brecht to describe how he wished his plays and production-techniques to jolt the theatre audience out of their accustomed, complacent ways of thought through the use of various jarring, incongruous or anachronistic details and events.

p. 49: 'Der Gute Mensch von Sezuan'. 'The Good Woman of Sezuan'; parable-play by Brecht deploying the above-mentioned kinds of alienation effect to drive home its point about the impossibility of being a simply 'good' or virtuous person in a bad or morally indifferent world.

p. 51: 'eros, city-builder'. Allusion to W. H. Auden's poem 'In Memory of Sigmund Freud'.

p. 52: 'Of Bloch's fine *Hoffnungsprinzip*'. Reference to the Frankfurt critical theorist Ernst Bloch, his book *The Principle of Hope*, and his lifelong quest to redeem utopian glimmers and gleams from sources across the widest range of 'high' and 'popular' culture.

p. 53: 'Teddy'. Affectionate nickname of Theodor W. Adorno, the Frankfurt School critical theorist whose 'negative dialectic' – or resolute insistence on facing up to the horrors and degradations of contemporary life – ensured his opposition to Bloch's utopian perspective until the brief period of their late (and very partial) reconciliation.

p. 53: 'as once by Trilling's students'. The critic Lionel Trilling tells of asking his students to read Conrad's *Heart of Darkness* and how their response, after dutifully peering into the abyss, was to register its depth and then write the requisite essay about it.

p. 54: *punctum* and *studium*. Latin terms given a special, highly personal significance in Roland Barthes' *Camera Lucida*, his text about the reading of photographs. *Studium* is the kind of detached, equable gaze that scans the photo as an object of scholarly or appreciative study, while *punctum* is the sudden arrested glance that responds to some detail uniquely specific to the encounter between viewer and viewed.

p. 55: *Umwelt*. Environment, surroundings, Heidegger's 'world'.

p. 58: 'Jakobson's my witness'. Reference to Czech structural linguist Roman Jakobson and his fantastically intricate analyses of the patterns of sound and sense in various poems, most famously a Shakespeare sonnet.

p. 61: *Seinsvergessenheit*. Literally 'forgetfulness of being'; alludes to the German philosopher Martin Heidegger and his brooding commentaries on how this supposed state of oblivion is manifest in the texts of 'Western metaphysics' from Plato to Nietzsche.

4

Shifters

The term 'shifter' was introduced into linguistics by Otto Jespersen to refer to those elements in language whose general meaning cannot be defined without reference to the message.

(*Encyclopedia of Lacanian Psychoanalysis*)

Language is possible only because each speaker sets himself up as a subject referring to himself as I in his discourse. Because of this, I posits another person, the one who, being completely exterior to 'me,' becomes my echo to whom I say you *and who says* you *to me.*

(EMILE BENVENISTE, *Problems in General Linguistics*)

His question then: how much of all that went
   Into those (face it) multiple decades
Of (say it) soul-companionship they'd spent
   Might yet hold firm against the gathering shades
Of nescience to witness what it meant
   And must still mean though all around it fades.
The trouble is, forgetfulness that lent
   A kind of self-forgiveness now just aids

The superego in its sole intent
    To substitute a memory-bank that trades
On a devalued coinage to augment
    The agenbite of inwit that invades
His every second thought. This means the bent
    Of self-esteem is also what degrades
The daily fainter messages he's sent
    From a shared past till almost it persuades
Him some mere tweak of hindsight might prevent
    Those thoughts from hitting him like stun-grenades.

OK, you know the signs: this thing's gone ways
    Around to cover up; just needs a few
Small changes here and there, e.g., rephrase
    To make it 'I' where it had 'he', and 'you'
For 'she', and – since first-person plural plays
    A major role – try out what you can do
To show the 'we' that masks behind the 'theys'
    Of my fake alibi. Then you'll see through
Each shifty switch of pronoun that betrays
    What's going on and bids you re-construe
My words as symptoms of an old malaise
    Still bugging me. They're now your biggest clue,
Just like in our onetime off-message days,
    By ringing not plain false but not quite true
While our shared frequency drifts out-of-phase
    Or increased error-rate contrives to skew
The sense until our signal strength decays
    And all the rest is noise. Yet though the two

Of us stayed partially in touch still there's
    The question I began with: how to tell
Just when – at what stage in the mind's repairs
    To self-inflicted harm – we'd better dwell
Less fixedly on everything that squares
    With our self-image, and not try to quell
Those memories that catch us unawares
    By emphasising how far short we fell

Of half-way good. If nothing quite prepares
    Us for this body-blow to thinking well
Of past and present selves – since now it spares
    No detail whose addition might compel
A harsher reckoning – it's because our shares
    (For 'our' read 'my and your') in that long spell
Of lives conjoined are why good sense declares
    A partial moratorium on the hell-
Bent quest for truth at which the heart despairs
    When everything incites it to rebel

Against so bleakly lucid a reprise
    Of *vita ante acta*. That's what I've
Been getting at, or leaving you to tease
    Out from between the lines: that in this drive
To purge our tale of what strict truth decrees
    The self-protective bits we may contrive
To lose, along with them, the bit that frees
    In us those counter-impulses that strive
For a shared story-line to which the keys
    Went missing. This might help us keep alive
A counter-truth that's without guarantees
    Although it tends most strongly to revive
Its claims on us when not forced to our knees
    By weight of self-reproach. So we arrive
That way at truths not always apt to seize
    On our (read my) worst attributes, or dive
Down to life-wrecks that all our expertise
    In salvage-work can't handle, or connive

With faults as yet unguessed-at to reveal
    How any sharing I might back-project
Onto our time together must conceal
    Those lies that most effectually wrecked
Its future chances. Better we should deal
    With so much guilt in ways that intersect
At some point well upstream from where we feel
    First tremors of the looming disconnect

Between that time and this, between how we'll
   Imagine things once were and how it's checked,
That fond remembrance, by the sorts of real-
   Time reckoning that would bid us redirect
Our wish-led errant thoughts. What might repeal
   Its harsh demand is coming to reflect
How such excess of conscience-driven zeal
   To render thought wish-free, and so effect
Its union with truth, might rather seal
   Their final separation through neglect

Of everything that failed to fit the bill
   Drawn up by our self-prosecuting need
For things to go against us and instil
   A sense that we shall do no good to plead
A case for the defence that fails to drill
   Itself in self-defeat. That's why we're keyed
Up to put recollection through the mill
   Of hyperactive conscience so as to feed
Our chronic guilt-addiction and to kill
   Our sense of other, kinder ways to read
The anamnestic signs. These say there's still
   Sufficient time for them to intercede
And show that all our memory-quizzing skill
   Went only to delude ourselves that we'd
Been wholly self-deluded. Thus we will,
   Or may at length, persuade ourselves to heed
Those shared-life intimations that – until
   The agenbite kicked in – we thought no deed
Of ours (for which read 'mine') could unfulfil.
   How soon the guilt-machine got up to speed!

Notes

p. 67: 'Shifters'. This poem has to do with matters of language,
identity (or personhood), memory, guilt, self-deception and – as

recent theorists have suggested – the extent to which these aspects of our lives may be products of verbal or narrative (re)construction. More specifically, it tries to evoke the way that certain decisive life passages – such as relationship endings or breakdowns – can have strange and unsettling effects on our sense of how those lives make sense or hang together.

Shifters (also known to linguists and philosophers as 'deictics' or 'token-reflexives') are words such as 'I', 'you', 'here', 'today', 'yesterday' or 'next year' that involve some irreducible reference to the person and/or time and place of utterance. From structural linguistics, where it figured centrally in the work of Roman Jakobson and Emile Benveniste, this topos migrated to Lacanian psychoanalysis and thence to the speculative discourse of literary theorists like Roland Barthes. If the shifter theme is doing further work in shifting attention from what is, or started out as, a distinctly personal verse-essay, then of course that is the point, or a large part of it. This relates to another running topic in these poems, namely the way that lyric utterance is complicated – perhaps even compromised – by its involvement with linguistic, textual or rhetorical devices that cannot but qualify any impression of 'direct' first-person address.

p. 68: 'the agenbite of inwit'. Middle English Kentish dialect phrase; title of fourteenth-century confessional/penitential work meaning 'the prick of remorse' or the 'gnawing of a bad conscience'.

p. 69: *vita ante acta*. 'Previous life', 'earlier life-history', usually implying the occurrence of some decisive or transformative event.

p. 70: anamnestic. Greek-derived term with distinctly Platonist echoes; 'tending to enhance memory or sharpen recollection'.

5

Picture of the elder R.B. in a prospect of mortality

My topic here is Roland Barthes' late text *Camera Lucida* with its haunted thoughts about the uncanny power of certain photographs – or seemingly trivial details thereof – to pierce eye and mind through an effect beyond the reach of any method of analysis, no matter how refined or resourceful. The poem, like the book, turns largely on Barthes's distinction between *studium* and *punctum*, the last of the many value-laden binaries (*écrivain/écrivant, lisible/scriptible, texte de plaisir/texte de jouissance*, etc.) that figure so prominently in his work. Where *studium* serves to denote all aspects of the photographic image that lend themselves to some kind of formal or structural decoding, *punctum* refers to precisely those occluded details whose none the less mesmerizing impact may be felt with special, whether painful or ecstatic intensity by just one uniquely susceptible viewer. I should like to think that an occasional line in these poems might have something like that *punctum* effect on the occasional responsive reader. Otherwise I trust that the more sedate interests and pleasures of *studium* – of theory, philosophy and civilized discourse – will be sufficient to compensate its absence.

The Winter Garden Photograph was my Ariadne, not
because it would help me discover a secret thing (monster

or treasure), but because it would tell me what constituted
that thread which drew me toward Photography. I had
understood that henceforth I must interrogate the evidence
of Photography, not from the viewpoint of pleasure, but in
relation to what we romantically call love and death.

Ultimately – or at the limit – in order to see a photograph
well, it is best to look away or close your eyes. 'The
necessary condition for an image is sight', Janouch told
Kafka; and Kafka smiled and replied: 'We photograph
things in order to drive them out of our minds. My stories
are a way of shutting my eyes'.

ROLAND BARTHES, *Camera Lucida: Reflections
on Photography*

The Winter Garden one it was that showed
    How far he'd gone in striving to subdue
The old desire for some great master-code,

Some old high-structuralist variant of the view
    From nowhere. Now this image found him out,
Revealed what *Maman*'s photograph could do

To signify not just the final rout
    Of that whole system-building enterprise
But the one truth that silenced every doubt

And all doubt-driven quests to theorise
    Its mute appeal. So *studium* gave way
To *punctum*, just as method in the guise

Of a once cutting-edge *activité*
    Structuraliste turned out (as now he thought)
Just one more routine in the cabaret

That academe came up with to abort
    All revolutions save the ones confined
To *bouleversements* of the textual sort

Or shake-ups of the semiotic kind
   That still gave scope for theory to inflict
Its patriarchal law. What limped behind

In that split second when her image clicked
   With everything to him most near and dear
Was theory and its claim to contradict

The evidence that otherwise stood clear
   To anyone sufficiently in tune
With such vast trepidations in the sphere

Of mind or soul incarnate. Those immune
   To image-reveries might then select
Some new post-structuralist option as a boon

To their still theory-hooked though jaded sect
   Since perfectly adapted to the need
Of waverers half-minded to reject

All commerce with that *passé* structuralist creed,
   Yet half-aware what help it might provide
For diehard structuralists inclined to read

Their Lacan, Barthes and Derrida beside
   Their lightly thumbed Saussure. Thus they'd reveal
Between the lines, by way of some applied

Linguisterie, how theory's old appeal
   Might be explained, though not explained with quite
Such pyrrhonist conviction as would deal

A fatal blow to its presumptive right
   As once and future king. This ruse allowed
Much wordplay in sub-Joycean mode despite

The need, as stern detractors soon avowed,
   For theory's aid in seeking to expose
Or deconstruct all versions of the proud

Yet self-deluding myth whose adepts chose
　　To make-believe a demiurgic power
Of *écriture* that promised to disclose

What transformations might be wrought by our
　　Utopian language-games. This notion seemed
To born-again post-structuralists and the shower

Of *Tel Quel* addicts something to be deemed
　　Just old high Modernism gone to pot,
Although they claimed a liberty undreamed

Of by that superannuated lot
　　Since premised on the *faux*-Saussurean wheeze
That somehow one could cut clean through the knot

That sutured word and world. Then one could seize
　　This chance to let the signifier float
Free of reality's prosaic squeeze

On everything that language might connote
　　Beyond the dull quotidian sense of things.
True, that's the gist of much that RB wrote

Way back when *plaisir* came from running rings
　　Round hapless Picard and those other last
Sad promulgators of a faith that clings

To relics of a reassuring past,
　　Like old-style *explication de texte*
Or other one-time *nouveautés* now cast

Impatiently aside. And yet what vexed
　　His restive soul was not so much the main
Concern of his camp-followers, 'What comes next

For us post-structuralists?', but more the pain
　　And pleasure mixed of what contrived to slip
Through theory's net since, like the vocal grain

Of Charles Panzéra, no apprenticeship
   In voice-production or *nouvelle critique*
Seemed likely to provide some handy tip

For figuring it out. So should we seek,
   In his case, something like a *passe-partout*
Or means, however subtle or oblique,

Of picking up on some essential clue
   As to what made him tick, we might do worse
Than go back and more thoughtfully review

The passages he chose to intersperse
   Throughout the reveries of *La chambre claire*
Where theory served as pretext to traverse

Those memories and desires that none could share,
   Though a few choice epigones might think
They'd direct access courtesy of their

Long-term apprenticeships in how to sync
   Each theory-change with some new trick by which
He'd hoped to throw them off or snap the link

With stupefying *doxa*. Better ditch
   The structuralists, post-structuralists, and all
Those starry-eyed young acolytes who'd hitch

Their project to whatever he let fall
   And then let drop, lest one amongst the range
Of his pet binaries should so enthral

The faithful as to veto any change
   And so (his greatest fear) immobilize
That semioclastic impulse to estrange

His thought from any that could compromise
   The liberation of the signifier
By letting on that what it signifies

Need not prohibit – might indeed require –
    Some reference-fixing *hors-texte*. Even so,
It's clear the sort of text they all aspire

To read or write is one that sanctions no
    Such parsimonious limits to the pure
Free-play of signs on which they can bestow

Those cherished terms of art like *écriture*,
    S*criptible*, *texte de jouissance* (rather than
Mere workaday *plaisir*), and other sure

Vouchsafers of their being in the van
    Of that great *revolution du langage*
That he and others of the *Tel Quel* clan

Believed would serve to detonate the charge
    Their own *nouvelle critique* once helped to prime.
This then was guaranteed to blow a large

Theory-shaped hole in each of those old-time
    Since classical or bourgeois-realist codes
Whose poor pretence to replicate or mime

A world outside their intratextual modes
    Of world-assemblage now becomes the pile
Of jigsaw pieces left when it explodes

And yet when each one carries, Magritte-style,
    Its fragment of a world that's somehow held
Intact despite those shards that all the while

Remind us how the shattered image spelled
    An end to *vraisemblablance*. Now he thinks
It strange his vagrant mind was once compelled

To find its fleeting pleasure in the chinks
    And gaps that might code-teasingly appear
In theory's smart attire, or missing links

Of discourse that transform *textes de plaisir*
   To *textes de jouissance*. Not so much enjoyed,
These latter, like some phenotext whose mere

Display of *lisibilité*'s deployed
   To keep our subjectivities in line,
But keenly felt like a speech-act devoid

Of any clue by which we might assign
   Sense, meaning, reference, intention, tone,
Or all those things that normally combine

To reassure us that we're not alone,
   That we're the addressees, and we're addressed
Not by some text-machine or writer-clone

But by a human being. Thus the test,
   Like Turing's in reverse, is to forget
Those fond illusions and decide it's best

To seek out texts of *jouissance* that won't let
   You trade that no doubt disconcerting mix
Of joy and pain for *plaisirs* that offset

Your isolation with a short-term fix
   Of human, all-too-human sentiment,
Along with a whole shop-worn bag of tricks

To kid you that its word-games represent
   Not just a *vrai monde* outside and beyond
The text but an authentic speech-event.

Then it's the reader's *plaisir* to respond
   As if pure empathy supplied the gift
Through this most intimate and special bond,

To catch the author's quintessential drift
   Or, by some occult secret-sharer's art,
Accomplish the deft hermeneutic shift

That takes them to a meaning-zone apart
    From all crass commerce with the surface sense
And leads them to the signifying heart

Even of texts whose Jamesian reticence
    Had so far shunned all comers. Myths like these
Once struck him as yet further evidence,

Were such still needed, of the sheer *bêtise*
    Involved in all short-cut manoeuvres aimed
At naturalising what Saussure decrees

L'arbitraire du signe, not to be tamed
    Or robbed of its full *scriptibilité*
By any limiting conception framed

In terms that bourgeois commonsense might lay
    Down ready-made in its appointed role
As order's champion against what they,

The semioclasts, took for their highest goal.
    Whence his old zeal to deconstruct all those
Fixed signatures and suturings whose sole

Function, he'd then thought, was to keep the prose
    Of stolid bourgeois realism free
From any *écriture* that might expose

The latent threat to its stability
    Contained, improbably enough, in such
Unreadable (on this the bourgeoisie

Might find themselves agreeing pretty much
    With him) productions of an *avant-garde*
Intent on prising lit crit from the clutch

Of explicators, scholars, or diehard
    Picardians. Yet some there were who'd been,
And not so long ago, amongst the card-

Carrying super-structuralists all keen
    To help with that *dérèglement de tous*
Les sens that he and they back then had seen

As prelude to the advent of a new,
    World-changing dispensation of the sign
That might, by textual agency, undo

All the power-laden binaries that define
    Not just the limits of what language lets
Us speak or think, but how it draws a line

To mark the point where social order sets
    Its 'here be dragons' flag. Blame his retreat
On mid-life hedging of those youthful bets,

Or else admire the perfectly discreet
    And delicately managed shift of gear
By which he made his peace with the defeat

Of hopes once raised at theory's far frontier
    And started out on a more inward quest
Where nothing of the sort might interfere

Since their appeal was not so much repressed
    As put to work in ways more apt to tease
Out all that his unconscious might suggest,

Along with what a subtilised reprise
    Of theory's image-repertoire might yield
By way of ideas suited to appease

An old desire. So he could hope to shield
    That repertoire against the theorist's drive
For concept-mastery of the kind revealed,

It struck him, in all systems that derive
    Their own appeal from some unguessed-at source
In eros's strange readiness to thrive

On modes of abstract reasoning whose force
   Comes solely of their will to sublimate
Whatever might deflect them from the course

Of pure askesis. So what we call 'late'
   Or 'post-post-structuralist' Barthes was maybe more
A case of theory transposed to the state

Of mind or mood now conjured by the *corps*
   S*onore* or *corps signifiant* – since this
And kindred binaries no longer bore

A moment's scrutiny – in texts of bliss
   Like fragments of an amorous discourse placed
As deftly on the page as any kiss

That lovers of the most fastidious taste
   Might delicately place and so evoke
The code-confounding imagery that graced

His textual/sexual reveries. This spoke
   More intimately of RB *lui-même*
Than all those rules he once routinely broke

So as to disconcert the likes of them,
   His *hypocrites lecteurs*, who thought to catch
Him out in just the error he'd condemn

By giving them some pretext to attach
   A *vouloir-dire* to floating signifiers
Whose pure *mise-en-abîme* would soon dispatch

That notion, like the author it requires,
   To obsolescence. Yet we find him now,
In his late texts, a prey to such desires

And perturbations as would scarce allow
   Either the sorts of reading here decreed
Scriptible or the sorts that show just how

Poorly since passively we opt to read
   When the *lisible* tempts us to defer
That fading of the subject-voice that he'd

Announced as the long wished-for *mort d'auteur*
   And raised to a post-structuralist shibboleth
Lest any waverers so gravely err

As to cling feebly to the life-in-death,
   The mere *arrêt de mort*, that helps them stave
Off theory's threat to choke the very breath

Of author-speech these necromancers crave
   To conjure up. Still the distinction cuts
Both ways since, though no doubt his late texts gave

The theorists succour, yet the ifs and buts
   Loom large as soon as we incline to scan
His writing less sharp-eyed for what it shuts

Up safe from those who think the style's the man
   In so direct a way that he who runs
May read. Then we're re-tuned to what began

In a new *scriptibilité* that shuns
   Self-revelation though it now contrives
To sidestep those, the theory-stickling ones,

For whom there's a lone *auteur* that survives
   Their purge of all such bourgeois residues.
This revenant it is whose ghost arrives

To keep them constantly supplied with clues
   As to whose accent, idiom, *timbre*, pitch,
Or vocal grain speaks through their texts, or whose

Own *écriture* preserves, beyond the switch
   From voice to text, a sense of how there might
Yet be some signified that serves to stitch

Things up. Thus may the twice-born *auteur* write
   His own self-ghosted epitaph that claims
At least some lingering power to reunite

What theory and the self-dismantling aims
   Of his and their once joint endeavour sought
To pull apart. Let's say it's this that tames

His radical *esprit*, bids him abort
   That early bid of RB to subvert
The bourgeois sign-regime, and so – in short –

Betray the revolution and desert
   Whatever fine imperative or zeal
For justice once impelled him to assert

The sheer iniquity of signs that deal
   In every kind of ersatz substitute
Or proxy term for 'nature' or 'the real'.

Enough, he'd thought, to strike all thinking mute
   When ideology thus gains the clout
To close off any prospect of dispute

By fixing in advance what they're about,
   Those signs by which the bourgeois code defends
The right of commonsense to silence doubt.

Yet there's another side to this that lends
   A different aspect to that turn-around,
If such it is, and says the story ends

With Barthes so far from having run aground
   On bourgeois ideology that he's
Now, after all his theorising, found

How writing may alleviate by degrees
   The pressure of those absolutes imposed
By the false notion that such binaries

As *texte* and *auteur* work within a closed
    Or strict disjunctive logic. This would leave
No room for *écrivain-penseurs* disposed,

Like him, to use the tricks up theory's sleeve
    Not (or not just) in order to demote
The author-myth and other such naïve

Ideas but more to keep the thing afloat,
    Or maybe keep its buoyancy just high
Enough for canny scriptors to devote

Such passions to their writing as would try
    Past breaking-point the theorists' flat demand
That readers see straight through the alibi

Of authorship or the mere sleight of hand
    With which the scholar-critics and old-school
Life-chroniclers got by. He'd let it stand,

That squib of his they'd raised into a rule
    Of authorcide, but also take his chance
That no such fixed decree would ever fool

The shrewd *lecteur* whose theory-led advance
    Beyond the vulgar hope that life-digest
Approaches might in any way enhance

Their reading still allowed a certain zest
    To animate the vectors of desire
Whenever textual symptoms of supressed

Or displaced ego let some few acquire
    A son's or lover's feel for what they meant,
Those shots that metonymically conspire

To hide in open view. And so it lent
    Each phrase the gentle force of that which first
Seized him in *Maman*'s photograph and sent

His thinking onto tracks which those well-versed
   In all the ways of *studium* might be last
To hit on since so thoroughly immersed

In codes, conventions, and all features classed
   As worth their study that the sign of signs,
The veritable *punctum*, never passed

Beneath their expert gaze. That which defines
   The *auteur* now, post-mortem, has to do
Far less with what the scholar-critic mines

From life and work than what sends tremors through
   The text when some stray detail first exacts
A stunned response and then the *après-coup*

Of time annulled. So memory contracts
   To just those moments when the reader's lost
All sense of any master-code which acts,

For cautious types, to amortise the cost
   Of *glissements* that could suddenly derail
The train of sense if not discreetly glossed

In case the splendid apparatus fail
   And all the codes be scrambled for the sake
Of textual bliss. Then nothing might avail

Against that endless power to make or break
   The bond of signifier and signified
Whose advent he'd divined in *Finnegans Wake*

But now, much nearer home and heart, descried
   In *Maman*'s photograph, or what it hid
From studious scansion of the sort applied

By his old structuralist *confrères*. Such their bid
   To bring the indefinable to book
Through sundry variations on the grid

Of abstract binaries that once they took
   (At his behest) as able to unlock
All those *ébranlements* of sense that shook

The faith of old-style exegetes in hock
   To rules encoded by the *derrière-garde*
Of some *ancienne critique*. They felt the shock

As did the fractured, x-rayed, tissue-scarred
   Balzac revealed by the *explosante-fixe*
Of every code in Barthes's *S/Z* which barred

An answer to such questions as 'Who speaks?',
   'With what authority?', 'How should we tell
What's true or false?', 'How know when fiction tweaks

The codes and lets its *effet de réel*
   Create such havoc with our waking sense
Of what's the case'. So, like the portrait's spell

On Dorian Gray, what starts as willed pretence
   Or make-believe insensibly transmutes
Into a text- or image-struck suspense

Of any referent save that which suits
   The *camera obscura* rather than
The *camera lucida* that he moots

As the best way we 20-20s can
   Get a good fix on this. It's like the mood
Evoked in those impressions of Japan

On his first visit when he understood
   Precisely nothing in that vast array
Of signs and so discovered how there could

Be *signifiants* without *signifiés*,
   A whole *empire des signes* that offered small
Reward to travellers who'd put away

The childlike gift to let such things enthral
     Their now well-disciplined *imaginaire*,
But held great promise of delight for all

Those sign-interpreters who, thanks to their
     Precosity or (as he'd have it) thanks
To gaps in the symbolic, came to share

With him a *jouissance* unknown to the ranks
     Of japanologists. They brought the trained
Perceptions of a *studium* that banks

On connoisseurship such as can be gained
     Only by strict suppression of the mind's
Quotient of bliss in all that's unexplained,

Unrecognised, unindexed in the kinds
     Of stuff worth indexing, or – as with Barthes's
Unlooked-for pleasures – counted happy finds

Precisely for not forming any part
     Of any culture-coded database.
That is, they figure nowhere on the chart

Of known unknowns that let the experts face
     Their *terrae incognitae* unassailed
By fears that some unknown unknown might trace

A yet more distant border that curtailed
     Their voyaging. And so it was he came
Long ways around to find his god that failed

In structuralism and the quest to tame
     By theory's means the limitless excess
Of signs that now he took it as his aim

To muse on, savour, celebrate, caress,
     And fail (next time fail better) to enfold
In theory's wraparound conceptual dress.

These he'd interpret just for what they told
 Of how interpretation's always played
Clean off the field when it attempts to hold

The line at bourgeois critics' stock-in-trade
 Idea of how the classic *pluriel*
Parcimonieux of Balzac might be made

The linchpin of a technique to dispel
 All thoughts of what he divinised in Joyce,
The prospect of a writing that would tell

A tale unspeakable in any voice
 Save one where monoglot or monophone
Authority gave way. This left the choice

To us, its reader-writers, to dethrone
 The author from his station *au-dessus*
The text or intertext and then atone

For our old servitude by paying due
 Hommage to his replacement in the mode
Of *écrivain*. Henceforth we should pursue

Our own, not his, conception of what's owed
 To writing by our freedom to suspend
The protocols of any master-code

That says no reader's licence should extend
 Beyond the best that patient scholarship
And perspicacity might do to lend

Us error-prone *lecteurs* a firmer grip
 On what reveals the author's *vouloir-dire*
And warns us off the textual ego-trip

We're prone to with no guard-rails there to steer
 Us back on course. And further: don't forget
The perils that ensue whenever we're

So far seduced as willingly to let
    The sheer *jouissance* of meanings *en abîme*
Subdue some passing impulse to regret

The author's loss of status as supreme
    Disposer in all questions as to what
The self-effacing exegete should deem

A faithful reading, or a decent shot
    At offering one. This draws the line at such
Excessive textual licence as would blot

The critic's copy-book, make double-dutch
    Of the plain sense, and substitute the thrill
Thus gained for that of getting back in touch

With the intention or expressive will
    Of some dead *auteur* whose unbidden ghost
The theorists laid to rest. And yet it still

Turns up, once in a while, and makes the most
    Of its rare opportunities to haunt
The semiotic banqueting of post-

And post-post-structuralists who think to taunt
    Its feeble apparition. Yet in fact
It was just when he reached that late *détente*

With the old virtues – hermeneutic tact
    Or feeling for the vocal-visual grain
Of texts and images – that he first tracked

The clues to how perhaps he might attain,
    Through this albeit reticent *retour*
De l'auteur, that which promised once again,

In *Maman*'s photograph, to reassure
    The subject (or what little's left of it
In theory's wake) that something might endure

Of her if one stray detail could transmit
    So punctually the scene, her face, the whole
Paysage tout transformé. No photofit

Of theory's *langue* to memory's *parole*
    Now seemed to offer the remotest hint
How this one image caught (let's say) the soul

Whose lineaments lay hidden from the squint
    Of any studious viewer, yet revealed
To the rapt gazer's startled eye by dint

Of that unlooked-for detail from left field,
    That *punctum* metonymically endowed
With everything a fleeting glance might yield

To one, like him, who'd long since disavowed
    The thought of occult senses beyond reach
Of his *sémanalyse*, but now allowed

That maybe they were all he had to teach,
    Or all that he'd now wish us to regard
As Barthes *lui-même*. And so the gist of each

Past stage in his long effort to discard
    Those false securities – the old supports
Of system, method, theory, all those hard-

Learned structuralist devices and retorts
    In face of a desired yet giddying *vide*
De signifiance – was that the only sorts

Of theory that could satisfy his need
    For theory's *au-delà* were those that glanced
Obliquely or aslant at all that he'd

So long and so resourcefully advanced
    As theory's gift to method. So it went
When his distracted album-browsing chanced

On that, for him, transfigural event
   Of her once having been there, having been
Not only there but then and there, now sent

From way-back-then across the gulf between
   Her now-time and his now-time. Such unwilled
Recherche du temps perdu propelled him clean

Across that other gulf fixed by the guild
   Of method-minded theorists who could see
No half-way manageable way to build

A bridge from what entranced the devotee
   Of all things past and passing to what held,
For hold-out structuralists, the master-key

To all those clear-cut binaries that spelled
   The prospect of a synchrony redeemed
From time's contagion. This it was that quelled

The old desire in him for that which seemed
   So handily to keep both thoughts in play
And use all the ideas whereby they schemed,

Those old Barthesians, to hold at bay
   Whatever might elude their regimen
Of theory whilst yet making sure to stay

One crucial jump ahead by now and then
   Engaging in so radical a type
Of self-critique that they were once again

Compelled, his many acolytes, to wipe
   All their slates clean. Then they'd run after him
In fresh pursuit of each new tune he'd pipe

So that his every latest wish or whim
   Would overnight take pride of place in some
New theory even if out on a limb

Of speculative fancy. Now he's come
  To a more temperate zone where those old swings
From dream of method to what strikes it dumb

Give way to a quite different sense of things
  Inflected by the Winter Garden snap
And how its long unnoticed *punctum* brings

A sudden understanding that the gap
  Between those theory-fixed antipodes
That he'd once steered by matters not a scrap

Compared with what her image does to ease
  His hankering for concepts to undo
Every last variant of the bourgeoisie's

Great master-trope. What if they still construe
  The cultural as natural and endow
The sign with nature's semblance of a true

Sens propre that would by degrees allow
  Its transformation from *signe arbitraire*
To one that made the customary bow

(Like bourgeois-realist fiction) to what their
  Fine-tuned antennae told them would conduce
Most aptly to augment their proper share

Of culture-capital? Not 'what's the use?',
  But now: 'how best more gently to campaign
Against ungentle kinds of sign-abuse?',

Is the subdued yet eloquent refrain
  Of those late texts where nature, or at least
Such feelings as (he half-suggests) pertain

To human nature, cannot be policed
  With that unflinching zeal to prosecute
Whoever dealt in them. This once increased

The stock of those engaged in close pursuit
  Of bourgeois ideology and its
Best ally or most pliable recruit,

The bourgeois *écrivant* whose discourse fits
  In perfectly with what the time demands
Of well-adjusted subjects or permits

The reader who correctly understands
  Its call-sign. Now his thought was, it could take
You just so far beyond the hinterlands

Of bourgeois thinking as at length to make
  It seem you've now fetched up at the far stage
Where only some great *coup de coeur* can break

Its hold and, in an instant, disengage
  The mind from that unending to-and-fro
Of theory's dialectic to assuage

Its chronic restlessness. What should bestow
  This late deliverance from Ixion's wheel
If not an idly chanced-upon *morceau*

Du temps passé that some weeks later he'll
  Have fixed in his mind's eye as he begins
To write *La chambre claire*, yet also feel

Compelled to say – lest any reader pins,
  Or seeks to pin, some semiotic tag
On its elusive sense that neatly twins

With their pet theory – how attempts to flag
  The key *signifiant* are sure to run
Up finally against a major snag.

Thus when the *studium* specialists have done
  Their utmost to disintricate the weave
Of codes decipherable, still there's one

Recessive trait no study can retrieve
    Since meant for him alone, or else dispersed
Amongst the codes so subtly as to leave

No purchase even for those deeply versed
    In structural *décryptage*. That's why he let
Drop such strong indications that the worst

Of all ways to view snapshots was to get
    Them perfectly in focus, rather than
(His way) try any odd trick to upset

That fixed perspective with its master-plan
    To ensure no photo-fetishist should zoom
Too close-up or no long-range *voyeur* pan

So far out that their viewpoints then left room
    For just those *déformations érotiques*
That all the best photographers assume

Must coarsen their fine art. View it oblique,
    He said, or sideways on, or in a Claude-
Glass upside-down, or using some technique

Of self-inflicted *trompe-l'oeil* to record
    Your take on it – indeed, just keep your eyes
Tight shut if that's the best way to afford

Yourself the time you need to recognise
    (Both see and bring to mind) what's here contained
When glimpsed aslant. No chance for one who tries

To view it either head-on or through trained
    And theory-nurtured habits of response
Whose aim may be to upset those ingrained

Or naturalised perspectives that ensconce
    The normal view yet whose effects conspire,
Through their devoutly studious *ambiance*

Du savoir, to extinguish all desire
    Save that which drives the scholar's feeble pen
Or lights some dusty commentator's fire

Only to quench it like Proust's madeleine
    Dunked in cold tea. Of course they'd get it wrong,
Those acolytes, and start to grumble when

The book appeared and what they'd all along
    Supposed would offer some ingenious twist
On theory's plot to date, or else some strong

Advice on how to go post-structuralist
    For photo-fanciers, then turned out to lack
All such high-rated items on their list

And seemed intent to put them off the track
    Of its conceptual genesis by turns
Of thought that still showed signs of his old knack

For winging it, though now in prose that yearns
    Beyond all that for what no writer's gift
Can ever yield. The reader then discerns

How absolute the loss that caused this shift,
    In his last text, from paradox as that
Which drove his agile mind along in swift

Thought-levitating fashion, to the flat
    Thought-quelling thought that, up against it, none
Of those *tropismes* he'd been so expert at

Could cushion that one photo's power to stun
    His practised gaze, annihilate his stock
Of figural devices, leave undone

His subtlest textual strategies, and knock
    Away the props of theory that, until
Just lately, countered or absorbed the shock

Of those events that else might quickly kill,
     As Freud hypothesised, the ego left
To its own frail devices. Any skill

He'd once displayed in that line through his deft
     Stylistic ploys to keep defences raised
Against such threats now leaves him quite bereft

Of stratagems to cope with what his dazed
     And dazzled subjectivity records
Of an *événement* that can't be phrased

Or conjured up by grace of magic words
     That once, like Ariel, sped at his command
On every errand. Now that power affords

No remedy that somehow might withstand
     The concrete evidence this image yields
Of how heart's intermittences expand

To blank each buffer-thought that theory wields
     Against them. What so captivates his eye,
And his alone, is also that which shields

Those others who incline to wonder why
     This snap had such a mesmerising force
Since *studium* supplies an alibi

And steers their gaze just wide of any source
     For that slight *tremor cordis* that provides
Sufficient clue that something in the course

Of photo-cruising may have slipped the guide's
     Shrewd notice since it marks the very point,
The *punctum*, where the signifier slides

From view. So any impulse to anoint
     Some one or other formal element
The one and only focus of their joint

Mind-riveting effect would circumvent
   The issue subtly yet intently faced
In his elusive text: how represent

The sense that in this image may be traced
   The outline, metaphorically condensed
Or (more like) metonymically displaced,

Of that which memory shored up against
   Its pending dissolution. What, then, would
They make of this from inside the ring-fenced

High concept-citadel where the pure good
   Of theory's not, as Stevens thought, the kind
Of saving notion every poet should,

At least in more reflective moments, find
   A source of strength. Rather it's one that struck
Him now as having back then struck him blind

To details that a punctual eye might pluck
   From the dense penetralia of some
Studium-encrusted image. This with luck,

Or by half-focused gaze plus rule of thumb,
   Might yield up secrets hitherto unguessed
Since too discreet and discrete to succumb

To any scansion of the palimpsest
   Accordant even loosely with the rules
Of structural analysis he'd pressed

So hard against the feeble-minded schools
   Of an *ancienne critique* whose leading lights
He'd deemed ideologues or downright fools.

No question now of setting that to rights,
   That old *querelle*, by saying he'd gone out
On some wild limb that led him to the heights

Of purebred theory, yet now come to doubt
  All those delusive notions that betrayed
(Or so his old antagonists would shout)

The very principles to which he paid
  Unwitting tribute by that sheer finesse
Of writerly accomplishment which made

The literary grade despite what stress
  He might place on repudiating those
Sure signs of bourgeois literariness

That, *malgré lui*, incessantly disclose
  His own affiliation to the brood
Of canon-aspirants. Witness that prose-

Style formed as if on purpose to exclude
  All that might link such exquisitely honed
Or Flaubert-worthy sentences with crude

Quotidian speech-acts of the sort disowned
  By every self-admiring turn of style
That marked him *écrivain* and thus atoned,

Or so they'd have it, for that infantile-
  Disorderly desire *pour épater*
The very readership that all the while

Made up his clientele. The one thing they
  Ignore in prosecution of their case
Concerning his supposed *complicité*

With those same institutions whose embrace
  The young RB shunned like the plague, is how
He apperceived that detail just by grace

Of a text-tuned sensorium that now
  Inflects his writing through such superfine
Eye-prompted shifts of idiom as allow

The photo-scriptor's gaze to cross the line
    From *studium*-based surveillance of the codes
To a new way of reading what each sign

May piercingly connote between the nodes
    Of culture-bound perception. Commonsense-
Approved significance then fast erodes

Down to a point where the mind's last defence
    Against that endless slide along the chain
Of errant metonyms held in suspense

By vagrant memory must prove a vain
    Though brave attempt since from the start condemned
To pitch camp on the perilous terrain

Of signs whose impetus, because close-hemmed
    By the sharp defile of unconscious drive,
Flows deathward on a rising tide that stemmed

From the first ruse of language to contrive
    The subject's self-undoing in that part
Of psyche's realm whose rule would long survive

Its denouement. If Pascal thought the heart
    Had reasons that mere reason failed to see,
Then let's suppose the reverie that Barthes

Fell into as the unique addressee
    Of *Maman*'s photograph and its *retrait*
De tous les codes was such as only he,

Their arch-cryptanalyst, could now essay
    'Post-theory', if you will, or from the far
Side of his up to now most *recherché*

Investigations. So it stood ajar,
    This portal framing all that hitherto
He'd failed to see for want of that *regard*

Eloigné that miraculously drew
   From fugitive sense-data what no store
Of culture-coded knowledge could construe

Or theory conjure up directives for
   Its structural undoing. As he gazed
At first intently, seeking something more

That might recapture memories erased
   By later memories, then made the switch
To a soft-focused scansion that amazed

Him with its analogue of perfect pitch
   In vision's realm, he came to recognise
At last whose punctual *trait* could so bewitch

The theorist as to let him trust his eyes.

Notes

p. 74: *studium/punctum*. Latin (scholastic) terms: on the one hand, a studious way of reading texts or photographs that patiently interprets their meaning in accordance with established (scholarly or convention-based) norms; on the other, a reading keenly responsive to certain utterly distinctive or idiosyncratic traits.

p. 75: 'trepidations in the sphere'. Approximate allusion to John Donne's poem 'A Valediction: Forbidding Mourning'.

p. 75: *Linguisterie*. Punning neologism devised by psychoanalyst Jacques Lacan to characterize the way that language – especially poetic language – enacts, performs or manifests the slippages and twists of the Freudian unconscious.

p. 76: *Écriture*. Simply 'writing' in everyday French usage, but for Barthes and post-structuralists *d'un certain age* it meant the kind of subversive, experimental, anti-realist, paradigm-breaking, world-transformative writing that challenged every convention of bourgeois literature and bourgeois common sense alike.

p. 76: *Tel Quel*. French journal of avant-garde criticism and theory, published between 1960 and 1982, which contained some of the most important early writing of Barthes, Jacques Derrida, Julia Kristeva, Philippe Sollers and other main proponents of post-structuralism and deconstruction.

p. 76: Picard. Raymond Picard, well-known practitioner of the old criticism (*ancien critique*), held up to structuralist scorn by Barthes in his early book *Critique et verité*.

p. 76: *Explication de texte*. Textual commentary of the traditional (scholarly, philological, explicatory) sort practised by critics like Picard and rejected by Barthes as naïvely 'positivist', bourgeois and tedious.

p. 77: Charles Panzéra (1896–1976). French–Swiss operatic and concert baritone, much admired by Barthes for the uniquely physical-erotic 'grain' of his voice, as opposed to the smoothed-out tonal perfection of a performer like Dietrich Fischer-Dieskau.

p. 77: semioclastic. In post-structuralist parlance: tending to unsettle, subvert or destroy the signifying regime of received (common sense) discourse as represented by the 'classic bourgeois-realist text'.

p. 78: *hors-texte* (Derrida). That which lies (or is taken by realists to lie) outside or beyond the text.

p. 78: *scriptible*. For Barthes, the kind of 'writerly' text that invites – or compels – the reader to become a writer herself by entering into the 'infinitized' semioclastic free-play of signs, codes and active restructuration. Contrasted with the *lisible* (readerly) text that prompts only familiar modes of sense-making procedure and invites only a routine, passive reading.

p. 78: *texte de plaisir/texte de jouissance*. Another of Barthes' cardinal binaries (cf. *studium/punctum* and *lisible/scriptible*, above). Contrasts the merely 'pleasurable' text (safe, conformist, straightforwardly enjoyable) with the ecstatic (orgasmic) text that unsettles and disturbs rather than affording such welcome reassurance.

p. 78: *vraisemblablance*. Having a plausible semblance of realism; seeming to represent the world accurately.

p. 79: phenotext. According to theorist Julia Kristeva, what pertains to the surface or manifest level of textual production, as distinct from the genotext where signification has its source or generative matrix. Clearly influenced by Noam Chomsky's transformational-generative theory of syntax, though here given a marked structuralist/post-structuralist spin.

p. 80: *L'arbitraire du signe*. The arbitrary, non-natural or non-motivated relation between signifier and signified which, according to Saussure, was a basic structural feature of all languages.

p. 81: *dérèglement de tous/Les sens*. 'Derangement of all the senses'; the state most conducive to poetic inspiration, as described by French symbolist poet Arthur Rimbaud.

p. 82: RB *lui-même*. Allusion to Barthes's artfully oblique third-person autobiography *Roland Barthes par Roland Barthes*.

p. 82: *hypocrites lecteurs*. Refers to line of Baudelaire, as quoted famously in T. S. Eliot's 'The Waste Land'.

p. 82: *mise-en-abîme* (or *abyme*). Term from heraldry; state of being plunged into an abyss, as by various kinds of infinite regress or figures-within-figures.

p. 83: *mort d'auteur*. References to Barthes's hugely influential and controversial essay 'The Death of the Author'.

p. 83: *arrêt de mort*. Alludes to Maurice Blanchot's untranslatably ambiguous title 'Death Sentence'/'Stay of Execution'/'Suspended State of Death' (etc.).

p. 84: 'proxy term for "nature" or "the real"'. Refers most directly to Barthes's early, high-structuralist analyses of bourgeois ideology and its semiotic workings in his book *Mythologies*.

p. 87: *explosante-fixe*. 1971/2 work by avant-garde composer Pierre Boulez; literally 'exploding-fixed', though metaphorically suggesting a combination of extreme (perhaps destructive) energy with momentary high-definition stasis. At this time there was a constant two-way exchange of ideas between Boulez, Barthes and the Parisian intellectuals gathered around the journal *Tel Quel*.

p. 87: 'Barthes's *S/Z*'. His elaborately coded, brilliantly speculative, utterly idiosyncratic reading of *Sarrasine*, a previously neglected but now (since Barthes) widely read novella by Balzac.

p. 87: *empire des signes*. Allusion to Barthes's *The Empire of Signs*, his traveller's notebook from a visit to Japan, often expressing

a kind of delighted quasi-erotic bafflement at the impenetrable
strangeness of Japanese customs, texts and sign systems.

p. 89: 'the classic *pluriel/Parcimonieux* of Balzac'. In *S/Z* Barthes
refers to the 'parsimonious plurality' of meanings to be found in
a 'limit-text' like *Sarrasine*, problematically poised at the point
of transition from classic 'bourgeois' realism to (albeit in the far
distance) Joyce's 'infinitely plural' *Finnegans Wake*.

p. 91: *langue* and *parole*. Saussure distinguishes *la langue* (the
total system of a language at any given time, that is, all its internal
structures of difference, contrast or opposition at the phonetic and
semantic levels) from instances of *parole* or individual speech acts
which presuppose the existence of *la langue* as their condition of
intelligibility.

p. 91. *Sémanalyse*. Activity of semiological analysis, theory and
critique as envisaged by Barthes, Kristeva, early Derrida and other
radical thinkers of the *Tel Quel* persuasion.

p. 91: *vide/De signifiance*. 'Void (or absence) of meaning'; thought
of by Barthes in his post-structuralist phase as occurring at certain
points in certain potentially radical texts that were capable, when
read aright, of generating crises in the classical (or bourgeois) order
of representation.

p. 94: 'Ixion's wheel'. Ixion was one of the great evildoers and repeat
offenders in Greek mythology. As punishment Zeus finally bound
the miscreant to a fiery wheel and sent him spinning for all eternity
across the heavens and the nether world.

p. 98: 'the pure good/Of theory'. Refers to poem of that title by
Wallace Stevens.

p. 95: 'in a Claude-/Glass upside-down'. I stole this joke from a
review by William Empson of Frank Kermode's book *The Genesis of
Secrecy*. My borrowing does justice neither to the joke in its original
context nor to these two great critic-thinkers.

p. 99: 'that marked him *écrivain*'. Barthes distinguished the
écrivain – a writer who worked creatively, inventively or
productively with language – from the *écrivant* who merely
transcribed a (supposed) pre-existent reality into some familiar and
ideologically conformist mode of discourse. These terms thus take
their place as yet another of Barthes' typically (post-)structuralist
binary pairs.

p. 100: 'the chain/Of errant metonyms'. Refers to psychoanalyst Jacques Lacan's understanding of the Freudian unconscious as 'structured like a language' and, more specifically, of metaphor and metonymy (Freud's 'condensation' and 'displacement') as its two principal axes or structural dimensions.

6

Hume a-dying: Notes from Boswell

On Sunday forenoon the 7 of July 1776, being too late for church, I went to see Mr David Hume, who was returned from London and Bath, just a-dying. ... I asked him if the thought of annihilation never gave him any uneasiness. He said not the least; no more than the thought that he had not been, as Lucretius observes. 'Well,' said I, 'Mr Hume, I hope to triumph over you when I meet you in a future state; and remember you are not to pretend that you was joking with all this infidelity.' 'No, no,' said he. 'But I shall have been so long there before you come that it will be nothing new.' In this style of good humour and levity did I conduct the conversation. Perhaps it was wrong on so awful a subject. But as nobody was present, I thought it could have no bad effect. I however felt a degree of horror, mixed with a sort of wild, strange, hurrying recollection of my excellent mother's pious instructions, of Dr Johnson's noble lessons, and of my religious

sentiments and affections during the course of my life.
I was like a man in sudden danger eagerly seeking
his defensive arms; and I could not but be assailed by
momentary doubts while I had actually before me a
man of such strong abilities and extensive inquiry dying
in the persuasion of being annihilated.

(from JAMES BOSWELL, 'An Account of my Last Interview with
David Hume, Esq., partly recorded in my journal, partly enlarged from
memory, 3 March 1777')

It seemed a chance too splendid to be missed.
    Johnson sent Boswell up there to report,
From Edinburgh, how the atheist
    And sceptic Hume would finally resort
To God in his last hours. That he'd resist
    And spurn such comfort the good Doctor thought
A crass conjecture so far down the list
    Of likelihoods that nothing now could thwart

The godly folk in their intent to spin
    Hume's long awaited death-bed change of heart
As showing both how 'the wages of sin
    Is death' and how divine grace can impart
Such nick-of-time redemption. Thus they'd win
    On points at last despite that dodgy start
When faith's best intellects had failed to pin
    Down where the errors lay in all his smart

Yet manifestly false (so faith decreed)
    Attempts to prove that miracles were just
The joint effect of priest-craft and our need
    For fictive recompense. This showed our trust
In revelation was a sign that we'd
    Been hoodwinked and – his clincher – that we must,
If capable of reason, pay no heed
    To schoolmen-books best left to gather dust

Since stuffed with metaphysics and the kind
   Of reasoning fit for fools. So Boswell took
Off speedily, perhaps in hopes to find
   A death-bed convert (though it doesn't look
The sort of mission he'd have most in mind,
   That reprobate), but maybe just to book
A bedside place amongst the others lined
   Up as eye-witnesses of how it shook

Hume's atheist creed, and then to take away,
   For his (not Johnson's) benefit, a nod,
Wink, jest, or anything that might convey,
   To minds alert, that he'd no time for God,
Now or in that mere emptiness that lay
   Just hours ahead. This meant the death-watch squad
Could carry off the pious fraud that they
   Came solely to promote while his long plod

All the way up from London hadn't been
   A waste of time since he'd be well supplied
With thoughts of that un-melancholy scene
   Whenever Johnson hit his moral stride,
Found some new sign that Boswell was unclean
   In thought or deed, and seized the chance to chide
His loyal yet wayward sidekick, caught between
   All those conflicting impulses that vied

In him for some brief moment of control
   Over what Hume would call the seamless flow
Of sentiments and Johnson the wracked soul
   Enslaved to its desires. Yet even so,
When the last act began, the leading role
   Was one the dramaturge would not let go
Since, despite all their stratagems, what stole
   A march on them by stealing the whole show

Was quite in character and went as Hume
   Intended, rather than the way they'd planned,

Whether the God-fixated lot with whom
    He'd long since learned to deal like an old hand
Or those, like Boswell, chiefly keen to plume
    Themselves on membership of that small band
Of fellow-ironists with mental room
    For any hint by which to understand

His subtler drift. Truth is, both parties went
    Astray along their preferential lines
In pretty much the different ways he'd meant
    Them each to go as readers of the signs,
The Christian lot ignoring his intent
    Since focused purely on their own designs
To make the very most of this event
    For godly purposes, while what defines

The Boswell error has far more to do
    With how interpretations tend to veer
Off-course when the sophisticated crew
    Of secular decoders choose to steer
A privy course known only to the few.
    Thus they suppose that any meaning clear
Enough to twig without a cryptic clue
    Must come across either as insincere

Or else as calling for the kind of gloss –
    Ironic, polysemic, hedged about
With queasy qualifiers – that would toss
    All literalist interpretations out
In quest of other codes that cut across
    That message and so license it to flout
The basic speech-act maxims. Any loss
    Of mutual understanding brought about

By this infraction of the normal modes
    Of social intercourse would then be more
Than compensated by the way such codes,
    Once brought to notice, prove an open door

Through which the literal sense of things explodes –
    To use the sort of hybrid metaphor
Much favoured in this context – till the nodes
    Of stable usage lose their guarantor,

Authorial or divine, and meaning spills
    Out on all sides. Absurd to saddle him,
Poor Boswell, with foreknowledge of the ills
    That follow when the merest verbal whim,
Once joined to certain dialectic skills,
    Enables the interpreter to skim-
Read with a fine dexterity that thrills
    The more for going way out on a limb

Of hermeneutic licence. Let's recall
    Hume's point about the Jesuits, how they said
One thing but thought another, or how all
    Their words and outward show could be misread
At any time since, as at a masked ball,
    Put on in order that the talking head
Belie the man within, or guile forestall
    The aim of those who'd surely see him dead

Did he but speak his mind. The point's best made
    By picturing the scene as he conversed
With friends on all the usual topics, played
    Another game of cards, calmly rehearsed
The practical arrangements, and conveyed
    His Epicurean message: that the worst
Of death's privations was no worse than they'd
    Non-suffered through for aeons before they first

Drew breath. Not (*vide* Larkin) quite the knock-
    Down argument it seems, but still the chief
Resource that helped the Humean sceptic mock
    That pious lot who thought he'd take a leaf
From some book in the amply furnished stock
    Of edifying tales whose main motif

Was Faust redeemed or how, just as the clock
    Struck twelve, and to the infinite relief

Of all beholders, the lost sheep was found,
    Or (if we cross to Graham-Greeneland) saved
Midway 'between the stirrup and the ground'.
    Yet he foiled all their projects and behaved
With such accustomed grace that most were bound
    To deem him neither pious nor depraved
But perfectly himself and still of sound
    Mind enough to perceive just what they craved

And turn it to ironic use despite
    The many clashing hopes and wishes pinned
On him by those who'd thought to overwrite
    His chosen script. They ended up chagrined
To find their godly shock-troops put to flight
    Or switched around by his good humour twinned
With a shrewd sense of how the whole thing might,
    In future, get believers to rescind

Their fideist allegiance rather than
    The atheists and sceptics to resile
From the beliefs by which their leading man
    Showed more adeptly how to hit the style
Required. This might persuade those who began
    Their vigil wishing solely to revile
His *vita ante acta* that their plan
    For its last scene was a non-starter, while

His civilizing irony eschewed
    Such sentiments and added just a touch
More wit to make its point. They might well brood,
    Like Johnson, on the consequence of such
Subversive thinking should it be pursued
    Beyond those Scots (who didn't count for much,
In the good Doctor's book) to what ensued
    Whenever folly kicked away the crutch

Of faith and – the catastrophe that loomed
   So hideous in the not-so-distant past –
Left social order and religion doomed
   To civil strife since nothing could hold fast,
He feared, unless our inner lives assumed
   The providential shape that their lot classed
Mere superstition. That's just why he fumed
   So much at Milton: God's decrees miscast

As politics became the very bane
   Of any soul, like his, resolved to seek
Its own salvation far from the profane
   Arena of a millenarian clique
Whose vaunted freedoms gestured to the reign
   Of Christ on earth but reached their devilish peak
When faith enforced no terrors to restrain
   The sceptic's final push. Let's not critique

His view of all this from a standpoint based
   On Humean principles but try to think
Just how a soul, like Johnson's, firmly braced
   Against its private demons came to link
That psychomachia with the terrors faced
   By a whole nation standing on the brink
Of some repeat disaster that would waste
   All their brave efforts to remove the kink

Of prejudice that drove the strongest minds
   To self-destructive zeal. What flipped their stance
From high to low was the same force that binds
   Affect to intellect and may enhance
The power of thought yet regularly blinds
   Our thinking selves to passions that might chance
To spur us into thought. If Hume then finds
   No choreographer behind the dance

Of streaming atoms jolted in the void
   And randomly assembling into some

Configuration soon to be destroyed
    By whatsoever clinamen might come
To break their fragile shape, it takes no Freud
    To figure out why he'd choose to keep mum
About all that as death approached, avoid
    The planned come-uppance, and prefer to thumb

His nose at pious types. This he did not
    By some shrewdly premeditated *coup*
De théatre but on account of what,
    By grace of sceptic intellect, he knew
Would later on ensure the other lot
    Belonged to unlamented *temps perdu*
And so in good time grant the genial Scot
    (No thanks to Johnson) all that should accrue

To mankind's benefactors. It's a tale
    Of how Hume's civil irony induced
A major shake-up on the Richter scale
    Of values, and – since I've just cited Proust –
How subtle shifts of feeling may prevail
    At length against the value-codes we're used
To holding sacrosanct. Then they'd derail
    Those one-track rulers of the moral roost

Who'd certainly have counted Boswell mad
    For any sceptic wavering he confessed
To later on although at first he'd had
    To keep them well concealed at the behest
Of his grave master. Plus, they said, his bad
    Past conduct was itself a manifest
And cautionary token of how glad
    He should be to embrace this as a test

Of his devotion to the truth of those
    Same doctrines Hume professed to hold in scorn
Yet surely must have clung to in the throes
    Of his last sickness. Scarcely to be borne,

By them at least, the idea that he chose
    Quite simply not to let himself be worn
Down by their constant rubbing of his nose
    In their bleak view of 'human nature' torn

From that blood-spattered ragbag of a text
    They took as holy writ, but to enact,
In dying, the humanity that vexed
    These pious scandal-mongers since it lacked
All sense of what so mightily perplexed
    Poor Boswell, let alone what terrors racked
His friend and mentor waiting for the next
    And last report. To Johnson, the mere fact

Of Hume's demise would also bring such news
    As either served more deeply to inure
His mind to self-assault or turned the screws
    Down hard and let him know he'd now endure
The utmost of its powers to disabuse
    His stricken faith of all that might procure
Brief respite, till some new vicarious ruse
    Of sceptic doubt regained its old allure.

Notes

p. 110: 'The basic speech-act maxims'. Refers to the performative
or speech-act philosophy of language advanced by thinkers like
J. L. Austin, H. P. Grice and John R. Searle. This holds that utterance
meaning is fixed by certain sociolinguistic conventions (such as
those involved in asserting, requesting, promising, excusing, etc.)
that serve to convey a speaker's intent and – so far as possible –
avoid linguistic 'misfires' or errors of communicative uptake.
This part of the poem has to do with the contrast between such a
straightforward, intention-based view of language and the various
possibilities of multiple meanings, irony, paradox, polysemy, textual
indeterminacy and so forth that have become the staple of modern
literary theory.

p. 111: 'the literal sense of things explodes'. Alludes to the post-structuralist idea – most strikingly developed in Barthes's *S/Z* – that certain literary texts may attain, or at any rate gesture towards, an open-ended plurality of meanings beyond the limits standardly imposed by bourgeois realism or authorial intent.

p. 111: 'not (vide Larkin) ...'. See Philip Larkin's poem 'Aubade', where he offers a glumly decisive retort to Epicurus's arguments against any rational basis for our fear of death.

p. 113: 'the catastrophe that loomed'. The mid-seventeenth-century English Civil War, looked back upon by Dr Johnson and many of his contemporaries as a calamitous since deeply divisive event in social, political, ethical and religious terms. This cautionary emphasis finds its way into Johnson's often unfavourable comments not only on the regicide-republican Milton but on pre-Civil War writers such as Shakespeare, Donne and other Metaphysical poets whose language he regards as licentious or obscure to the point of potentially fomenting civil discord.

p. 113: millenarian clique. Alludes to the various heterodox religious movements and sects, many with remarkably progressive or visionary social and political views, which emerged during the Civil War period.

p. 113: psychomachia. Struggle or conflict within the mind or soul.

p. 113: 'streaming atoms jolted in the void'. Refers to the ancient materialist doctrine first promoted by Epicurus and versified by Lucretius. The *clinamen* is that random swerve from the atoms' otherwise totally predetermined downward path by which these thinkers strove – somewhat confusedly – to make room for free will and moral agency.

7

This be the life

The poetic impulse is distinct from ideas about things or feelings about things, though it may use these. It's more like a desire to separate a piece of one's experience & set it up on its own, an isolated object never to trouble you again, at least not for a bit. In the absence of this impulse nothing stirs.

(PHILIP LARKIN, *Letters to Monica*)

What's he like?
Christ, I just told you. Oh, you know the thing,
That crummy textbook stuff from Freshman Psych,
Not out of kicks or something happening -
One of those old-type natural fouled-up guys.'

(LARKIN, 'Posterity')

Dear, I can't write, it's all a fantasy: a kind of circling obsession.

(*Letters to Monica*)

Well, something fucked him up, but let's not take
  His word for it that it was Mum and Dad.
Whatever fucking-up it took to make

His views and attitudes turn out that bad
   Was likelier not to lie so deep or so
Far back that listing 'all the faults they had',

Those most maligned of parents, might then go
   Some way toward explaining all that stuff
Biographers now dwell on. Yes, we know

From them (the life-accounts) that he'd enough
   To put up with from childhood through to teens,
Not just because those pre-war times were tough

For families, like his, of finite means
   Who yearned for something better, but because
(And here he spilled some titillating beans

To tempt the scholars) one of Dad's small flaws
   Was loudly echoing the *Daily Mail*
On Hitler, race, and (what drew most applause)

The Jewish question. Still these reasons fail
   The test of telling us precisely why,
After we've followed that domestic trail

Right back to source, it leaves us high and dry,
   At least if we're expecting something more
Than might (as Auden said) let us get by

With shilling-lives that managed to ignore
   What lay beyond the facts. Dad's not to blame
For that sub-tabloid stuff, nor even for

The rank misogyny, the taking-aim
   At all things socialist, the plain desire
To scandalize, and everything that came

At last as second nature. To enquire
   More closely what hard lessons might have set
Him off or bitter reckonings could conspire

To yield the unforgiving self-vignette
    That frames a Larkin poem may then lead
To questions like: how far can poets get

From all the basic decencies yet plead
    Some special dispensation, or again –
More to the point – how far can they exceed

Those bounds by some trick of the poet's pen
    That overwrites all judgments brought to bear
On moral grounds? The biggest question's then

One that your critic and life-writer share
    With others who'd make sense of how a freak
Linguistic knack so fixes things that there

Seems no clear way to tell some special peak
    Of human creativity from some
Unwholesome trait or downright nasty streak

That, as with Larkin, gradually we come
    To take on board as yet another case
Of *méchant* genius just as apt to plumb

The depths as scale the heights. Should we embrace
    This all-forgiving creed, so Orwell thought,
Then we'll give scoundrels license to debase

Not only art but morals since the sort
    Of artist who required it – and his prime
Example here was Dali – fell way short

Of conduct that once fitted us to climb
    Out of the primal mud. Still it has force,
That Orwell argument, and may well chime

With those of Larkin's readers who endorse
    The view that puts him up there with the best
Of recent poets but would add: 'of course

There's the whole question whether such a messed-
    Up misanthrope has any right to gain
That title if he fails the simple test

Of human decency'. Let's now refrain
    From dragging in his Mum and Dad, and pose
The issue squarely: why should mind or brain

In gifted types so frequently disclose,
    As if by root affinity, those traits
That prove (what any Larkin reader knows)

Old Possum's rule which deftly separates,
    In his and our best interests perhaps,
The 'man who suffers' and 'mind that creates',

Thus quarantining any moral lapse
    From the word go. And yet, the old idea
Of genuine poetry as that which taps

Into a realm where motives are unclear
    Or moral judgments somehow in suspense
As language-norms recede is one that we're

Much better off regarding with some sense
    Of what those compartmentalists would hide
By shielding work from life or in defence

Of lives that might look less than bona fide
    If viewed in art's clear mirror. Then the whole
Thing comes down finally to what's supplied

By expert verse-craft under the control
    Of thoughts and feelings properly in touch
With all things once describable as 'soul'

But now more commonly put down to such
    Demystified alternatives as meet
The need of critics anxious not to clutch

At outworn certitudes yet keen to greet
    The same high virtues Arnold bid us use
As touchstones. Thus they offered sticks to beat

Those small-fry Leavis said we should refuse
    All claim beyond their having penned some well-
Made verses or to being poets whose

True life-affirming greatness we could tell
    By certain tests. Yet then it seems we're stuck
Up Larkin creek with nothing to propel

Our creaky moral boat since – just our luck! –
    His verse has all the self-restraint and checks
On sentiment that likely went to fuck

Him up the more completely or to hex
    His double love-life but that Leavis took
As a sure mark of adulthood in sex

And likewise – in his *echt*-Lawrentian Book
    Of Life – as shown by every textual sign
That here's a grown-up poet who won't brook

Self-dramatizing stuff or shows of fine
    Though excess passion. Trouble is, they fit
The poet Larkin down to every line

Of self-directed irony or wit
    Turned back satirically against the least
Suggestion that his idiom might admit

Themes, thoughts, or feelings deeper than those pieced
    Together from the detritus of days
Spent half-envisaging his soul released

At last from the quotidian malaise
    Inflicted by that old toad, work, and half-
Inventing more sardonic ways to phrase

His toad-taught disposition just to laugh
    At fantasies so idle as to rate
A like reaction from his fellow-staff

Of Hull librarians. Still we'd understate
    The problem if we thought to get around
It simply by presuming to equate

The self-negating sentiments and sound
    Of Larkin's verse – where everything that can
Goes slowly off the boil and nothing's found

To halt the entropy – with how a man
    Like Leavis made it simply *de rigueur*
That poets worth their salt uphold the ban

On unchecked feeling-floods and not incur
    The charge of such indulgence as may pass
For truth, if anywhere, then in the blur

Of image and emotion that he'd class
    As all too common in the loitering heirs
Of Shelley's Milton. Truth is, the cracked glass

Of Larkin's poems yields a view that squares
    With none of the perspectives that find room
In any larger picture such as theirs,

The critic-moralists', who must presume
    That there exists at least some basic link
Between those *Lebensfragen* like: for whom

Could such bleak words not bring them to the brink
    Of terminal despair? and questions like:
What are we textual analysts to think

Of poems that immediately strike
    The expert eye as satisfying all
The preconditions for a hefty hike

In critical esteem? They just don't fall,
   His poems, under any handy rule
Of text-to-life translation that would call

The bluff of old subscribers to the school
   Of pure-bred exegesis or subscribe
For its part to the view that one good tool

Of textual scholarship (*pace* their tribe
   With its absurd taboos) is that which draws
On writers' lives rather than circumscribe

The text-domain so far as to give pause
   To life-and-times retailers. Yet despite
Their brandishing that perfect get-out clause

These critics still seem preordained to bite
   Off more than they can chew or end perplexed
When contemplating what and how to write

Of that which takes them out beyond the text
   To speaking of the life. Not that we lack
For commentaries that dwell on just this vexed

Relationship. Yet then they tend to tack
   Haphazardly across or try to steer
A course far off the moral radar-track

Which sticks to lit-crit stuff but needs to veer
   Off that course too if it's to meet the kind
Of question raised by those who think it mere

Evasiveness to read his stuff with mind
   Foreclosed to these big questions. For we've not,
So far, done much to show what lies behind

The use of terms like 'Larkinesque', or got
   Much further on in trying to explain
How it can be that that such a hateful lot

Of prejudices commandeered the brain
   (Or gut) of one whose amply proven gift
For empathy goes clean against the grain

Of all those crass remarks the tabloids lift
   From dashed-off letters or the scholars hoard
As evidence. Most likely he was miffed

At some choice outrage-stirrer from 'abroad'
   In the day's news, or goaded by some pal
And egger-on, like Kingsley, to record

Those same *obiter dicta* that we shall
   From now on find it difficult to screen
From memory since Amis *fils* et al

Held forth on what exactly it might mean,
   This strange conjunction of a mind attuned
So well to shared afflictions with a spleen

Spasmodically enlarged by every wound
   Whose suppurating stink induced the crew
To leave him, like Philoctetes, marooned

On a far island. Granted, mine's not too
   Secure a vantage-point from which to press
This case for leaving off the great to-do

About our need to face and reassess
   That psychic split since, after all, I've done
My share of such ill-judged but none the less

Intriguing speculation. So I've spun
   Another tale of dubious worth to boost
The dodgy trade in anecdotes begun

By Larkin *ipse* when he introduced
   Us first to Mr. Bleaney, then the troupe
Of shiftless types whose faults came home to roost

As soon as chroniclers took leave to snoop,
  Like Murdoch dustbin-sleuths, through every last
Poor scrap of evidence they'd count a scoop

And one set fair to overturn all past
  Ideas of life and work. Still there's this point
I'd differ on: place him amongst the cast

Of his own show by all means, yet the joint
  Effect of all those dull or wasted lives
Played out in verse does nothing to anoint

The anti-hagiographer who strives
  To do him down as the sole legatee
Self-authorized to process what survives

Of scenes imagined, sift through the debris,
  And finally emerge with some new twist
On the old narrative. Then we shall see

In it a dark significance we'd missed
  The last time round or managed to regard
More kindly by attributing some gist

Less apt to leave all exits firmly barred
  Except those signposted: this way if you'd
Prefer to know not just the facts that marred

This proto-Bleaney's life but would include
  In that sad reckoning everything that went,
From childhood on, to constitute a screwed-

Up life and one – as he well knew – that lent
  A special force to those prophetic lines
Of his which have the screwings-up augment

Each time they're handed on. But it combines,
  The current taste for treating poems more
Like cries of self-contempt, with all the signs

That these hard-bitten critics know the score
    Only so far as lets them comprehend
The poem-text as one where metaphor,

Verse-rhythm, rhyme, parsimony with end-
    Stopped lines, and so forth, go for naught beyond
A means to bang the point home or extend

Identikit assumptions to the bond,
    If such it is, between the life and work.
More likely it's between how some respond

To complicating undertones that lurk
    In certain lines or stanzas and suggest
That we not count him such an utter jerk

And, flat opposed to that, what's mostly stressed
    In all those live dispatches from the front
That heed no verbal nuance in their quest

For headline news. If this requires they shunt
    The poetry aside and just go straight
To what impels the Larkin scandal-hunt

Then best admit there's no way to translate
    From work to life or life to work without
A standing bias prone to overrate

Some way of figuring what it's all about
    And slighting or repressing any bits
Of counter-evidence. These might cast doubt

On their interpretation whether it's
    One that goes work-to-life so nothing slows
The rush from words to world or one that fits

The words to what the world already knows
    About the life and so ensures ahead
Of reading that their view of things will close

Off other possibilities. Instead,
 Why not accept – like anyone who's strung
Some few choice words together on the thread

Of rhyme and meter – that surprises sprung
 By Freudian slips or parapraxes aren't
The only way our speech-designs are swung

So far off-course. These verbal misfires grant
 Us means, let's not deny, to vent some wish
So dark or shameful that its content can't

Be consciously acknowledged, so we fish
 Around for means of putting them across
In ways that stop well short of gibberish

While not allowing sense to win the toss
 Outright and nonsense move so far backstage
That it provides no last redemptive gloss

Of word-derangement that might help assuage
 Our watchful superego. Yet we'll stray
Far wide of Larkin-land if we engage

These questions on the mind-terrain that they,
 The Freudians, have staked out and (Larkin held)
Thus made a space where charlatans could play

Their infant games. In his case, what compelled
 Those pointed deviations from the flow
Of straightforward *vouloir-dire* was better spelled

In words less charged than those that undergo
 Some wrenching parapraxis that the loyal
Freud-follower might bring to light and so

Reveal how id so shrewdly works to foil
 Our conscious vigilance. Much better hitch
A language-lift along that other 'royal

Road to the unconscious' where each glitch,
    Each Freudian slip or signifier loosed
From ego's hold might suddenly unstitch

The serial *points de capiton* that used
    To let their signifieds seem well within
The poet's grasp. Here it's the shocks induced

By a *dérèglement* where senses spin
    Not way beyond the radar, Rimbaud-style,
But more, in Larkin's case, when we begin

Doubting that all those efforts to compile
    A life-to-work concordance, or to treat
The life in ways not hard to reconcile

With details of the text, are quite as neat
    As might appear. No problem if you're one
Of those psycho-biographers complete

With vulgar-Freudian handbook who'll not shun
    Methods devised way back by Ernest Jones
For fitting work to life. Thus should some pun,

Stray metaphor, odd pair of homophones,
    Syllepsis, chiasmus, or suchlike trope
Show up and point to unfamiliar zones

Of sense you'll count it past the proper scope
    Of good life-writing, even after Freud,
To give practitioners sufficient rope

To hang themselves. Then poetry's left void
    Of any life bar tropic motions apt
To make it seem we'd best be re-deployed

As rhetoricians or with those who mapped
    The language-structures that, through Lacan's take
On Freud, would see the speaking subject zapped

And signifiers seize their chance to stake
   A strictly prior claim. It's not the chief
Concern here that we know just what to make

Of such high-structuralist notions since belief
   In them's no basic part of what's required
If we're to see how it might come to grief,

That life-work project. Even if we're wired
   Up differently from how the structuralists think,
Still it may strike us how events conspired

With certain formal requisites to sync,
   Not life and work, but how the poet felt
That sense and sound effects should interlink

In striking ways. These he'd account best dealt
   With by the kind of reader most prepared
To focus on them, and not one who dwelt

Too closely on such facts as might be shared
   Across the shadow-zone that fell between
Those formal traits meticulously bared

By structuralists and all that might have been
   Imputed to life-history on the crude
(As it must seem) presumption that the scene

Of writing can most naturally be viewed
   In just the optic that gives highest power
Of resolution when its lens stays glued

To factual detail. If we still devour
   Lives of the poets with the relish due
To pop-star lives whose pages we could scour

And find no phrase worth noticing it's through
   The same reductive drive that makes us fool
Ourselves with the idea that we can do

A good job on the poet's work and tool
    Up adequately for the critic's task
By putting ourselves principally to school

With readers who'd in kindred fashion ask
    No more than that both parties just relax
Those structural constraints and drop the mask

Of formal artifice. When life-hounds wax
    Indignant over that supposed excess
Of rigor that would hide the poet's tracks

By making verse a verbal game of chess
    With arbitrary rules then it's the same
Objection that chess-master fans might press

Against those stricter adepts of the game
    Who strive to say which strategies and moves
Led them, not others, to the hall of fame,

Just as it's formal mastery that proves
    The poet's gift and not their happening
To have lived lives that somehow it behooves

The chronicler to log. Though he may bring
    Some circumstance to book that just might shed
A little light, or even hope to spring

Surprises here and there, still if we've read
    The poetry with ear and eye alert
To everything that's shown as well as said,

Then factual stuff's unlikely to divert
    Us from the stubborn details that hold out
Against our utmost efforts to insert

Them each in its appointed place and scout
    The sources for whatever helps to fill
The few remaining gaps. For then we flout

The first rule of good reading through a will
　　To bypass anything the text may thrust
Unasked-for at us and deploy our skill

As narrative tacticians to adjust
　　Those details as required by the demands
Of proper story-telling. These we must

Obey, so habit tells us, if the strands
　　Of life's-work and life-history are meant
To coalesce for one who understands

The plot-type. What they have to circumvent,
　　These synthesizers, is the awkward truth
That anything which poets represent

As fit material for the bio-sleuth
　　Is, read aright, more likely to provide
Such evidence as goes to show, in sooth,

That poetry's most apt to cast aside
　　All mere fidelity to what concerns
Those adept chroniclers of time and tide

And listen rather to the unsought turns
　　Of rhythm, rhyme, and that which appertains
To verse-craft. This the canny poet learns

As their best way to break the sullen chains
　　By which the rules of evidence consort
With a prose etiquette that so restrains

The biographic muse. That's why they're short
　　Not just of poetry but all that lets
Close-reading of the subtler kind comport

More intimately with whatever sets
　　The poet's mind in motion than do those
Life-studies that place all their leading bets

On the slim chance that digging might expose
 Some work-revealing truth. This asks no more
Than that the trained detective trust their nose

For useful stuff and maybe not explore
 Too closely any words that could derail
Their narrative, disturb the close rapport

Of life and work, and leave them prone to fail
 In their main task of smoothing out the odd
Discrepancy whose notice might entail

The thought that maybe Homer didn't nod
 So much as tip the wink to critics who
Read more intently than the see-through squad

Fixated on the prospect of some coup
 En dehors du texte. They're liable, let's say,
To nod themselves or look somewhat askew

At textual details likely to betray
 A meaning or a subtext out of line
With what biographiles have stashed away

For use in showing how the two combine,
 The life that bodies forth some stock idea
Of poet-life and readings that define

Poetic 'form' and 'meaning' to cohere
 Most readily with just that *idée fixe*
Of how things went. This tends to disappear

Once we apply more sensitive techniques
 Of verbal exegesis and reveal
How much gets lost when criticism seeks

To shortcut such complexities and deal
 Directly with the life as it takes shape
In keeping with a myth that may conceal

Far more by letting formal traits escape
   Its watch than shows through all the scholarship
It brings to bear. If, then, the scholars scrape

Around for factual stuff that lets them skip
   The business of close-reading then it's most
Of all in Larkin's case you find them zip

From work to life-event and then move post-
   Haste on to some reflection *à propos*
The linkages between them that's supposed

To warrant such procedures yet may show
   More tellingly how vain the wish that art
And life should hang together so that no

Anomaly could drive the two apart
   Or give the reader pause by tripping up
That otherwise sure-footed run from start

To close of writers' lives. Twixt lip and cup,
   The saying goes, there's room for slips enough,
Or for suspecting we've been sold a pup

When the view shifts from all that life-time stuff
   To comments in an old-style lit-crit vein
Whilst striving, lest the gear-change feel too rough,

To smooth the passage or dispel the strain
   By filtering out all evidence except
The formal details they can entertain,

Those chroniclers, just so long as they're kept
   Within the hermeneutic circle drawn
By exegetes well-primed to intercept

The kinds that don't so fit and else might warn
   The trustful reader that her credence now
Needs scaling down. Should these become a thorn

In the well-padded flesh of that cash-cow,
    The literary life, it's on account
Of their so forcefully insisting how

Implausible it is that one could mount
    A reading of the life on words as prone
As poetry's to agitate the fount

Of true first-person witness with its own
    Life-complicating artifice. This means
We're never safe in thinking to atone

For past excess by changing our routines,
    Restraining the interpretive desire
To test our exegetic word-machines,

And letting details of the life inspire
    Henceforth a way of reading more in key
With its broad contours. These may well require

Mere ingenuity to curb its free-
    Style commentary and let the life inflect,
If not dictate, what readings we should see

As valid or what meanings we detect
    By way of textual strategies less strained,
Or protocols more strict and circumspect,

Than those whose sheer inventiveness once gained
    A sympathetic hearing from the crew
Of old Empsonians or post-structuralists trained

On Barthes or Derrida. Yet it won't do
    A lot of good, this will to moderate
Such bygone fashions, if it helps to skew

The sense of things toward a steady state
    Where life-events can always be construed,
On a selective view, as lending weight

To pretty much whatever story you'd
   Already fixed on. Meanwhile the reverse
Technique deploys close-reading to conclude

With some new life-account that they rehearse,
   These new life-writers, principally by grace
Of certain methods sure to reimburse

Their practised users with the gift to trace
   Whatever subtle ironies or not-
So-subtle twists of meaning might displace

More orthodox accounts and find a slot
   For episodes or views of them aslant
The orthodox account. Or, if they trot

Out something more conventional, this can't
   Be held a fault in them since here again
It's new life-writing's privilege to grant

Its choice exponents liberty to pen
   The kinds of history that best comply
With their desires by making sure that when

Life and work meet they'll manage to get by
   Through some such shrewd expedient that frames
The meeting so as deftly to shanghai

Its outcome. New plan: let's combine the claims
   Of both and hope to strike that equipoise
That most effectively unites their aims

By warding off all sense of what destroys
   The pre-established harmony through its
Refusal to deemphasize the noise

That typically results when certain bits
   Of certain poems stubbornly abjure
Such smoothing-over. That which so misfits

Them for it is the very thing they're sure
    To spurn, those smoothers, when they seek to mute
Discordant rhymes or moments of impure

Verse-melody that hold the threat of brute
    Disruption to the otherwise precise,
Ear-flattering concordances that suit

The purpose of revisionists or twice-
    Born chroniclers. For them the turn to some
New-style historicism's just the price

One has to pay if anything's to come
    Of all that Larkin scholarship whose sole
Intent is to persuade us we can plumb

The poet's meanings, motives, and the whole
    (They think) integral kit of parts that build
Up steadily – since under the control

Of a shrewd life-interpreter well skilled
    In suchlike work – to satisfy the specs
Laid down for lives that properly fulfilled

The rule. This said: let no obstruction vex
    Those readers chiefly out to recompense
Themselves with stories (preferably sex-

Related) telling them that things make sense,
    That narratives cohere, that lifetimes scan
Like poems, and that therefore our defence

Against life's chaos is one that began
    With bed-time stories deftly brought around
To some foregone denouement that who ran

Might read and verse-forms whose beguiling sound
    Recalled not just the world of nursery-rhymes
But a plot-structure that would firmly ground

Itself in a domain where music chimes
   With myth and offers meanings guaranteed
To resonate with later lives and times

In ways well-known from Homer down. Take heed,
   The Larkin lesson goes, how flat it falls
On modern ears, that echo of a creed

That may long past have issued clarion calls
   To true believers in the power of words
But now struck him as just a load of balls

Fit only for the avant-gardiste nerds
   Or idiot subscribers to the just
As self-deluding crap that led those herds

Of modernists to think all poets must,
   Beyond age twenty, harken to the voice
Of classical tradition and not trust

To individual talent or rejoice
   In poems gifted merely at the whim
Of some Romantic genius spoilt for choice

Amongst strange gods. Anathema to him,
   That Eliotic doctrine by whose lights
His stuff would rate as merely *Lucky Jim*

In verse, or as an instance that invites
   The charge of substituting private quirks,
Mythologies, neuroses, hang-ups, flights

Of fantasy, and so forth, for those works
   Where true poetic discipline prevails
And no such taint of 'spilt religion' lurks

To cloud our view. Should, suddenly, the scales
   Fall from our hoodwinked eyes, then chances are
We'll come to think the antidote entails

A treatment more rebarbative by far,
    Since teaching us – what the strict classicist
And rapt romanticist must likewise bar

Outright – that our best efforts to enlist
    The poem in support of this or that
Life-reading or recruit the text as grist

To lit-crit mills are apt to come up flat
    Against the warning signs of an intent
That's swung far wide of what it first aimed at

And let the sense-deflecting tropic bent
    Of language throw a spanner marked 'Beware:
Detours ahead!' into each word-event

Along the way. Whatever special care
    The poet took, perhaps a few lines back,
To pre-secure their import or prepare

Fit readers with fit meanings to unpack,
    Still they'll encounter the unlooked-for jolt
Of a chance rhyme, or metric shift of tack,

Or other such inducements to revolt
    Against the mind's conviction of its firm
Self-governance till signifiers unbolt

From signifieds and mark the end-of-term
    For any school of thought that would adopt
A midway stance. Thus it might seek to worm

Its way out by professing to have stopped
    Well short of those dogmatic or extreme
Echt-formalist positions, and so propped

Up some great pillars of the old regime –
    Intention, meaning, poets' lives, the sorts
Of notion no post-structuralist would deem

Worth resurrecting – while good sense exhorts
  That it provide a formal get-out clause
Allowing it to counter their retorts

By stressing how inventively it draws
  On recent transformations in the field
Of Eng Lit Crit. Thus it might blunt their claws

And show how poets' lives may stand revealed
  Through formal-structural analyses
So long as nothing stipulates their yield

Should then require we throw away the keys
  That once (we thought) afforded us the deep,
Life-mediated sense it took to tease

The poet's meanings out. For then – too steep
  A price – they'd banish outright any sign
Of the biographer's old mission-creep

That let the life-and-work brigade combine
  Their partial insights and so boost their trade
In joint-stock goods. However you incline

To think about it, still let's grant they've made
  A valid point, the sceptics, when we give
An ear and eye to just what made the grade

About those poets who, like Larkin, live
  On principally by way of what they wrote
And how they wrote it, not by what we sieve

From their biographies and then devote
  Our critic-selves to winnowing for clues
Which highlight just those details that promote

Our favored view of things. So if we choose
  To think *poeta nascitur non fit*,
Or if – for just that reason – we refuse

To recognize how deep it runs, the split
    Between his art and life, then we'll avert
Our tender gaze each time we chance to hit

Some further proof of how the kinds of hurt
    He caused himself and others through the tale
Of furtive lusts and cruelties – all the dirt

Those shrewd biographers dig up to nail
    Their man – were woven from the same hair-shirt
Of self-contempt troped by the coarse chain-mail

Of blokish talk. And should it disconcert
    Some readers, viewing that unholy grail,
Let them reflect that poets' just desert

May often lie well off the moral scale
    That holds for life-transactions and exert
Its strongest claim where different norms prevail,

Where the worst sin's that language go inert
    Or words not wound. Although the serpent's trail
Lies over everything, yet ears alert

Enough may hear how turns of phrase convert
    The language-curse to sound more like a frail,
Rhyme-granted blessing that would bid us skirt

Those truths the plain-prose chroniclers unveil.

Notes

p. 117: 'something fucked him up'. Allusion to Philip Larkin's well-known poem 'This Be the Verse'.

p. 118: 'a shilling life'. See W. H. Auden's poem 'Who's Who' ('A shilling life will give you all the facts').

p. 119: 'his prime/Example here was Dali'. Refers to George Orwell's essay 'Benefit of Clergy', where he attacks the Romantic idea that artists should enjoy some special dispensation from normal standards of moral or social responsibility.

p. 121: 'high virtues Arnold bid us use/As touchstones'. In his essay 'The Study of Poetry' the Victorian critic Matthew Arnold advised readers to memorize certain lines from classic texts such as those of Virgil, Dante, Shakespeare and Wordsworth and use them as 'touchstones' – or intuitive standard-setters – for assessing the value of other poetry.

p. 121: 'that Leavis took/As a sure mark'. Refers to the (at one time) hugely influential Cambridge critic F. R. Leavis who evaluated poetry and fiction primarily in terms of moral criteria such as 'maturity', 'sincerity', 'character' and 'reverent openness before life'.

p. 121: '*echt*-Lawrentian Book/Of Life'. See F. R. Leavis, *D.H. Lawrence: Novelist*, where he takes Lawrence as a great example of the above-mentioned literary-moral virtues.

p. 121: 'that old toad, work'. Refers to Philip Larkin's poem 'Toads' ('Why should I let the toad work/Squat on my life?').

p. 122: 'the loitering heirs/Of Shelley's Milton'. T. S. Eliot disliked Milton's poetry, purportedly for what he considered its artificial, rhetorical and somnolent word-music (a criticism taken up by Leavis), but also – no doubt – on account of Milton's republican politics, heterodox religious beliefs and leading role on the radical wing of Civil War politics. Eliot also deplored Shelley's poetry, again on nominally stylistic grounds (the poet's vague and unfocused imagery), but again – one suspects – even more for his vigorous atheist views, his scientific-materialist outlook and his 'far-left' secular humanism. The point here is to stress these links – in Larkin's case likewise – between 'literary' issues of style, language or form and issues of cultural history and politics. There is an echo of Eliot's line about 'the loitering heirs of city directors' (from 'The Waste Land'), just to press that point.

p. 122: *Lebensfragen*. 'Life-questions', 'existential problems'.

p. 123: '*pace* their tribe/With its absurd taboos'. Refers to the long-running debate – from the US New Criticism of the late 1940s to present-day post-structuralism – about whether interpreters can (or should) appeal to authorial motives, meanings or intentions.

The New Critics placed a doctrinal veto on 'the intentional fallacy', 'the biographical fallacy', 'the psychological fallacy' and other such signs of misplaced subjectivist thinking. Post-structuralists followed Roland Barthes in proclaiming, more dramatically, the (achieved or imminent) 'Death of the Author'.

p. 123: 'life-and-times retailers'. A classic statement of the anti-biographical case is Marcel Proust's unfinished polemical book of essays *Contre Sainte-Beuve*.

p. 124: 'Kingsley'. Kingsley Amis, novelist and poet, Larkin's lifelong friend and sharer of his right-wing views, prejudices, grudges, off-key jokes, etc.

p. 124: 'Amis *fils*'. Martin Amis, Kingsley's son and well-known novelist, has written a good deal (not all of it admiring) about Larkin as poet, family friend and (albeit unwilling) public figure.

p. 124: 'Philoctetes, marooned/On a far island'. Greek warrior abandoned by his companions on the island of Lemnos while they were en route to Troy. In one version of the tale, this was because he suffered a snakebite to his foot, after which the wound festered and the smell became too bad for his shipmates to tolerate.

p. 128: *points de capiton*. Alludes to Jacques Lacan's structuralist-inflected Freudian account of those occasional 'stitching-points' or 'suturings' between signifier and signified whereby the unconscious – 'structured like a language' – momentarily arrests their otherwise incessant slippage or decoupling.

p. 128: Ernest Jones. Early British proponent of Freudian psychoanalysis who pioneered its application to literary texts, most notably in an essay on *Hamlet*.

p. 132: *en dehors du texte*. Refers to Jacques Derrida's notorious (though widely misconstrued) statement that 'there is nothing outside the text' (more accurately: 'no "outside" to the text'). Best understood as a call for meticulous and well-informed close reading rather than an ultra-textualist spin on idealist (or solipsist) themes.

p. 136: 'New-style historicism'. The (mainly) US New Historicism and, to some extent, its (mainly) British counterpart Cultural Materialism were both of them movements in literary criticism from the mid-1980s on that strove to redress the perceived 'textualist' fixation and anti-historical excesses of post-structuralism and deconstruction. This they did by retaining the same close attentiveness to texts – literary and non-literary alike – but conspicuously broadening the range of what counted as relevant 'context', or claiming simply to collapse that distinction.

p. 137: 'the voice/Of classical tradition and not trust/To individual talent'. Allusion to Eliot's well-known essay 'Tradition and the Individual Talent' where he decries the (somewhat typecast) Romantic emphasis on inwardness, subjective self-expression or sincerity of feeling and commends a more disciplined tutelage in the virtues of classical self-restraint. See remarks about Eliot on Milton (Note to p. 113 above) for more on the implicit cultural politics of all this.

p. 137: 'Amongst strange gods'. Eliot's book *After Strange Gods: a primer of modern heresy* (1934) is his single most explicit doctrinal statement of those conservative views about religion, politics and literature that often come across as strongly prejudicial and (at times) repellently anti-Semitic.

p. 137: 'spilt religion'. A phrase used by the early twentieth-century poet-critic T. E. Hulme to describe what he thought was ethically, doctrinally and culturally wrong with Romanticism and to recommend – in company with Eliot and other conservative modernists – a return to classical precepts and values.

p. 139: *poeta nascitur non fit*. 'The poet is born, not made'; a Latin proverb that stresses individual talent or native genius as opposed to craft or acquired poetic skills.

p. 140: 'the serpent's trail/Lies over everything'. Biblical allusion by which the American pragmatist philosopher William James conveyed his belief that everything we know is a product of human perception, cognition and evaluative judgement, so that we should learn (in good pragmatist fashion) to let go of objectivist illusions about truth and knowledge.

8

A plain man looks at the angel of history

This is another verse-essay on jointly philosophical, aesthetic and political themes. It takes the form of an extended and in some ways rather baffled meditation on Walter Benjamin's well-known short text inspired by Paul Klee's painting *Angelus Novus* and posthumously published as the ninth of his *Theses on the Philosophy of History*. The 'plain man' of the poem's title may be thought of, if you like, as a handy *persona* drafted in to raise some naïvely formulated questions concerning the far-from-obvious relationship between text and image, the uses (and abuses) of allegory, the perils of over-interpretation and the way that this particular piece has become a kind of sounding board – or echo-chamber – for commentators bent on reading life into work and vice versa. Or again, you can count it just a strategy to pass off my own puzzlement with regard to Klee's (so all the experts agree) singularly thought-provoking image as well as the enormous weight of exegetical comment that it has lately come to bear.

The poem also reflects on the tug of priorities in Benjamin's thought between political (Marxist or communist) commitment, with Brecht as the dominant if fluctuating influence, and his strong attraction to that strain of Jewish mysticism expressed in the tradition of Talmudic exegesis and embodied by his friend Gershom Scholem. This links up at various points with that much-discussed topic 'the politics of theory', one that is equally pressing for those on the present-day 'cultural left' with similar problems about finding some direct – or more often, as it works out, decidedly oblique – connection between their activist involvements and theoretical concerns. Undeniably there is a good deal of personal reflection bound up with all this, some of it barely disguised or displaced and much of it (I find) in a rueful key. Most likely this is in part a result of what Benjamin diagnosed as the contagious strain of 'left-wing melancholy' that characterizes a good deal of Marxist thought, and Benjamin's writings, in particular.

> A Klee painting named 'Angelus Novus' shows an angel looking as though he is about to move away from something he is fixedly contemplating. His eyes are staring, his mouth is open, his wings are spread. This is how one pictures the angel of history. His face is turned toward the past. Where we perceive a chain of events, he sees one single catastrophe which keeps piling wreckage and hurls it in front of his feet. The angel would like to stay, awaken the dead, and make whole what has been smashed. But a storm is blowing in from Paradise; it has got caught in his wings with such a violence that the angel can no longer close them. The storm irresistibly propels him into the future to which his back is turned, while the pile of debris before him grows skyward. This storm is what we call progress.

> BENJAMIN, 'Theses on the Philosophy of History', in *Illuminations*, pp. 253–64; pp. 257–8.

'Creative licence' and all that, but still
    It's clear enough, at any rate to my
Sub-Benjaminian subtlety of eye
    And intellect, that no degree of skill

In eking out a limited supply
  Of visual cues could possibly distil,
From the Klee drawing, everything that will,
  In his last text, elude all those who try

To grasp it or communicate its gist
  In terms that go along with this or that
Choice hermeneutic slant. I'd say it's flat
  Impossible, but then perhaps I've missed

The picture's point just as the arcane chat
  Of commentators manages to twist
His words into some view of things that's grist
  To any meaning-mill they're grinding at,

Whether they take the Brechtian line and rate
  His Kabbalistic ventures something best
Paused over briefly with a sigh then pressed
  Into materialist service, or translate

His Marxist talk as just the manifest
  And vulgar form of what we'd desecrate
If we gave such mere fads of his the weight
  Of Benjaminian scripture. So the test

Is one that catches them, the exegetes
  Of either party, in an awkward spot
Since his idea of history's master-plot
  Was an unending pile-up of defeats

Whose import, to the angel's eye, was not
  The kind of tragic uplift that completes
Soul's odyssey nor yet the kind that meets
  The standard bunch of requisites for what

Should count as a last-act redemptive turn,
  For some the promised end that signified
God's covenant, for others that which tied
  Their thought in dialectic knots to learn

How a materialist reading might provide
 Them with a better optic to discern
Truths less occult in kind. Thus they'd adjourn
 The end-days so intently prophesied

By readers of a messianic bent
 (Albeit, as the cautious ones require,
Just 'weakly messianic') and aspire
 So shrewdly to translate or reinvent

His Talmudic motifs that their entire
 Text-centred eschatology seemed meant
To herald not so much a non-event
 That still, perversely, set some minds afire

With god-intoxicated thoughts but now
 Its secular equivalent that placed
An unillusioned faith in what embraced
 Such thoughts with a good Brechtian grasp of how

Their valid kernel might not go to waste
 Once shot of its old shell. So they allow,
Like him, that history may perchance endow
 Ideas long since abandoned or outpaced

By the brisk march of progress with a sense
 That their time's come around at last, or their
Presumed attachment to some *derrière-
 Garde* movement stuck in the pluperfect tense

At last been found to signal, *au contraire*,
 How they had just the genius to condense
Futurity by holding in suspense
 Those rules that drew a *cordon sanitaire*

Between what falls within our rear-view scope
 Of reckoning and what lies so far beyond
Our present grasp that these could 'correspond'
 Only in Baudelaire's sense. Thus shattered hope

Re-constellates to form a fragile bond
  Of trans-world correspondences that cope
With all that debris through a will to trope
  The stubborn literality of *monde*

Quotidienne and thereby show a way
  To keep the whole catastrophe in view
Yet from an angle so far out of true,
  By all the optic codes, as to convey

How such a slant perspective might imbue
  The angel's vision of a groundhog day
Nightmarishly transformed with that which Klee
  Perhaps meant its beholders to construe

In terms less dire or ominously fraught
  Than Benjamin supplied. No doubting its
Compulsive power to exercise our wits
  By thwarting all the methods we've been taught

To try till we come up with one that fits
  And so dispels our fear of being brought
Up short by an odd piece like this or caught,
  Like shell-shocked angels, in the endless blitz

Of meanings driven by a wind that blows
  From some lost hermeneutic paradise
Where the diviner's art could still suffice
  To bring us peace. The text might then disclose

All kinds of deep enigma to entice
  Our curious minds yet free us from the throes
Of doubt at last, not lead us by the nose
  Until we find some recondite device

By use of which to make his cartoon out
  The very image of apocalypse
Or raise the genre-stakes till fancy tips
  The scales that way. More evidence, no doubt,

Of inability to see what grips
    The eyes and minds of those who talk about
Klee's angel-sketch like this, or like to tout
    Its lines and planes as shot through with the chips

Of messianic time that Benjamin
    Conceived as lying close concealed through all
The debris-strewn millennia in thrall
    To a mystique of progress that had been

(Or so he read those remnants that appal
    The angel) an infernal wind-machine
Whose wrecking powers are most distinctly seen
    By those who know the worst that can befall

Their lives or work. That's why he'd have us shun
    That false idea of homogeneous time,
Or history so conceived, as apt to chime
    All too thought-numbingly with every one

Of those cyclic catastrophes whose prime
    Role – as the victors saw it – was to stun
Hope's vestiges by stressing the long-run
    Sad chronicle of falls by all who'd climb

To heights where they could spare themselves the sight
    Of that bad history and so lose touch
With history full-stop. Else they'd take such
    A Whiggish vantage-point as to invite

His charge of falling back into the clutch
    Of crass triumphalists whose heirs would write
Them out of every history-book despite
    Their having for so long now done so much

To help secure the apostolic line
    Of victors. Let's allow, since it resounds
Throughout his work, that what exceeds the bounds
    Of literal sense will often prove a mine

Where the best digger's one who best expounds
    Not only subtle details that refine
Our textual grasp but truths we should assign
    To the Derridean *hors-texte*. This confounds

All efforts to establish just where tact
    Or good procedure should have fixed the *non*
Plus ultra beyond which the text alone,
    If not in some way adequately backed

By extra-textual sources, formed its own
    Self-referential world that clearly lacked
Firm anchorage in the territory of fact
    Whatever its cross-linkage in the zone

Of intra-textual sense. Let's further yield
    The point to those who say that, in the case
Of thinkers such as Benjamin, the space
    Presumed to separate life and text is sealed

Against the very doctrines that would base
    Their separation on the truths revealed
By lives that, unlike his, lay unconcealed
    Or not at every stage compelled to face

Such threats of inward or external source
    As otherwise would drive him to the brink
Of terminal despair. Still those who think
    To see prefigured in his texts the course

His life took in its last few weeks, and link
    His life-text to Klee's image, may endorse
No less an error than the strict divorce
    Insisted on by purist types who'd shrink

The hedgehog text secure within its rolled-
    Up prickly tenement and so enjoy
An unrestricted freedom to employ
    Those same techniques to shrink and then enfold

The world safe in the text lest it destroy
    Their fine-tuned instruments. Yet readers sold
On life-and-times and captive to the hold
    Of Klee's mesmeric angel should alloy

The elements that go to allegorize
    Those last death-haunted weeks by turning back
To ask if Klee's creation might not lack,
    Judged simply on what's there before one's eyes,

The sorts of quality whose sum could stack
    Up close to what he'd have us recognise
In its blank gaze. More likely this supplies
    The exegetes with just sufficient slack

To compensate the angel's deficit
    With value-added features that might lend
Themselves, thus amply viewed, to the chief end
    These readers have in mind of bringing it

And Benjamin's life-history to blend
    By text-osmosis. Should it not submit
At first attempt, the very lack of fit
    Between Klee's image and the fragments penned

By Benjamin about it goes to make
    More working space for just that hybrid mode
Of commentary whose aim is to decode,
    Through every mazy detour it might take,

The language of analogies he showed,
    In Baudelaire, to link the wide-awake
Of consciousness with images that break
    Through from oneiric regions and explode

All the ensconced conventions we perceive
    To constitute the real. Still we'd do well
Not to fall quite so much beneath the spell
    Of Klee's beguiling image, but take leave

To query some of what they have to tell,
    Those dreamworld-emissaries, and retrieve
Only some portion of the web they weave
    From history's stray threads. Else we may dwell

Too fixedly upon it and become,
    Ourselves, so many angels left behind
Yet driven forward by some brute impulse blind
    To past and future, or possessed by some

Resistless drive that leaves the reeling mind
    Deprived of motive or intent to plumb
Its own inchoate depths and therefore dumb
    To give their dumbstruck angel voice or find

Some apter idiom to convey what's past
    Its gobsmacked power to tell. Just look once more
At Klee's *ange de nos jours* and then, if you're
    Still one by whom image and text are cast

In co-star roles, then by all means ignore
    This (you'll think) vain endeavour to contrast
The two by striving – as he'd say – to blast
    A hole in that too intimate rapport

Between the two. If, on the other hand,
    Your inclinations run *contre Sainte-Beuve*
For something like Proust's reasons, it may serve
    To help you more resolvedly withstand

The knack they have of touching a raw nerve,
    Those reading-protocols that take a bland
Or rough-hewn image linked to an unplanned
    Event or chance catastrophe, then swerve

Into a realm of figural excess
    Where last days and late writings each assume
The sense of some far-back prefigured doom
    That no such graven image could express

Unless one so unformed that you could zoom
   Right in yet be no better placed to guess
What the thing signified, which points to stress,
   Or even – like some garbled code – for whom

It's meant. My point is, Benjamin was far
   Ahead of his interpreters in just
The ways and means required if we're to trust
   The subtle exegete, while there's a bar

(Or should be) on our craving to encrust
   Those texts and images that bear the scar
Of lives destroyed or ruined with what are,
   In truth, projections of a kind we must

Put down to our own wishes rather than
   Project onto the author's *vouloir-dire*
Or *vie hors-texte*. This might apply if we're
   So eminently well-equipped to scan

Their import that there's no life/text frontier
   To cross or need for us to heed the ban
On any misplaced notion that we can,
   By gift of divination or by sheer

Telepathy, gain insight such as struck
   A note of charlatanry with the likes
Of 'old' New Critics, and more lately strikes
   The same false note to those who'll have no truck

With an *echt*-Heideggerian turn that hikes
   Its self-ascribed capacity to pluck
Deep meanings out while others remain stuck
   With surface sense, till some gross error spikes

Its hermeneutic guns. For it's the mix
   Of life-historic truth with allegory's
Long-licensed swerves from it that render his
   Example not the best by which to fix

Our working notion of how history's
  Or life's demands might stipulate what ticks
The vital boxes, rather than the tricks
  Of *n*-fold exegesis that some whiz

Life-allegorist might make out to contain,
  In nuce, every episode of note
Which their close-reading skills may then promote
  By textual magic to a higher plane.

A far cry, this, from what the Brechtians wrote
  In their Marx-tutored efforts to restrain
The angel's flight by hitting on the vein
  Of *plumpes Denken* aptest to connote

Their message that, wherever fancy's bred,
  Its offspring yield their secrets only when
Pressed to reveal, beyond the author's ken,
  Such meanings as could properly be read

By good materialists alone, and then
  Just those of them not prone to be misled
By each new allegoric go-ahead
  To that deceiving elf. Compare again

Klee's image with the commentary it drew
  From this most rapt and erudite among
The many who've been drawn, enticed, or stung
  To write about it and you'll get a clue

As to why some brave exegetes have clung
  To literal sense against the larger crew
Of intertextual lemon-squeezers who,
  From ancient times, habitually flung

Such hermeneutic caution to the wild
  Shape-shifting winds that tangle all the codes,
Mix up historical and fictive modes
  Of discourse, and – through meaning-strata piled

Heaven-high – ensure their pious labour loads
    Each rift with sacred lore. The Fathers styled
Their four-fold method that which reconciled
    Our tongues post-Babel through God-granted nodes

Of mutual comprehension that relieved,
    From time to time, the cacophonic din
And promised to undo old Adam's sin
    (Plus the tower-building exploit that so peeved

A jealous God) by speech-events akin
    To those that Benjamin himself conceived
As bearers of the one gift that reprieved
    Our fallen language-state. They helped us win,

Like his authentic poet-allegorist,
    A post-Edenic glimpse of how things stood
Back then when no tight bonds of nationhood
    Or speech-community contrived to twist

Our meanings out of true. Since now there could,
    He thought, be no sound method to assist
Translators in attaining what they missed
    Nine times in ten, and brought off only should

Some miracle permit, the task they had
    In Benjamin's hard teaching was to pass
Through and beyond the sense-refracting glass
    Of language, like the magic writing-pad

Of Freud's analogy, and – what they'd class,
    Those Brechtians, just another quirk to add
On his Talmudic debit side or fad
    Picked up from Scholem's company, alas –

By that means come as near as we're allowed,
    Us post-lapsarians, to the language-game
That Adam played. This gave each beast a name
    By which it stood distinct amongst the crowd,

Since name and nature signified the same
    Divine intent that all things be endowed
With just that *haeccitas* that did them proud
    By showing how their nomination came

Through God's decree and not – *pace* the rule
    That holds for mortal languages – as laid
Down by those proto-structuralists who made
    It a first rule of entry to their school

That one maintain no sense can be conveyed
    Except by use of that all-purpose tool,
The arbitrary sign. This way the pool
    Of communal-linguistic usage paid

Its debt to structures far outside the reach
    Of conscious grasp or way beyond the pale
Of what might figure in the fictive tale
    Contrived by those who far preferred to teach

(Like him at times) a mysticism stale
    Through centuries of abuse. Adamic speech,
As Benjamin conceived it, rendered each
    Of structuralism's tenets sure to fail

The test of language-faith which said that no
    Mere act of meaning-transference across
Two languages, however small the loss
    Of literal sense involved, could ever show

That third dimension shadowed by the gloss
    The allegorist supplies. Such claims may go,
For scholars, way beyond what's apropos
    But for text-gleaners separate the dross

Of literal gist from the rare gleam of pure
    Or pre-discursive language that reveals,
To souls attuned, a sense that sense conceals
    Since the forked tongues of men work to obscure

What so exceeds their compass or repeals
      The law of plain intent. That helped assure
Loquacious mortals – when the talking cure
      Misfired – that good communication heals

The wounds of fractured sense without the least
      Assistance from those peddlers of abstruse
Hermetic doctrine who might so seduce
      Our waking minds that all the bits we'd pieced

Together in some roughly fit-for-use
      Communicative order promptly ceased
To signify at all when some off-piste
      Interpretation or some fast-and-loose

Analogy drove thought clean off the tracks
      And into a lost-soul-frequented maze
Of allegoric meanings. These might craze
      The seeker's wits or else so greatly tax

Their hermeneutic skills that every phrase
      Becomes one more inscription in the wax
That holds, as in Freud's writing-pad, the stacks
      Of past inscriptions that our minds erase

Yet whose material traces still engrave
      The archive of what memory retains
At some unconscious level. Here the brain's
      Ancestral wiring bids it always save

For future use whatever it disdains
      To memorise or even seeks to stave
Off at all costs where the occurrence gave
      So great a shock that now it too much pains

Remembrance to record. That's why I say,
      Or said way back when this thing started out,
That probably the best, most useful route
      (US pronunciation) to essay

Such questions is by taking leave to doubt,
    Contra the commentators, whether Klee
In any real sense managed to display
    The tiniest part of what his deep-devout

Ekphrastic *Uebersetzer* sought to parse
    In terms so eloquent that they provoked,
In turn, the kind of meta-gloss that yoked
    Its speculative compass to the stars

Of some remote sense-constellation cloaked
    In figural deep space. This firmly bars
The way for those whose 20/20 mars
    Their chance of having egos nicely stroked

By coming up with an eccentric slant
    On meanings or appearances that makes
Of their strabismic gaze just what it takes
    To see things clear or, like his angel, grant

A visionary power to raise the stakes
    Of exegetic faith. Thus they implant,
In the more literal-minded – those who can't
    Quite get their eyes or heads around what breaks

With all the rules – a notion that it's their
    Defect of brain or vision that's the cause
Of this, or some endemic range of flaws
    On their part that must shoulder the main share

Of blame. Yet if one thought should give us pause
    In saying this, or bid us take more care
Before we heirs of Benjamin declare
    On his side of the question, it's that clause

In all such mystical or cryptic creeds
    That makes a watchword, then a shibboleth
Of what, if known, becomes the very breath
    Of life but, if unknown, sends him who reads

In ignorance straight off to dusty death,
    Or (less dramatically) for special-needs
Sense-ampliative training which then breeds,
    In some, such devious spells as drove Macbeth

To that conclusion. Let's ourselves conclude,
    More hopefully, that there's room to extend
Our critical horizons and suspend
    Those cautionary maxims that obtrude

Too much on our ambitions to transcend
    The commonplace without things getting skewed
To such a point that only ultra-clued-
    Up allegorists can hope to comprehend

What's going on. Then all the rest are lumped,
    Like the unclued-up types who, Jesus said,
Lacked ears to hear, with those who lose the thread
    Of some soul-saving parable that stumped

Their feeble intellects since poorly read,
    Or read in ignorance of that which trumped
The overt gist and so cast those who plumped
    For literal sense amongst the living dead

Of cloth-eared infidels. It's this that throws
    A sharper light on Benjamin's wire-drawn
Klee-commentary and how it's apt to spawn
    Yet wilder flights of fantasy from those

Who think that understanding starts to dawn
    Only at that far point where reading goes
Beyond the utmost limits of plain-prose
    Interpretation and becomes a pawn

In some text-game more erudite by half
    Than any trial of wits that might result
From sights fixed wisely short of those occult
    Meaning-coordinates way off the graph

Of shared intent. So, rather than exult
  In getting the last anagogic laugh
Or writing literal sense's epitaph,
  These thinkers tend more often to consult,

If not the 'common reader', then her near
  Relation who reads closely and in full
Cognizance of how words can sometimes pull
  New wonders up from thought's unconscious sphere,

Yet also of how this can pull the wool
  Over the eyes of allegorists who'd peer
Asquint or upside-down at texts for fear
  Of acting like the hermeneutic bull

In meaning's china-shop. What may have done
  Its share to pile sky-high the wreckage hurled
At the angel's feet, to keep its wings unfurled,
  And give the wind called 'progress' power to stun

Or mesmerise its gaze is what lay curled,
  Like agenbite of inwit, in each one
Of those choice texts whose eisogetes had spun
  Around them such an intertextual world

Of gloss and commentary that nothing seemed
  Revision-proof enough to stand against
The blitz of meaning-fragments that commenced
  Its sense-unravelling work each time they dreamed

Of some transcendent vision that dispensed
  With modes of discourse so obliquely themed
As further to fragment the mass that streamed
  From paradise. So if he finds condensed

In Klee's *unheimlich* angel such a deal
  Of pent significance, perhaps that's less
Because the thing has such power to compress
  Multum in parvo, but in hopes that he'll

Have some small chance to parlay the distress
    That comes of knowing this *Glasperlenspiel*
A game forever lost with no appeal
    To any saving vision that might bless

Us finally by showing how the storm
    Of progress must at some point cease to rage
Or, by some very marvel of backstage
    Plot-fixing, grant intelligible form

To the mere piling-up of age-on-age
    Calamities that constitutes the norm
As viewed from any place within the swarm
    Of tempest-driven debris. Let us gauge

How deep it was, that allegory that held
    Him fascinated like the death's-head tropes
Of *Trauerspiel*, by seeing how he copes
    Not only with such life-events as spelled

Defeat for all his dearest private hopes
    But also with the history that compelled
His angel to a *Rückwärtsblick* that quelled
    Even the flickering faith of one who gropes

For long-range consolation. What he shared
    With the skull-gazers whose unhinged pursuit
Of vengeance left them and their victims mute,
    By the last act, to say why we'd been spared

No devilish atrocity *en route*
    To that denouement is the thought that there'd
Be something fake about a plot that squared
    With just desert or turned out to commute

Our final verdict on the bloody farce
    To a more meaningful since tragic sort
Of moral uplift. Though this might comport
    More readily with sentiments that pass

For truly human it would so distort
    The moribund revenger's *coup de grâce*
That we'd have just a Beckett-type impasse
    Of failed apocalypse that fell far short

Of such redemptive power. The angel's curse,
    It then appears, is that which figures all
Our lives and histories as one long-haul
    Deluded odyssey from bad to worse,

A message more than likely to appal
    Those thinkers temperamentally averse
To such gloom-mongering but which some rehearse,
    As if apotropaically, to stall

Catastrophe and turn the thing around
    At last. Then a few fragments might be snatched
From chaos and, by patient sifting, matched
    With a few others so as to propound

A view of things not too securely latched
    To hope's rickety wagon nor yet bound,
By gloomy predilection, to confound
    All thoughts of progress with a doctrine hatched

By *Kulturpessimismus* from the wreck
    Of the old Europe Pound once called 'a bitch
Gone in the teeth'. So if he chose to ditch
    Its cherished values as not up to spec

And, at the Spanish frontier, unhitch
    His own life-burdened wagon where the trek
Ran into one last fatal border-check,
    Then it's Klee's mute apocalypse to which

We dwellers in the aftermath had best
    Direct our not too sharply focused gaze
If we're to grasp why such communiqués
    As his and Benjamin's are not addressed

To expert eyes well practised in the ways
    Of eisogesis but to those unblessed
With any special skill save that expressed
    By everything about it that betrays

The angel's having nothing to impart
    Like news of virgin births or other themes
In arch-seraphic style. Rather than streams
    Of light celestial tricked out by art

Into some true epiphany that seems
    To find its way to every viewer's heart,
Klee simply says: no vision here apart
    From an angel-shaped thing that neither screams,

Like Munch's shocker, nor assumes a look
    Of rapture whether sacred or profane,
Nor, like a Buddha-face, seems to contain
    All these brave opposites since it can brook

Their discord undisturbed. More it's the plain
    Uncomprehending blankness that so shook
Klee's expert draughtsmanship and left the book
    Of life, for Benjamin, a text-domain

Where allegory contrived to cock a snook
    At any symbol-seer who hoped to gain
Such insight as the angel sought in vain
    Through every tropic twist the storm-path took.

Notes

p. 147: 'Whether they take the Brechtian line'. Commentaries on
Benjamin tend to divide – as did his own thinking – between a
Marxist-oriented and strongly Brecht-influenced political emphasis
and the quasi-scriptural, mystically inclined exegesis of texts in
which Benjamin was encouraged by his friend Gershom Scholem.

p. 148: 'weakly messianic'. Refers to the kind of speculative thinking proposed by Benjamin, and more recently by Jacques Derrida, which adopts a certain eschatological (even quasi-prophetic) standpoint and tone while avoiding anything more explicit in the way of doctrinal commitment.

p. 148: '"correspond"/Only in Baudelaire's sense'. Reference to the French nineteenth-century poet and his symbolist doctrine of arcane metaphorical, imagistic and mystical correspondences.

p. 150: 'that false idea of homogeneous time'. One of Benjamin's cardinal distinctions was that between a conventional, ideologically inert conception of time – where events occur only as orthodox thinkers (and political victors) perceive them – and a temporal dimension where past events may always 'flash up' under new pressures of circumstance or be rescued from oblivion by the urgency of present revolutionary hopes and desires. This theme is central to his 'Theses on the Philosophy of History'.

p. 153: 'to blast/A hole'. Benjamin writes elsewhere in the 'Theses' about the power of revolutionary thought to blast a hole in the continuum of history, or to explode that 'homogeneous' conception of time that he regards as inherently opposed to revolutionary change.

p. 153: '*contre Sainte-Beuve*/For something like Proust's reasons'. Refers to Marcel Proust's unfinished book of polemical essays attacking the biographical or life-and-works approach to literary texts practised by scholar-critics like Charles Augustin Sainte-Beuve.

p. 154: 'the author's *vouloir-dire*/Or *vie hors-texte*'. Roughly, 'the author's intention and their life outside [or beyond] the text'. Alludes to various well-aired topics of dispute in recent and contemporary literary theory.

p. 154: '*echt*-Heideggerian turn'. Reference to Martin Heidegger's practice of depth-hermeneutic (or depth-ontological) interpretation as applied to poetic and philosophical texts. For political and personal as well as philosophical reasons, the relationship between Heidegger's and Benjamin's thought is fraught with difficulty.

p. 155: '*plumpes Denken*'. 'Rough-and-ready thinking' or 'down-to-earth thought'. A phrase of Brecht, one that clearly appealed to the Marxist-materialist (though not so much the 'other', theologically inclined or Kabbalah-inspired) Benjamin.

p. 155: 'intertextual lemon-squeezers'. T. S. Eliot once took a
gentle potshot at the 'lemon-squeezer' school of criticism, referring
(presumably) to William Empson and his less talented followers.
Many of them happily acknowledged a debt to Eliot's critical
practice, so this may have been a piece of rueful self-directed irony.

p. 156: 'their four-fold method'. The four codes or interpretative
levels of scriptural exegesis in the patristic tradition, namely the
literal, allegorical, moral and anagogical (this latter having to do
with matters of our ultimate destiny or last judgement).

p. 156: 'the magic writing-pad/Of Freud's analogy'. Allusion to
Freud's 'Note on the Mystic Writing-Pad' where he compares the
processes of unconscious repression or sublimation to the trick
device involving multiple layers of wax paper where inscriptions can
apparently be erased by lifting a leaf but are preserved in a latent
state, so to speak, on underlying sheets.

p. 156: 'the language game/That Adam played'. See especially
Benjamin's essay 'On Language As Such and the Languages of Man'.

p. 157: *haeccitas*. Scholastic (medieval philosophical) term for the
unique quality, essence or quiddity of something; whatever makes it
that particular thing and no other.

p. 158: 'the talking cure'. Freud's description of psychoanalysis once
he had (at any rate provisionally) given up on his early hopes that it
would rejoin clinical psychology and neurophysiology on the path
towards a secure science.

p. 159: 'ekphrastic *Uebersetzer*'. *Ekphrasis* = detour from image or
picture into passage of textual or verbal explication; *Uebersetzer* =
translator. Hence – at a stretch – this idea of Benjamin performing
just such an act of ekphrastic translation on Klee's cryptic painting.

p. 160: 'such devious spells as drove Macbeth/To that conclusion.'
See Shakespeare, *Macbeth*, Act V, Scene 5: 'And all our yesterdays
have lighted fools/The way to dusty death'.

p. 161: 'the agenbite of inwit'. Title of fourteenth-century penitential
work meaning 'the prick of remorse' or the 'gnawing of a bad
conscience'.

p. 161: 'eisogetes'. Textual commentators, critics or interpreters who
offer their own, perhaps skewed or idiosyncratic reading of passages
rather than striving – like faithful exegetes – for fidelity to author's
intent or original sense.

p. 161: 'Klee's *unheimlich* angel'. *Unheimlich* = 'uncanny'; the topic of a nowadays celebrated essay by Freud that launches some typically far-reaching speculations about the role of repetition in phenomena or experiences that strike us as somehow spooky or disturbing.

p. 162: *Glasperlenspiel. The Glass Bead Game*; title of novel by Hermann Hesse. This fiction has to do with a future (sort-of) utopia where music enjoys a privileged cultural-political role, but where the masters of 'composition' are secluded in an island-world apart from the rest of humankind. Moreover, their 'creativity' is restricted to the perpetual analysis and re-combination of formulas derived from pre-existing music since it is thought that – after so many works of genius – there can no longer exist the possibility of inventing/discovering new melodies, harmonies or forms.

p. 162: 'the death's-head tropes/Of *Trauerspiel*'. Benjamin's *Habilitationschrift* – his postdoctoral thesis – was an intensely theoretical and speculative work about German seventeenth-century revenge drama. He argued that these plays didn't so much fall short of tragedy as refuse the idea of tragic transcendence through their morbid dwelling on death's-head imagery and other insistent reminders of mortality. There are clear parallels with the English revenge plays of Webster, Tourneur, Middleton, Ford and others in relation to a tragic drama like *Hamlet*.

p. 162: *Rückwärtsblick*. 'rearward gaze', 'backward-fixated stare'.

p. 163: 'apotropaically'. 'as if to ward off some mortal threat by outfacing and hence averting or annulling it'.

p. 163: *Kulturpessimismus*. 'Cultural pessimism'; refers most often to those doctrines of sociocultural decline and ultimate collapse fashionable in the early years of the twentieth century, especially among conservative intellectuals in the Austro-German empire. Despite his in many ways radical-left allegiances Benjamin was by no means immune to such ideas.

p. 163: 'And, at the Spanish frontier, unhitch'. Benjamin committed suicide by poison pill at the Franco-Spanish Pyrenees border-crossing when (perhaps temporarily) refused permission to continue his journey.

p. 164: 'where allegory contrived to cock a snook/At any symbol seer'. Alludes to debates around the rival claims of symbol and allegory, the one a hallowed Romantic trope supposed to give immediate access to transcendent or eternal truths beyond reach of mere prosaic understanding, the other deemed an intrinsically inferior (since time-bound and overly literal) mode of expression. Such was at any rate the mainstream view among Romantic poet-philosophers and pre-1970 academic critics alike. It has, however, come increasingly under challenge from more recent literary theorists often influenced by deconstructive readings of the symbol/allegory distinction like Paul de Man's 'The Rhetoric of Temporality'. Walter Benjamin's work has also been central to these debates and, as will be seen, they have left their mark on my thinking in the present verse-essay.

9

Doors and pictures: Wittgenstein

This poem about the philosopher Ludwig Wittgenstein has its generative source, as regards both topic and rhyme scheme, in the two words 'say' and 'show'. Wittgenstein's early philosophy – as likewise, in a different way, his later thought – turned crucially on that contrast whether pushed in a linguistic, metaphysical, ethical or quasi-mystical direction. My poem reflects on the multiple ironies of his life and work, among them the fact that, so far from 'giving philosophy peace' by getting philosophers to drop all those futile since merely abstract disputes, his writings managed to spawn an academic cult and a full-scale industry of Wittgenstein scholarship and exegesis. It is constructed around that resonant pair of rhyme sounds (say/show), which of course runs the risk of becoming a protracted and rather tedious technical tour de force. However the poem is redeemed, I hope, by conveying a sense of how Wittgenstein deployed his own intellectual and temperamental traits – austere, rigorous, obsessive-compulsive, self-disciplined to the point of self-torment – in some highly creative and idiosyncratic (if philosophically bewilderment-inducing) ways.

It is, I should say, a very far-from-reverential piece that aims to puncture a few of the pomposities that currently surround his work and have allowed some very dodgy or questionable arguments to gain widespread currency. On the other hand it does try to honour what is impressive – even in an odd way exemplary – about Wittgenstein's facing up to his private demons and managing to keep them from doing more in the way of harm to others. Still one can't help wishing that he'd given them a bit less grief and that the Wittgenstein commentariat hadn't so often emulated the worst aspects of his character in their dealing with others and among themselves.

A picture held us captive. And we could not get outside it, for it lay in our language and language seemed to repeat it to us inexorably.

       (LUDWIG WITTGENSTEIN, *Philosophical Investigations*)

A man will be imprisoned in a room with a door that's unlocked and opens inwards; as long as it does not occur to him to pull rather than push it.

       (WITTGENSTEIN, *Culture and Value*)

I think I summed up my attitude to philosophy when I said: philosophy ought really to be written only as a poetic composition.

       (*Culture and Value*)

> He had this thing about what you could say
>   And what you couldn't say but only show.
> To make that point, he thought, the only way
>   Was to push 'say' as far as it would go.
> With that in mind he'd put up an array
>   Of reasonings *more geometrico*,
> Along with a meticulous display
>   Of numbered parts that made it seem as though
> The thing was too well-built to go astray.
>   This would ensure that those chaps in the know,
> Bertie and his lot, had their role to play
>   As dupes in Ludwig's stratagem to blow

A T-shaped hole in everything that they,
   Like his Tractarian double, took as so
Self-evident as strictly to convey
   No more than syllogistic might bestow
By way of sense or content. Yet dismay
   Set in when those same chaps proved far too slow
To take his point, or eager to essay
   Some risk-containment exercise that no
Depth-rumblings might disturb. This helped allay
   Their nagging sense that he'd contrived to stow
Something in his oblique communiqué
   That threatened to upset the status quo
Of language, truth, and logic. Anyway
   They picked it up, the cryptic undertow
In this strange work of Russell's protégé,
   But made sure it was kept so far below
Deck in the first translation as to stay
   Disarmed of any spanners it might throw
Into the works. For there they'd ricochet
   And cause no end of philosophic woe
To Russell and those heralds of the day
   When mystics would repay the debt they owe
To logic. Then they'd see fit to obey
   Such rational demands as bid them toe
No line where superstition's apt to prey
   On trust or faith says reason should forego
Its privilege. Keep saintliness at bay,
   His colleagues thought, lest worldly wit lie low
In deference to it and extend the sway
   Over weak minds of any holy joe
With some new crack-brained gospel to purvey,
   Or any US-style politico
With God on board. That stuff was now *passé*,
   So Russell thought, that Sunday-School tableau
Got up with all the faux-naiveté
   By which the firm of Jesus Christ & Co

Had managed so adroitly to portray
   Their potentate as power's most powerful foe.
Yet this ignored Saint Ludwig's *dieu caché*,
   His hidden god (think Pascal, think Godot),
Whose failure to arrive as promised may,
   To souls elect, reveal the vapid flow
Of saying's intellectual cabaret
   Struck dumb. Thus having nothing *à propos*
To say – and falling silent – might defray
   The cost of all those endless to-and-fro
Discussions spawned, he thought, by the decay
   Of what once found expression (think Rousseau)
In sentiments that showing might relay
   Once all the saying's done. On this plateau
The tribe of *bons sauvages* join Mallarmé
   In savouring only fragrances that blow
From flowers that have their place in no bouquet,
   Or hues that vanish in the gaslight glow
Of rainbows shadowed by the grey-on-grey
   That passes muster in the Savile Row
Of logic-suited thought. The first rule: pay
   No heed to anything we cannot sew,
Us stitchers-up, to standards checked OK
   For sticking to the proper ratio
Of words to thoughts and things lest words outweigh
   Truth's currency and thinking undergo
Such figural bewitchments as betray
   Its old malaise. His message: we should grow
Alert when language 'went on holiday'
   Since here it often held in embryo
All the misshapen progeny that lay
   Athwart the path to thinking's *vrai niveau*
Of common speech. Such were those *recherché*
   Linguistic idioms that he thought *de trop*
Since parasitic on the DNA
   Of communal accord, or the escrow
That underwrote our forms of everyday
   Folk-usage. This he showed us, *modulo*

The need for umpteen exegetes to say
  Just what it was his words were meant to show,
As witness the shelf-bending dossier
  Of monographs and endless *de nouveau*
Renditions of old themes whose overstay
  He'd hoped his *Tractatus* would long ago
Have laid to rest. Last irony: that they,
  His acolytes, should be the ones whom no
Strict rule, like his, against such making hay
  With words and concepts could persuade to throw
The habit off despite its threat to fray
  The bonds of communal accord and so
Permit such verbal licence (aka
  Delinquency) to twist the quid pro quo
That constitutes a true *communauté*
  De langue et vie. His tragedy: to know,
If dimly, that he'd pointed them the way
  And sounded the linguistic tallyho
That led his followers to a disarray
  Of language-games as likely to kayo
That prospect as the mutants on display
  In some linguistic isle where Doc Moreau
Spliced metaphors like genes. And so, *malgré*
  His dearest wish, this anti-Prospero
Saw monstrous life-forms bred out of Roget
  By language-games from his own portmanteau.

Notes

p. 170: *more geometrico*. 'In a geometrical manner'; refers to the
numbered paragraphs, sections and sub-sections of Wittgenstein's early
Tractatus Logico-Philosophicus, no doubt intended – by him as by
Spinoza and other philosophers before him – to establish (or suggest)
a degree of deductive rigour comparable to that of Euclid's *Elements*.

p. 170: 'Bertie and his lot'. Bertrand Russell, Wittgenstein's mentor
and champion during his early years at Cambridge but later on
sharply opposed to the new direction of his thinking.

p. 171: 'T-shaped hole. ... Tractarian double'. Commentators differ on the question how far – or how much of – the *Tractatus* is intended to undermine its own appearance of logical rigour by gesturing towards a transcendent realm of meaning, significance or value. This would have to do with what cannot be said (conveyed by statements or propositions) but only shown (as lying beyond the power of logic or language to articulate).

p. 171: 'far too slow/To take his point'. Russell and C. K. Ogden (its first translator) took the *Tractatus* as basically a version of the logical-positivist doctrine which held that the only genuinely meaningful statements were logical truths and empirically verifiable statements of fact. For them its final few passages – which seemed to undermine that doctrine and turn towards a quasi-mystical idea of revelatory 'showing' – were regrettable but minor aberrations. Nowadays the consensus among commentators is that this gets things completely upside-down and that Russell/Ogden were out of their depth.

p. 171: 'Of language, truth and logic'. Refers to the title of A. J. Ayer's 1936 book popularizing the programme of logical positivism.

p. 171: 'When mystics would repay the debt they owe/To logic'. Alluding to Russell's essay collection *Mysticism and Logic*.

p. 172: 'dieu caché/His hidden god (think Pascal ...'. Refers to the *deus absconditus* of seventeenth-century Jansenist theology and its influence – as argued by Lucien Goldman – on the thinking of Blaise Pascal. This connects with the subsequent allusion to Beckett's forever non-arriving Godot and with Wittgenstein's gesturing towards that which eludes any adequate statement or representation.

p. 172: '(think Rousseau)'. Compares Wittgenstein's 'saying'/'showing' dichotomy to Rousseau's elevation of a conjectural proto-language of feeling above the refinements of 'civilized' (articulate) discourse.

p. 172: 'flowers that have their place in no bouquet'. The phrase comes (modified) from Stéphane Mallarmé's Preface to René Ghil's *Traité du verbe* (*Treatise on the Word*, 1886).

p. 172: *bons sauvages*. 'Good (or noble) savages': refers to Jean-Jacques Rousseau's idealized conception of (so-called) primitive peoples as living in a perfectly natural, pre-'civilized' and therefore as yet uncorrupted state of pre- or proto-social existence.

10

The winnowing fan

'The Winnowing Fan' is a more straightforwardly narrative-thematic piece about Odysseus's wanderings after the main events of Homer's poem and the first homecoming to Ithaca. It was sparked off by a passing reference to the titular phrase – I think in a newspaper article – which sent me to Google and thence to the story of Teiresias's prophecy and the idea of Odysseus travelling further and further until the people he came across were so thoroughly landlocked that they mistook his oar for a harvesting implement. Where the poem touches most directly on issues literary-theoretical is by offering thoughts about genre and the cultural transition from epic with its predominantly martial, masculine and seafaring ethos to georgic (or pastoral) with its strongly – that is, gently – opposed set of values and priorities. The rhyme scheme here is particularly tight, especially towards the end where the intention of all those reiterated rhymes, again, for what it's worth, was not any kind of virtuosic display but a point about the quality of consonance achieved by a life lived in keeping with the latter (georgic and peaceable) rather than the former (epic and warlike) sort of code. The poem also picks up on issues of literary reception-history and reader-response theory though these are more to be glimpsed between the lines. The epigraph from Homer has Odysseus in conversation with Penelope.

I will tell you, hiding nothing, though your heart will gain no pleasure from it, and nor does mine. Teiresias told me to travel through many cities of men, carrying a shapely oar, till I come to a race that knows nothing of the sea, that eat no salt with their food, and have never heard of crimson-painted ships, or the well-shaped oars that serve as wings. And he gave me this as a sign, one I could not miss, and now I tell it you. When I meet another traveller who says that I carry a winnowing-fan on my broad shoulder, there I must plant my shapely oar in the ground, and make rich sacrifice to Lord Poseidon, a ram, a bull, and a breeding-boar. Then leave for home, and make sacred offerings there to the deathless gods who hold the wide heavens, to all of them, and in their due order.

And death will come to me far from the sea, the gentlest of deaths, taking me when I am bowed with comfortable old age, and my people prosperous about me. All this he said would come true.

'If the gods really intend a more pleasant old age for you,' said wise Penelope, 'there is hope this will set an end to all your troubles.'

So they conversed ...

> HOMER, *The Odyssey*, Bk XXIII:247–299,
> trans. A. S. Kline

Just like the last time, and the time before,
    And times as many as the years that ran
Back to the time his wanderings began
    The second time around. He'd kept the score
Since then, the tally that he'd often scan
    Despairingly, of those by whom his oar,
Though pluripotent as a metaphor,
    Was never taken for a winnowing fan.

Teiresias the seer it was, 'old man
    With wrinkled dugs', etc., who thrice swore

That fate would drive Odysseus from the shore
    Of Ithaca again, despite his plan
To quit Penelope's embrace no more
    Throughout the remnant of his mortal span.
No chance, the prophet said, since other than
    Her having been his steadfast guarantor

Of hearth and home, she could impose no ban
    On his fresh-kindled impulse to explore
Way past the bounds of all that heretofore
    Restrained his *Wanderlust*. From frying-pan
To fire, he knew, and something they'd deplore,
    The *nostos*-lovers and their landlocked clan,
But his last chance to stay out in the van
    Of sea-adventurers and not close the door

On other lives and loves. Yet it was not
    Just down to him, this renegade desire
To sail, but what the rules would soon require
    As part of any well-formed epic plot
Once Homer got to work. Although he'd tire
    Of wandering and lament his vagrant lot,
They fixed it that he never quite forgot
    How blind Hermaphrodite could inspire

Yet further odysseys, until the knot
    Of his old love pulled loose. Lest we admire
Too much this seeking-out of perils dire
    In lands unknown, let's just recall that what
First set his curiosity afire
    Was old Teiresias' cryptic parting shot,
The bit that said no X would mark the spot
    Where he could put his oars up and retire

From journeying till eventually he got
    To some place where the natives would enquire

Whether his winnowing-fan were now for hire,
　　Since the gods fixed this season as the slot
For threshing. When he reached that furthest shire
　　He'd know these inland folk cared not a jot
For sailors' tales so long as he could pot
　　Fine grain from chaff and keep the yield entire.

The point was, they'd no use for things that fell
　　Under the heading 'oar' when so defined
As to pick out just objects of the kind
　　'Long paddle, mostly wood, used to propel
Water-borne vehicles'. Though once designed
　　Solely for that, as means to brave the swell
And give the traveller more tales to tell,
　　Now they revealed him strangely more inclined

To see them as proclaiming his farewell
　　To all those yarns he wished to leave behind
As relicts of a distant time and mind.
　　Here we might think him mastered by the spell
Of Dionysus, lately intertwined
　　With winnowing-fans and a new clientele
Mad keen for any psychotropic smell
　　Of Eleusinian mysteries. Resigned

No longer to drop anchor, but to dwell
　　For keeps in this safe haven, he'd the blind
Sooth-sayer now to thank who once divined,
　　Way back, how no port in a storm could quell
His storm-tossed soul. Still we might wish to find
　　Our twice-born hero with a mind to sell
His oar as winnowing-fan, and so dispel
　　The hormone-heavy *mythos* that assigned

The straying male to zones remote while she,
　　Stitched up and stitching, hangs around and waits
For him to call. Agreed, spot-checking dates
　　Seems like the merest piece of pedantry

Compared with everything the hostile fates
    Contrived for his undoing. Yet we'll see
The whole thing in a different light if we
    Switch angles and enquire how that stuff rates

Against a counter-myth that might just be
    The one that most convincingly translates
Into a tale that he and his shipmates
    Would scarcely relish though it held the key
To their deliverance from the rocky straits
    That presaged doom each time they put to sea.
On this at least the oarsmen might agree:
    That just as 'beat your swords to ploughshares' states

A precept kindlier than the harsh decree
    That drove them on, so when this yarn relates
Their oarsmanship to harvest, or equates
    His strong-arm stuff to skilful husbandry,
The truth of what that counter-myth narrates
    Lies in its georgic turn. His epic spree
Might then end up not with Penelope,
    Whose fabled constancy perhaps now grates

On his promiscuous ear, but with him free
    To find his *nostos* far beyond the gates
Of those uncivil realms where war rotates
    From clan to clan in perpetuity.
That scene he now uncertainly locates
    In some half-known, half-dreamed pre-history,
Or some inextricable potpourri
    Of fact and fiction, as his mind conflates

The mythic tales with images that he
    Finds redolent of past-life loves and hates.
And so blind Homer's story-line creates,
    Like blind Teiresias, the narratee
Of this first-person tale who now awaits
    His own denouement or peripety

As one no prophet ventures to foresee
    Or final twist of epic plot dictates

By law of genre. That whole odyssey
    Then seems to him a tale that conjugates
The factual with the fictive and mandates
    No sifting of his true life-history
From what Homeric scholarship notates
    As one part truth to nine mythology,
And therefore not at all the cup of tea
    Of inkhorn types for whom this designates

The grossest kind of impropriety.
    My point is, all these late-born rustic traits
Are of a pastoral kind that elevates
    Him far above his old-time company
Of rabid sea-dogs ravening the baits
    Of treasure, sex, and all the wild whoopee
That came of voyaging. Apostasy
    Of this sort's no bad thing. The tale updates

In ways unknown to that old poetry,
    As new-born georgic gently intimates
How he'd do best to tend his own estates
    And make the most of what long vagrancy
Did to ensure that their coordinates
    Should intersect far from the territory
He once called home. Or, less nostalgically,
    It says: see how Odysseus navigates

With an oar cut from some familiar tree
    Whose strength and suppleness he estimates
By gift of peace-bred skills, and so negates
    Those martial arts their one-time devotee
Set sail to prove. Now the old mood abates,
    That mood of troops waved off from many a quay
By many a cheering crowd when victory
    Abroad meant peace at home between the spates

Of civil strife. So he's no detainee
    In a new land where *physis* regulates
The *nomos*-driven will that else inflates
    To claim all lands as sovereign property.
This then seems fit conclusion: that the greats
    Of our and their blood-chequered history
Are those who get the thing off to a t
    When whittling oars to fan-shape indicates

Not some retreat to mankind's infancy
    Or lotus-eating pastime that sedates
The warrior-spirit, but what correlates
    With every real advance in the degree
Of man's humanity to man. Let potentates,
    Swashbucklers, sea-wolves, and all wannabe
Odysseus-types heed well this allegory
    Of pure nostalgia that no *nostos* sates.

Notes

p. 177: *nostos*. home or homeland.

p. 178: *Eleusian mysteries*. Ancient Greek secret rituals performed every year at Eleusis in the name of Demeter and Persephone.

p. 179: *Narratee*. Term from narrative poetics; technically a named or unnamed character within a frame narrative to whom the story is addressed. Here it is meant to suggest how Odysseus has become both protagonist-narrator of his own tale (as told to Penelope) and one whose role – whose history of wanderings – seems predestined (plotted in advance) by the demands of the epic genre. Muriel Spark did marvellous things with this sort of trick in her novels, the point being (I suppose) that it applies less self-consciously to all fictional characters.

p. 179: *denouement* and *peripety*. Terms from formalist poetics, first introduced by Aristotle; upshot or outcome of a plot, moment of reversal or abrupt change of fortunes.

p. 180: *law of genre*. Alludes pointedly to Jacques Derrida's essay of that title.

p. 181: *physis* and *nomos*. Roughly, Greek for 'nature' or 'natural growth' as opposed to 'law' or 'custom'. The first recorded instance of *physis* (referring to natural growth) is, appropriately enough, in Homer's *Odyssey*. Most likely Dylan Thomas had this etymology somewhere in mind when he wrote 'The force that through the green fuse drives the flower'.

11

Life, love and theory: A chronicle

There follows a sequence of thirteen pieces in villanelle form, or rather – most of them – in extended and modified versions thereof. They have epigraphs from Descartes, Leibniz, Heidegger, Adorno, Benjamin, Lacan, Derrida, Lévinas, Deleuze, Althusser, Agamben, Badiou and de Man leading into poems that are, I suppose, somewhat more 'personal' than other items here but which nevertheless ('emotion recollected in tranquillity') are formally, tonally and thematically pretty remote from any first-person or – perish the thought – confessional mode. The villanelle form is of particular interest in this regard because the tight rhyme scheme and the pattern of insistently repeated refrains have, for many readers, a strongly felt affective impact while clearly involving too much in the way of highly conscious poetic artifice to strike the mindful ear as products of directly passional or lyric inspiration.

For what it's worth, and indulging that favourite eighteenth-century rhetorical figure *zeugma*, these pieces were written in a shortish (five-week) period, a melancholy mood, and emulation of certain very striking successes with the form achieved by W.H. Auden, Elizabeth Bishop, William Empson, Douglas Houston, Sylvia Plath, and Dylan Thomas, among others. It is a lovely form in many ways but apt to have a certain opiate effect on the critical faculties if not supplied with some adequately mind-stretching content. The epigraphs are there to do just that, or – in crudely dualist terms – to give the verse music a running counterpoint of ideas. They are also (I hope) informative enough to justify providing only minimal endnotes.

Descartes

I am indeed amazed when I consider how weak my mind is and how prone to error.

(DESCARTES, *Discourse on the Method*)

It is only prudent never to place complete confidence in that by which we have even once been deceived.

(DESCARTES, *Meditations on First Philosophy*)

It stood to reason, but can reason stand?
    All the best indicators say not so.
One thing's for sure: it will not go as planned.

Time was when good solutions came to hand.
    You searched, and when you found one, you would know.
It stood to reason, but can reason stand?

We fly on instruments but still crash-land.
    They run for cover now who watched below.
One thing's for sure: it will not go as planned.

Margins of error constantly expand
    To show how far off-beam our flights can go.
It stood to reason, but can reason stand?

And you, whose finer instruments once scanned
    My thoughts sky-wide, now track just those that show
One thing's for sure: it will not go as planned.

The gap's too large: Descartes's pineal gland
  Won't help our minds and bodies say hello.
It stood to reason, but can reason stand?
  One thing's for sure: it will not go as planned.

Leibniz

Modal logic: the logic of necessity and possibility.

Modal realism: the view that all possible worlds are real, that is, objectively existent though non-actual. This means that we can have no knowledge or experience of them since the only world that is actual for us is the one that we ourselves inhabit, albeit – from our own epistemic standpoint – one that includes every past, present and future state of the entire cosmos. Thus 'actual' should be treated as a deictic, or as referring – like 'I', 'you', 'here', 'over there', 'yesterday', or 'next year' – to some specific person, place or time of utterance. These were claims first developed in the seventeenth century by Leibniz and currently espoused (in extreme realist form) by David Lewis. Leibniz notoriously held that our actual was the best of all possible worlds since a benevolent God would necessarily ensure that such was the case.

Actualism: modal anti-realism, or the view that reality extends no further than the actual (this-world) cosmological totality of objects, properties, states, attributes, processes, events or whatever. So possible-worlds talk is just that – a convenient way of talking about modal issues but not to be taken as making any reference to objectively existent (though non-actual) realia.

Ersatzers (and *ersatzism*): Lewis's less than flattering term for those philosophers, especially modal logicians, who help themselves liberally to possible-worlds talk but shy away from endorsing its realist entailments for fear of breaking Ockham's rule that entities (here: worlds) not be multiplied unnecessarily. In that case, he argues, they have no entitlement to, for example, causal explanations involving counterfactual-supporting hypotheses ('event x would not have occurred if necessary condition y had not obtained').

(Of course, my poem makes very free and fanciful use of these
ideas, as likewise of terza rima form.)

> I fear the actualists have got it right.
>> They say that possibilia can't be real
> Since might-have-been is simply out of sight.

> *Echt*-realists like Lewis take delight
>> In other worlds the actual may conceal.
> I fear the actualists have got it right.

> I'd love to see those killjoys put to flight,
>> Though as things stand I rather tend to feel
> The might-have-been is simply out of sight.

> Then thinking those worlds real must seem the height
>> Of folly, best lopped off by Ockham's steel.
> I fear the actualists have got it right.

> Count me a would-be realist, despite
>> Their saying 'it's your old Achilles' heel:
> The might-have-been is simply out of sight'.

> Yet when I see them sailing off in tight-
>> Rigged vessels on a perfect even keel,
> I fear the actualists have got it right.

* * * * * * * * * * * * * * *

> What if the actual's hit by such a blight
>> That those nay-sayers get the rawest deal?
> Then might-have-been's lush coastline greets our sight.

> It's this that saves us when the facts are quite
>> Determined they've no blessings to reveal:
> Let's hope the modal realists turn out right.

> They say our counterfactuals should invite
>> A realist spin since, if we use them, we'll
> Have might-have-been's lush coastline greet our sight.

And lest we wavering ersatzers take fright
    When Ockham strops, let's trust to its appeal
And hope the modal realists turn out right.

Modality's what separates the might-
    Be-worlds from actual worlds where facts congeal
Till might-have-been's lush coastline greets our sight.

For those whose actual or whose factual plight
    Is such as other worlds alone may heal,
Let's hope the modal realists turn out right.

* * * * * * * * * * * * * * * * * * * *

The actualist comes back: such thoughts excite
    Only those fantasists who'll make a meal
Of might-have-been although it's out of sight.

His point is, mere good sense begs we indict
    Such waking dreams as so much *blosses Spiel*
Though ersatzers may parse things roughly right.

Still realists insist: why reignite
    Old feuds or reinvent the Ockham-wheel
Just to keep might-have been safe out of sight?

If possibles are real then they shine bright
    On fractured lives their rays might yet anneal,
So let's not say the ersatzers are right.

The question is how thought could reunite
    Those worlds and set a life-redeeming seal
On any might-have-been that's out of sight

Just now, though modal thinking may requite
    The realist's wish and tame the sceptic's zeal
To prove that actualists have got it right.

* * * * * * * * * * * * * * * * * * *

What then if they're the ones who so benight
　　Our firmament that it decrees we kneel
To what's flat obvious or in plain sight?

Let modal realists nowise turn contrite
　　If Ockham's stroppy mood's not what they feel:
Leibniz's God will see things come out right.

He thought pure reason shed sufficient light
　　To show how doubters could be brought to heel
By grasping truths found nowhere in plain sight.

Make him your multiverse-crusading knight
　　Of modals and you'll not seem imbecile
To say the Leibniz doctrine must be right.

Still the thought nags: what if this soaring kite
　　Of possibilities spins off the reel
And vacancy's the one thing in plain sight?

On doldrum days that thought's most apt to smite
　　The modal realist with such doubts as she'll
Then fear not even Leibniz can put right.

That is, unless wanhope requires she bite
　　Off more than ersatzers can chew, and steal
A glimpse of real worlds nowhere in plain sight
　　Yet such as *a priori* prove him right.

Heidegger

'What was Aristotle's life?' Well, the answer lay in a single sentence: 'He was born, he thought, he died.' And all the rest is pure anecdote.

Now the German people are in the process of rediscovering their own essence and making themselves worthy of their

great destiny. Adolf Hitler, our great Führer, created ... a
new state by which the people will assure itself anew of the
duration and continuity of its history.

(MARTIN HEIDEGGER)

Quite simply, 'He was born, he thought, he died'.
    These facts, you said, suffice to tell the tale.
All else is idle talk, best set aside.

Birth-dates and death-dates: these can be supplied,
    Though thought alone sets out on Being's trail.
Quite simply, 'He was born, he thought, he died'.

Such is thought's piety, so woe betide
    Those whom it summons but to no avail.
All else is idle talk, best set aside.

They take your *Daseinsfrage* as their guide
    To truth although its rudiments entail,
Quite simply, 'He was born, he thought, he died'.

Should we enquire just how the rule applied
    In your case, Herr Professor, we should fail
And fall to idle talk, best set aside

Since then we'd ask – for instance – why you tried
    To cover Nazi thought-tracks so that they'll
Show simply 'he was born, he thought, he died'.

Let's rather say the question's bona-fide
    Although addressed to you by surface mail
And rated 'idle talk, best set aside'.

For while the factual-everyday may hide
    Deep truths, yet deep-truth talk may serve to veil
All facts save 'he was born, he thought, he died'
    As yet more idle talk, best set aside.

Adorno

If negative dialectics calls for the self-reflection of thinking,
the tangible implication is that if thinking is to be true –
if it is to be true today, in any case – it must also be a
thinking against itself.

(THEODOR ADORNO, *Negative Dialectics*)

He who has loved and who betrays love does harm not
only to the image of the past, but to the past itself.

(ADORNO, *Minima Moralia*)

He who integrates is lost.

(*Minima Moralia*)

Particulars alone should rivet thought.
    Let's have no concept cast its abstract spell.
By each catastrophe the lesson's taught.

Maybe it helps us get from is to ought,
    Sets value free of its fact-hardened shell:
Particulars alone should rivet thought.

This pleads that haecceitas not go for naught,
    No scheme of things its vibrant thinghood quell.
By each catastrophe the lesson's taught.

All history shows that lesson dearly bought
    When heavenly concepts conjured earthly hell.
Particulars alone should rivet thought.

So it was on negation's side he fought
    For space where exiled intellect might dwell.
By each catastrophe the lesson's taught.

Forgive me if I cut this discourse short
    Since it's already bid that rule farewell:
Particulars alone should rivet thought.

One gift of yours was helping me to thwart
   Such thoughts of you as habit might compel.
By each catastrophe the lesson's taught.

To my conceptions came your swift retort,
   Some gesture more exact than words could tell.
Particulars alone should rivet thought.

And now you're gone how should I not resort
   To *idées fixes* at which you'd soon rebel?
By each catastrophe the lesson's taught.
   Particulars alone should rivet thought.

Benjamin

(This poem has to do with Walter Benjamin's cryptic yet lapidary 'Theses on the Philosophy of History', and more specifically with the section from it that discusses Paul Klee's painting 'Angelus Novus'. For the full text of this passage, see my epigraph to 'A Plain Man Looks at the Angel of History', p. 127 here.)

Face backward where the wreckage piles sky-high.
   That storm's called 'progress', so his *Theses* said.
Unfold your wings, but do not think to fly.

No use now for your expert weather-eye,
   Nor for your flying skills: you'd best instead
Face backward where the wreckage piles sky-high.

There's too much debris cluttering the sky,
   Along with parts by other angels shed.
Unfold your wings, but do not think to fly.

No second thoughts: however hard you try
   To fold them down the gale keeps them outspread.
Face backward where the wreckage piles sky-high.

He says it blows from paradise, but I
    Think that's from some Kabbalah-text he read.
Unfold your wings, but do not think to fly.

No point postdating when things went awry
    Though that's the kind of myth we're always fed.
Face backward where the wreckage piles sky-high.

On every scale this lesson must apply:
    Be not by thoughts of Eden so misled;
Unfold your wings, but do not think to fly.

Paradise lost is our stock alibi;
    It's putting dates to break-ups that we dread.
Face backward where the wreckage piles sky-high.

No primal bliss, nor reason to ask why.
    Back then catastrophe lay far ahead.
Unfold your wings, but do not think to fly.

The storm's still raging, that we can't deny.
    Through wings it whistles fit to wake the dead.
Face backward where the wreckage piles sky-high.

No way our breaking-up can justify
    This stretch of his fine parabolic thread:
Unfold your wings, but do not think to fly.

Applaud the exegetes when they decry
    My lacking their angelic fear to tread:
Face backward where the wreckage piles sky-high.

Still you alone might see the point of my
    Attempting such dissimilars to wed.
Unfold your wings, but do not think to fly.

Some hope things might make sense before we die
    Is why these tales are here thus interbred.
Face backward where the wreckage piles sky-high;
    Unfold your wings, but do not think to fly.

Lacan

In man, there's already a crack, a profound perturbation
of the regulation of life. That's the importance of the death
instinct. ... [Freud] was forced to introduce it so as to
remind us of a salient fact of his experience just when it
was beginning to get lost.

Here there's a radical difference between my non-
satisfaction and the supposed satisfaction of the other.
There is no image of identity, of reflexivity, but a relation
of fundamental alterity.

JACQUES LACAN, *Seminar* II (1954–5)

'There id shall be', is how the message goes.
    Read Rimbaud ('j'est un autre') and concede:
Id knows the gaps in all that ego knows.

Theorists depend on Lacan to disclose
    This truth though, if it's true, then what's the need?
'There id shall be', is how the message goes.

'I' may propose, but signifiers dispose.
    The rule brooks no exception, since indeed
Id knows the gaps in all that ego knows.

Our gaps grow ever wider, and it shows.
    Your silences are what I most should heed.
'There id shall be', is how the message goes.

Our case is not so hard to diagnose
    Since Freud and Lacan taught us how to read.
Id knows the gaps in all that ego knows.

Quite simply, it's the problem that arose
    When Descartes pushed his ego-sponsored creed.
'There id shall be', is how the message goes.

What's lost when poetry's reduced to prose
   Is crucial here, both masters seem agreed.
Id knows the gaps in all that ego knows.

For it's in poetry that language slows
   The rush to sense and non-sense takes a lead.
'There id shall be', is how the message goes.

So listen well, and with most care to those
   Whose words mere sense-propriety exceed:
Id knows the gaps in all that ego knows.

Still gaps are gaps and this is one that throws
   Us way off-course, no *nostos* guaranteed.
'There id shall be', is how the message goes.

Which hurts the more, to think that ego chose
   The break-up or that it's what id decreed?
Id knows the gaps in all that ego knows.

Though id-pressed ego begs we not foreclose
   The case its voice sounds scarcely fit to plead.
'There id shall be', is how the message goes.

The iceberg's tip may show yet still it froze;
   How should lost warmth the permafrost impede?
Id knows the gaps in all that ego knows.

Should some small part unfreeze then this it owes
   To what's by lethal climate-change now freed.
'There id shall be', is how the message goes.
   Id knows the gaps in all that ego knows.

Derrida

Prickly with spines, vulnerable and dangerous, calculating
and ill-adapted (because it makes itself into a ball, sensing
the danger on the autoroute, it exposes itself to an

accident). No poem without accident, no poem that does
not open itself like a wound, but no poem that is not also
just as wounding.

JACQUES DERRIDA, 'Che cos'è la poesia?' ('What is poetry?')

Each time headlights approach I curl up tight.
    The roar of tyres crescendos, then recedes.
So I outlive your road-kill night by night.

My spines do splendid service in a fight
    With any animal that wounds and bleeds,
But when the lights approach I curl up tight.

See here: my spines still bristle though the sight,
    Mid-carriageway, is one no driver heeds.
Yet I outlive your road-kill night by night.

You tossed me from the verge; for you I write
    This hedgehog-poem as you judge their speeds
So that when lights approach I curl up tight.

Let's not pretend you don't enjoy my plight
    Out here where every near-miss surely pleads
I might outlive your road-kill night by night.

Should not such fluke longevity invite
    Some greater care for my survival needs?
Yet still when lights approach I curl up tight.

Now they pass inches from me left and right
    Where every speeding vehicle exceeds
The law. Outlive your road-kill night by night
    I shall, but lights approach: I curl up tight.

Lévinas

The Other, whose exceptional presence is inscribed in
the ethical impossibility of killing him, marks the end

of powers. If I can no longer have power over him it is
because he overflows absolutely every *idea* I can have of
him.

The calling in question of the I, coextensive with the
manifestation of the Other in the face, we call language.
... This voice coming from another shore teaches
transcendence itself.

   EMMANUEL LÉVINAS, *Totality and Infinity*, trans. A. Lingis

An alter ego's what the Other meant.
     'Tout autre est tout autre' can't be true.
Sheer Otherness would be a non-event.

Let's then resist the segregating bent
     That bids the *moi haïssable* shrink from you.
An alter ego's what the other meant.

I'd say it's too much otherness that went
     To knock our fragile likenesses askew.
Sheer Otherness would be a non-event.

Though sometimes its reserves were overspent,
     Still it's the empathy that got us through.
An alter ego's what the other meant.

What room for ethics if the dictate's sent
     Each time by who-knows-whom to who-knows-who?
Sheer Otherness would be a non-event.

Despite the Lévinasians intent
     On letting no first-person spoil their view
An alter ego's what the other meant.

Truth is, those over-ready to accent
     Alterity give no event its due:
Sheer Otherness would be a non-event.

The law their tablets stonily present
     Is apt to give mere humans little clue
An alter ego's what the other meant.

Recall how it was growing discontent
  Brought otherness, not egos we outgrew.
Sheer Otherness would be a non-event.

Real happenings spring from all that's different
  When one plus one's both more and less than two.
An alter ego's what the other meant.

Past tense, you'll note, since everything that lent
  That status once now ceases to accrue.
Sheer Otherness would be a non-event.

Alterity showed change was imminent
  And warned those old self-comforts wouldn't do:
'An alter ego's what the other meant';
  'Sheer Otherness would be a non-event'.

Althusser

The individual is interpellated as a (free) subject in order
that he shall (freely) accept his subjection, i.e., make the
gestures and actions of his subjection 'all by himself'.

(LOUIS ALTHUSSER, 'Ideology and Ideological State
Apparatuses')

Marx was constrained to think within a horizon torn
between the aleatory of the Encounter and the necessity of
the revolution.

(LOUIS ALTHUSSER, 'Philosophy of the Encounter')

A tendency can bifurcate under the impact of an encounter
with another tendency, ... take a path that is unforeseeable
because it is aleatory. (ibid.)

On that night in 1980, possibly as the result of drugs,
mania or even sleepwalking, Althusser massaged Helene's
neck to the point of asphyxiation. Two victims followed –
the dead woman herself and Althusser's theories, fatally

wounded and useless in his subsequent attempt to make
sense of his monstrous experience.

(STEVE WATERS in *The New Statesman*)

It seemed those swerving atoms held the key.
    No theory has a chance once chance takes hold.
Truth speaks, but who's to tell the addressee?

It's by their clinamen alone that we
    Might slip from ideology's tight mold.
It seemed those swerving atoms held the key.

Time was when, by his structuralist decree,
    We stood to it as subjects pre-enrolled.
Truth speaks, but who's to tell the addressee?

Ay, there's the rub: the more you think you're free,
    The more your every thought is thought-controlled.
It seemed those swerving atoms held the key.

One lurch from normal and you're all at sea,
    Misled by some fine theory you've been sold.
Truth speaks, but who's to tell the addressee?

Back then his concepts seemed a guarantee
    Of truth itself, but now they left him cold.
It seemed those swerving atoms held the key.

Sage Epicurus got it right when he
    Gave chance the lead in letting things unfold.
Truth speaks, but who's to tell the addressee?

That's why, post-Plan A, there was no Plan B:
    Too many chance occurrences, all told.
It seemed those swerving atoms held the key.

Too late to *épater* the bourgeoisie
    With concepts scientifically patrolled.
Truth speaks, but who's to tell the addressee?

What if, perchance, the theorist's *parti pris*
    For proving falsehood proved itself fool's gold?
It seemed those swerving atoms held the key.

Maybe their chance collisions meant that she,
    His partner-victim, had no cause to scold:
Truth speaks, but who's to tell the addressee?

The judge and shrinks all questioned his i.d.:
    Get sane, quit theorizing, they cajoled.
It seemed those swerving atoms held the key.

Perhaps his thought was: aleatory
    Events brought hell to pass; now I'm paroled
Truth speaks, but who's to tell the addressee?

So much hinged on the chance trajectory
    Envisaged by the atomists of old.
It seemed those swerving atoms held the key.

Best put the word out now to all would-be
    Materialists, lest theory grow too bold:
Truth speaks, but who's to tell the addressee?

On this at any rate they might agree:
    That chance alone lets matter seem ensouled.
It seems those swerving atoms held the key.

Two thoughts he may have plucked from the debris
    Of ravaged life, two fragments that consoled.
Truth speaks, but who's to tell the addressee?
    It seems those swerving atoms held the key.

Deleuze

We're tired of trees. We should stop believing in trees,
roots, and radicles. They've made us suffer too much. All

of arborescent culture is founded on them, from biology to
linguistics. Nothing is beautiful or loving or political aside
from underground stems and aerial root, adventitious
growths and rhizomes.

GILLES DELEUZE, *A Thousand Plateaus: Capitalism and
Schizophrenia*

How should the rhizomes not destroy the trees?
   Their growth is rank, it spreads from root to root.
What once stood strong must perish by degrees.

They blame it on some airborne bark disease,
   Those experts, but their figures don't compute:
How should the rhizomes not destroy the trees?

At times like this I feel the rhizomes squeeze
   More tightly lest our branches yield good fruit.
What once stood strong must perish by degrees.

Come Winter they'll survive the sharpest freeze
   Deep down but up above kill each new shoot.
How should the rhizomes not destroy the trees?

Let's grant, trees rot; yet nothing guarantees
   Their death until root-sickness grows acute.
What once stood strong must perish by degrees.

Such, then, the grim prognosis we reprise
   Each time some new root crisis strikes us mute:
How should the rhizomes not destroy the trees?

Time was when careful tending might appease
   The threat, but now they find no cure to suit.
What once stood strong must perish by degrees.

The arborologists say 'time to seize
   Our chance', but still they leave the question moot:
How should the rhizomes not destroy the trees?

Truth is, the rhizome-network's one that she's
   Entangled with, like me, their forced recruit.
What once stood strong must perish by degrees.

If both of us are now part-time trainees
   With rhizome's army, what's there to dispute?
How should the rhizomes not destroy the trees?

At least we'll then do nothing to displease
   Those who make trees their evil absolute.
What once stood strong must perish by degrees.

Best treat us two as shell-shocked refugees
   Shot up at every crossing-point *en route*.
How should the rhizomes not destroy the trees?

Or maybe their assault will help us tease
   Out finally which maxim's more astute,
'What once stood strong must perish by degrees',

Or its brave opposite? You're one who sees
   To what new depth their pathogens pollute:
How should the rhizomes not destroy the trees?

And our dead branches shredding in the breeze
   Yield one hard truth Deleuzeans can't refute.
What once stood strong must perish by degrees
   As rhizomes tangle roots of words, thoughts, trees.'

Agamben

If poetry is defined precisely by the possibility of enjambment,
it follows that the last verse of a poem is not a verse.

'... as if the poem as a formal structure could not and
would not end ...'

GIORGIO AGAMBEN, *The End of the Poem*

The endings of the last verses are most beautiful if they fall
into silence together with rhymes.

DANTE, 'On Eloquence in the Vernacular'

Verse-closure throws the whole thing out of gear.
    With tensions unresolved it stays alive.
Signs of convergence mean the end is near.

Unrest's endemic to the poem's sphere.
    When meter vies with syntax, then they thrive;
Verse-closure throws the whole thing out of gear.

If metric skill's enabled us to steer
    A crash-free course, still soon we'll take a dive.
Signs of convergence mean the end is near.

Caesura and enjambement make it clear
    These things are poems, till last lines arrive.
Verse-closure throws the whole thing out of gear.

That's why, when synchronicities appear,
    A dying fall's what poets must contrive:
Signs of convergence mean the end is near.

And so it is with us when first we hear
    Our cadences too perfectly connive:
Verse-closure throws the whole thing out of gear.

If only our two beats would interfere
    We might some quick-fix counterpoint derive:
Signs of convergence mean the end is near.

As poetry declines to prose, so we're
    Flat-liners no caesura can revive:
Verse-closure throws the whole thing out of gear.

All that we know of this we know by ear
    As accents lose their negentropic drive.
Signs of convergence mean the end is near.

Syntax and meter finally cohere
  Though prosody requires they strain and rive.
Verse-closure throws the whole thing out of gear.

All options fail and yet we persevere
  With forms that still for Dante's blessing strive.
Signs of convergence mean the end is near.
  Verse-closure throws the whole thing out of gear.

Badiou

A truth is always that which makes a hole in knowledge.

(ALAIN BADIOU, *Being and Event*)

Love can only consist in failure on the fallacious assumption
that it is a relationship. But it is not. It is a production of truth.

(BADIOU, *Conditions*)

All resistance is a rupture with what is. And every rupture
begins, for those engaged in it, through a rupture with oneself.

(BADIOU, *Metapolitics*)

Where truth meets knowledge, it's to punch a hole.
  We thought we knew for sure but new truths say
All knowledge comes to play a walk-on role.

Old bits of it pile up: just take a stroll
  Down science lane and relish the display.
Where truth meets knowledge, it's to punch a hole.

Knights of the known look splendid on patrol
  Till the giants Doubt and Error block their way.
All knowledge comes to play a walk-on role.

Some think that growth in wisdom should console
  For knowing less, yet still these words dismay:
Where truth meets knowledge, it's to punch a hole.

I steered by you like my magnetic pole
    For years on end, but it led me astray.
All knowledge comes to play a walk-on role.

Each theory falsified exacts its toll;
    Each time we up sticks there's a price to pay.
Where truth meets knowledge, it's to punch a hole.
    All knowledge comes to play a walk-on role.

Paul de Man

Verba volant, scripta manent (spoken words fly off,
written words remain).

(attr. CAIUS TITUS, Roman senator)

Prior to any generalization about literature, literary texts
have to be read, and the possibility of reading can never be
taken for granted.

(PAUL DE MAN, *Blindness and Insight*)

By calling the subject a text, the text calls itself, to some
extent, a subject. The lie is raised to a new figural power,
but it is nonetheless a lie.

(PAUL DE MAN, *Allegories of Reading*)

Why is it that the furthest-reaching truths about ourselves
and the world have to be stated in such a lopsided,
referentially indirect mode?

(DE MAN, *Aesthetic Ideology*)

When it was learned, after de Man's death, that he had
written during the war for two Belgian newspapers
controlled by the Nazis more was at stake than the
reputation of a deceased academic. Two former students of
de Man's ... spread the news among the de Manians, all of
whom were stunned.

(LOUIS MENAND, *The New Yorker*)

Speech-acts take wing but written words constrain.
   No exit-clause from text-commitments made.
Regret comes late and eats our words in vain.

No question but those things I wrote contain
   Some passages where better judgment strayed.
Speech-acts take wing but written words constrain.

From now on I must read against the grain
   And deconstruct what *vouloir-dire* conveyed.
Regret comes late and eats our words in vain.

Changed circumstance is every writer's bane
   Whose perlocutions leave them self-betrayed.
Speech-acts take wing but written words constrain.

They'll say: the gist comes through, the meaning's plain,
   So why not call this textual spade a spade?
Regret comes late and eats our words in vain.

Good sense would plainly counsel us abstain
   From texts that might not make the moral grade:
Speech-acts take wing but written words constrain.

They said: let's have no more of those arcane
   Text-games, your deconstructive stock-in-trade.
Regret comes late and eats our words in vain.

God knows it's true: I managed once to feign
   A second marriage-vow that law forbade.
Speech-acts take wing but written words constrain.

If that's the case, then better we refrain
   From writings whose denouement's long delayed.
Regret comes late and eats our words in vain.

And yet, that premise granted, how explain
   My later texts, the difference they made?
Speech-acts take wing but written words constrain.

My answer was: let language take the strain,
   Use its persuasive arts to unpersuade.
Regret comes late and eats our words in vain.

I might have wiped the record clean again
   If only certain scenes could be replayed.
Speech-acts take wing but written words constrain.

It seems there must have been some close-linked chain
   Of truths no subtle reading could evade.
Regret comes late and eats our words in vain.

Then all my cunning in the text-domain
   Might be by some plain truth of things outweighed.
Speech-acts take wing but written words constrain.

Still my texts hold some lessons you might deign
   To learn once truth-talk grows a touch clichéd.
Regret comes late and eats our words in vain.

Read closely, then you'll see how I arraign
   Myself along with the naïve brigade.
Speech-acts take wing but written words constrain.

It's to my errant past they appertain,
   Those readings sharp as Ockham's lethal blade.
Regret comes late and eats our words in vain.

If, then, I seem to say 'Just engage brain
   Before you write', it's my rash hand that's stayed.
Speech-acts take wing but written words constrain.

Pay heed to this precautionary campaign
   By one on whom false certitudes once preyed.
Regret comes late and eats our words in vain.

For only if truth's advocates re-train
   In error's ways can truth's debts be repaid.
Speech-acts take wing but written words constrain;
   Regret comes late and eats our words in vain.

Notes

p. 187: *blosses Spiel.* German 'mere game'; here signifying 'idle word-play', 'empty verbiage'.

p. 189: *Daseinsfrage.* Literally 'being-there question'; Martin Heidegger's idiosyncratic coinage intended to convey a more profound questioning of existential concerns than anything expressible in the inherited language of humanism or 'Western metaphysics'.

p. 190: *haeccitas.* Medieval scholastic-philosophical term meaning 'thisness'; the distinctive or uniquely identifying set of features that characterize some particular object.

p. 196 *moi haïssable.* 'Le moi est haissable': 'the "me" is hateful'; one of the *Pensées* of Blaise Pascal, the French seventeenth-century philosopher, mathematician and speculative thinker.

p. 198: *to épater the bourgeoisie.* 'To shock (or scandalise) the middle classes'.

p. 199: *parti pris.* A foregone bias, partiality or prejudice, for or against, that is apt to influence judgement for the worse.

12

Performatives
(Yeats/Heaney)

This is another verse-essay concerned, like 'Ectopiques', with issues of politics, action, violence and the grimly ironic twists of outcome or consequence that are liable to wait upon commitments undertaken in ignorance of what changing circumstance may do to thwart our original aims and intentions. In other words, it has to do with just those unpredictable factors that Sartre, in the *Critique of Dialectical Reason*, so vividly evoked through his concepts of 'counter-finality', the 'practico-inert' and the 'coefficient of adversity' that confront our various projects, individual or collective, as soon as they encounter a stubbornly non-compliant world. More specifically, I broach that theme via philosophy of language (speech-act theory and the question: what becomes of performative commitments in poetry?) along with two short epigraphs – from poems by Yeats and Seamus Heaney – which struck me as between them raising some exceptionally sharp and challenging issues in that regard.

I will arise and go now,
    And go to Innisfree...

(W. B. YEATS)

Some day I will go to Arhus
    To see his peat-brown head...

(SEAMUS HEANEY)

Lake isle or peat-bog? One the sort of place
　　You'd want to visit once you'd made the pledge,
The other more the sort you'd go to face

Whatever demons drove you to the edge
　　Of some brute reckoning or dread surmise
Worse than the worst you'd ever hope to dredge

Up from the blood-choked seam that underlies
　　Our thin civilities. Let's think that Yeats
Fared forth as prophesied ('I will arise

And go now'), since mere honesty dictates
　　The words should have some future-binding force
Beyond the test of euphony that rates

Word-music of that Yeatsian strain the source
　　Of such deep truths as poetry conveys
By redirecting language from the course

Of dull quotidian sense to what obeys
　　A higher law. Still, if he then arose
And went, his heading off at least displays

A decent understanding of what goes
　　With what if promises and other kinds
Of speech-act in a poem still impose

Some illocutionary force that binds
　　The utterer straightforwardly to mean,
Intend, or purpose just the act that minds

More literal ascribe to the routines
　　Of common usage. Granted, some are junked
Or relegated to the might-have-beens

Of good intent derailed, or will defunct,
　　Or else (more often) speech-acts reconstrued
In consequence of some big test we've flunked

The first time round and so completely screwed
    Things up that our last hope's to redefine
What sets the pass-mark so as to exclude

All chance that the examiners assign
    A second test by which our efforts fail
To make the grade. Truth is, you might incline

Or disincline to think that Yeats set sail
    For his fair lake-isle since the mythic spot,
Like the verse-music, works so to regale

Our fancy that we tend to lose the plot
    Commitment-wise, or simply to forget,
While swept along, that finally there's not

So much to choose between the way we let
    That music work its charms on us, and how
We make our peace with challenges unmet

In ways that self-forgivingly allow
    A generous reckoning with the fact that we're
Just transient dwellers in the here-and-now,

And therefore not so much to blame if mere
    Post-facto change of circumstance or mood
Be cited to account for acts that veer

Far wide of first intent. These might include
    (Just might, since we're encouraged not to dwell
Too much on this) what factually ensued

When need for travel-planning broke the spell
    Of that impassioned vow and let him weigh
The risk his boat might capsize in a swell

Against the risk that, should he long delay
    The visit, or decide to call it off,
Then local gossip might at length betray

The tale to some grant-hungry US prof
　　So that it did the academic rounds
And gave the cynics ample room to scoff

At how that old-school rhetoric rebounds
　　On its past master. Not at all his style,
Our second mental voyager, who sounds

A note unheard on Yeats' enchanted isle
　　Since here the trip in prospect offered none
Of those fine consolations that beguile

The dreams or idle fantasies of one
　　In whom the *Wanderlust* might well be laid
To rest once the poetic work was done.

That is, the trick was simply to persuade
　　Poet and reader that the sorts of act
Most vital here were speech-acts that gainsaid

All trivial concern with truths of fact
　　Or questions such as: Did he make the trip?,
And opted rather for the mutual pact

That made it easier for both to skip
　　Such tedious inquisitions for the sake
Of prising loose brute fact's tenacious grip

And thereby giving poets room to take
　　Whatever liberties their muse required
By way of mock-performatives that break

Those humdrum rules. No so what later fired
　　The travel-yearning of a poet bred
In times less grand-heroic that conspired

With his own sense of all those mighty dead,
　　Like Yeats, whose power to move he held in awe
Yet resolutely kept at bay for dread

That any word of his should help to draw
     Whole cartloads of fresh victims to the shrine
Of some blood-boltered goddess. Whence the law

That, then as now, said killing should define
     The tribe's true lineage or placate its gods,
And so decree no end to the malign

Enchantment that impelled the restless squads
     Of killers to take out 'the cap, the noose
And girdle' without reckoning the odds

That some day they or theirs would reproduce
     The scene with roles reversed. That's why he makes
No song and dance about it: though Aarhus

Is where he means to go, this time the stakes
     Are pitched much lower, like a flattened note,
To signify that even if he takes

Time off to make the trip just as he wrote
     In promissory mode, still those words lack
The force of perlocution to promote

The word-turned-deed. Else they might point us back
     To atavistic killing-rites that link
With headline news, and so demand we track

The old blood-craving through that merest blink
     Of hindsight suturing the gap between
Ourselves and everything we choose to think

Primeval, savage, brutish, or obscene.
     So dig a few feet down and what's revealed
Is the same sanguinary truth that's been

So long if intermittently concealed
     By all our fine contrivances to keep
The peat-bog victims in the killing field

So that they won't disturb the restful sleep
    Of us fine specimens whose self-esteem
Depends on letting no such image creep

Into the depthless mindscape of our dream.
    This leaves room for returns of the repressed,
But only on condition they should seem

Just like-ourselves enough to pass the test
    Of human motivation by our own
More civilized criteria or best

Idea of what should fall within the zone
    Of claims to shared humanity, and what
Can't by the utmost mental stretch be known

In that empathic way since simply not
    Us-like enough to count as having started
On the long up-hill trek whose master-plot

Of *Geist* and its *Geschichte* Hegel charted.
    So we enjoy the moral alibi
Of having out-evolved and far outsmarted

The ancient savagery of eye-for-eye,
    Or (worse) the even more contagious kind
Of pure mimetic violence that we try

To thrust down deep beneath what comes to mind
    By digging since it's apt to skew the aims
Of Hegel's progeny and those inclined

To lend an ear to such uplifting claims.
    That's why his poem finds no need to flout
The speech-act rules, and why its music shames

Our chronic inability to doubt
    Those well-intentioned narratives whose gist
Concerns how not to rub our tribal snout

In the harsh truth that one big thing we've missed
    From this self-favouring vantage-point is just
The thing that, if we'd hope to coexist

Henceforth on half-way civil terms, we must
    Take well on board. It tells us there's not much
To choose between that peatbog victim trussed

In cap, noose, girdle suffering the clutch
    Of ritual strangulation and the sorts
Of violence that at any time may touch

The lives of all alike. This then comports
    Quite nicely with the paramount *donée*
Of modernist poetics that exhorts

The poet not to let clock-time betray
    Their vision but keep all times in review
By treating them as if *sub specie*

Aeternitatis. Let them then eschew
    The comfort-zone of factual guarantees
And have a better chance of staying true

To an elect vocation that decrees
    They spurn such vulgar truths-of-fact as chance
Just happens to throw up, but rather seize

Those truths that rise above mere circumstance
    And make a mockery of what the slave
To *vie quotidienne* stoops to advance

As his sole *verité*. Still we should save
    Some plaudits for those others of a less
Prophetic turn of mind who think that they've

Their work cut out just trying to redress
    Some small part of the ancient wrong that weighed
On every word and syllable whose stress

Fell in with that crude metric to persuade
     The killing squads that no accentual shift
To milder tones distract them from their trade

Or new-found gentleness of diction lift
     The spirit in a way unknown to those
Old tribalists. For them the poet's gift

(As Plato taught) should properly disclose
     The martial virtues and thereby ensure
The errant soul's not tempted to suppose

The arts of peace more likely to procure
     Its health and strength than arts of war that long
Accustomed strife showed fittest to endure

And find their call-sign in the poet's song,
     Such as that stirring music which (Yeats feared
Or boasted) may have sent out some among

Those men the English shot. Perhaps he cleared
     His conscience by reflecting how the sense
Of speech-acts wasn't quite what it appeared

Once versified, since shorn of the pretence
     That they have any consequence beyond
The artifice that holds them in suspense

As between 'meaning' = what the bond
     Of word, intent and purpose has the thing
Expressly mean, and what the magic wand

Of quasi-illocution has us bring
     To a suspension-point short of the stage
Where acts ensue. For otherwise they'd sing,

Those poets, songs whose promise to assuage
     The killer's itch came of their power to stoke,
Not lay to rest, his long case-hardened rage

And use whatever words might best provoke
      New blood-lust under cover of an old
Speech-covenant with the word-ways of the folk.

He played a safer game, if truth be told,
      Our Yeatsian ephebe whose verse-music found
No room for such fine promises or bold

Assertions of a will expressly bound
      To follow through on its avowed intent
And see its noble protestations crowned

With actions truly and sincerely meant,
      Whether the lake-isle visit or those lines
The rebels might have uttered as they went

To face the English guns. What best defines
      The change is how he puts it: that 'some day'
He'll make the visit, learn to read the signs,

See Tollund Man, consider how this may
      Connect with tribal passions nearer home,
Evoke (not re-enact) the scene, and pray

That their connection stretch through some rhizome-
      Like spread of tangled tubers to embrace
Those fresh-laid corpses. In the Irish loam

Such intimate revenges leave their trace
      On each new victim killed to antedate
The uncreated conscience of their race

So that the singling-out of those whose fate
      It was to ride the tumbril had them lie
Unmarked in peat while others lay in state.

Still let's not think he's out to justify
      That ancient, now state-sponsored lie that tells
The victims words like 'justice' don't apply

In cases where a blood-sealed pact compels
    Some reckoning more primordial than pertains
To any sense of due desert that dwells

On individual merit and complains
    If, by some brute impersonal decree
Of fate, the most excruciating pains

Are borne by those least guilty. What we see
    In his aversion to the Yeatsian style
Of speech-act is his striving not to be

A poet of the sort who might beguile
    His reader with performatives that bend
Sense, sound and context to their purpose while

Perfecting means to sort out foe from friend
    By all-or-nothing speech-acts. These require
Unquestioning assent since they depend

On mustering the muscle to inspire
    Such faith as will admit no move to check
The force of that inveterate desire

That leaves its votaries wholly at the beck
    And call of every two-bit tribal bard
Whose words decide who gets it in the neck

And who directs the squaddies. So the tarred
    And feathered girls conspire with Tollund Man
To catch him momentarily off-guard

Out there in Jutland, as the travel-plan
    So cautiously drawn up ('Some day I'll go')
Now brings him out amongst the peatbog clan

Of killer-victims whose remains bestow
    At least the sense that he'd done right to make
A virtue of the need to turn down low

That old-style Yeatsian rhetoric and take
    A duly chastened view of what his art
Might manage once delivered from the lake-

Isle dreamworld. For its darkside counterpart
    Enabled some performatives to work
A magic that could captivate the heart

Then turn it stony through a lethal quirk
    That cast its potent spell so as to leave
Small cognisance of all those threats that lurk

Beneath their overt sense. Yet we deceive
    Ourselves most gravely – so he has the skill
Obliquely to suggest – if we believe

Ourselves or him quite blameless for the ill
    That comes of that collusive *entre nous*
By which we readily allow the poet's will

And way with words to execute a coup
    Of *trompe-l'oreille* by crypto-Cratylist
Word-magic where fortuities on cue,

Like rhyme and rhythm, constantly insist
    On how, despite all caution to surround
His speech-acts with those hardly-to-be-missed

Quote-marks of hesitation, still the sound
    Of strong precursors echoes through the verse
And tells another tale. That's why we're bound

To hear his vow as if the lines rehearse
    Afresh, though in a muted tone, the same
Key-shift by which the blessing turned to curse

So that, as seasons changed, the peat-man came
    To switch his scapegoat role from one elect
Amongst the horde to one they deemed fair game

For that time-cancelling ritual of unchecked
   Yet calculated bloodshed that's once more
Evoked by picturing the rail-tracks flecked

With four young brothers' blood. What they ignore
   In rightly praising all that skill and tact
Is how the very things they praise him for

Are such as always come discreetly backed
   By the spell-worker's gift to perlocute
From nascent wish to word and thence to act,

Their own or others', that can serve to mute
   All doubts, misgivings, second thoughts, or fears,
Or else persuade us not to follow suit

And, like him, wish away a thousand years
   Of social evolution. Then the strife
Seems something that in consequence appears

More like an emanation of bare life
   Or force that through the peatbog drives the juice
And so keeps Tollund Man, the killer-wife

Of Heaney's vision, girdle, cap, and noose
   There at the poet's mythopoeic call
And summons up for time-negating use

Rhyme, rhythm, symbol, metaphor and all
   The sound-and-sense accoutrements that chime
So nicely with his purpose. These forestall

At source the very notion that mere time,
   Change, history, or politics might need
Attending to before some ancient crime

Or some primeval, god-placating deed
   That's meant to fit our here-and-now yet bids
Us take the point through an imagining freed

From reason's grip since here remembrance skids
   Clean over such constraints. So we might ask:
Why summon 'the mild pods' of those eye-lids

As if behind the fen-juice fretted mask
   Some errant Buddha or his avatar
Assumed once more the old unending task

Of teaching by example how we mar
   The soul's perfection when our thoughts revert
To mere particularities. These are,

The image has us feel, a cause of hurt
   More grievous than the instruments devised
For his dispatch since apt to reassert

The claim on us of all those human-sized
   Conditions, circumstances, changing modes
Of love and war, and social detail prized

By fact-informed decipherers of the codes.
   Here that prosaic stuff seems quite beside
The soul-perfecting point because it bodes

No good for such ambitions to provide
   A failsafe alibi by which the past
Might yet be called to memory, not denied,

And those old killing parishes at last
   Allowed to show up plain in survey maps
Just on condition that the tale's recast

With proper care to suture all the gaps
   In its selective record by appeal
To mythic time. Then centuries elapse

And nothing alters save the changing styles
   Of ritual, weapons used in due accord,
And – whether uttered *en route* for lake-isles

Or far off in the bogs beneath the sward
    Where nations mingle blood – the exact strain
Of pulse-attuned verse-music that the horde,

Primal or present-day, allows to gain
    A wider resonance or rhythmic power
To sway the motions of some tribal brain

To lethal deeds. So Guyon in the Bower
    Of Blisse created havoc and laid waste
To all about him, every tree and flower,

Because (or so the myth-debunking taste
    Of current exegetes tends to conclude)
The whole catastrophe's best seen as based

On Spenser's deeply felt though deeply skewed
    Sense of a late-come coloniser's guilt
At Ireland's grief. Yet that's an attitude

Where any tears the poet may have spilt
    As witness to events were far outweighed
By the material benefits long built

Into that grievous state of things. This made
    Those hard-nosed New Historicists apply
The best tricks of their intertextual trade

To taking down a peg or two the high-
    Romantic claim that poets only dealt
In such transcendent truths as scorned to vie

With plain-prose literalists whose readings dwelt
    On just the kinds of detail Spenser strove
To hold beyond the frail protective belt

Of platonizing allegory that drove
    Clean out of mind all fact-related thoughts
Or wrinkles in the cloth that fiction wove

From its delusive thread. These are the sorts
   Of strategy deployed by those, like Yeats,
Who grasp whatever doctrine best supports

Some latest fake mythology that skates
   So close to eccentricity or sheer
Stir-craziness that then the case mandates

A switch of strategy by which to steer
   Things back on course. This bids us take a view
Less tolerant of any cavalier

Myth-driven resolution to construe
   All history as slung between the poles
Of just those mythemes which, as Yeats well knew,

Would easily take over the controls
   By countermanding reason, then direct
The folk to track their lineage back through soul's

Metempsychoses rather than inspect
   That claim against the myth-averse demands
Of plain good sense backed up by intellect.

Still it's a point he fully understands,
   Our cautious non-subscriber to the tribe
Of Yeats epigones: that language hands

Down some performatives that may prescribe
   Those deaths enacted in the peatbog seams
As well as speech-acts that more aptly jibe

With all the high-toned literary themes
   Whose safe rendition none the less requires
An ear alert to how the poet's dreams

Of freedom, love, or anything that fires
   His ardent soul is just as prone to spark
Far different passions once the dreamer tires

Of non-fulfilment and so turns to dark
    Imaginings of what might bring about
The wished-for end. Yet should we now embark

For Jutland, haunted on the voyage out
    By those remembered lines, then it may strike
Us suddenly that there's some room for doubt

Whether this far from tourist-favoured hike,
    This quest for what unites our tribe with theirs
In consanguinity, might yet – just like

The lake-isle travelogue of Yeats that shares
    Its vagrant wish – cast doubt on our intent
To make the trip and see how it compares,

That killing-field, with others that he went
    There partly to erase, partly to fix
In memory. Then maybe it's the bent

Of one bred up in word-ways that would mix
    The will to act with a will to suspend
From speech-act to enactment. They'd endorse

In earlier, let action-time distend
    To thought's own measure as events unfold
And so allow the poet's words to lend

Some deeper meaning to the story told
    By opting, Hamlet-like, this time to let
No firm decision exercise its hold

So mind can recognise its endless debt
    To mere contingency. Then Tollund Man
May seem to pose less of an outright threat

To what's laid out in reason's master-plan
    For civil concord, and instead become
The very prototype of what began

As thought's dull stirring to a tribal drum
　　Before it set out on the age-long trek
To just that point where finally the sum

Of knowledge and experience served to check
　　Those atavistic cravings. Then the rate
Of human betterment goes neck-and-neck

Not just with nature's fumblings to update
　　Our gene-pool but with poetry's long haul
From far-off times, when epics might narrate

Acephalous heroics yet enthral
　　The listening throng, to this more nuanced phase
Of consciousness when speech-acts may forestall

Such deeds as way back then the ancient craze
　　For sacrifice just left to run their course.
So it may be that poetry displays

A counter-perlocutionary force
　　Whose special gift it is to slow the rush
From speech-act to enactment. They'd endorse

Such wavering thoughts as go against the crush
　　Of mob-desire and by example show
The native hue of resolution blush

At its crass lack of forethought. Still there's no
　　Ignoring how the very urge to meld
Wish, word and speech-act in his 'I will go'

Betrays a kinship with the acts that spelled
　　A tale of victimage from Viking times
To the near-present of those labourers felled

By deeds of war the state once titled crimes
　　But now inclines more tactfully to deem
'Political' since this description chimes

More sweetly with both sides. Then it might seem
    That, after all, the peat-bog's not so far
From the lake-isle since both invoke a dream

With denouement distinctly below par
    Since aptest either to go way off track,
Or fade away, or conjure acts that are

So utterly remote from what might stack
    Up to the consequence a vow decrees
That the poetic way of hanging back

From perlocution and the fatal squeeze
    Of present fixed intent on future choice
Might well appear the greatest gift that he's

Enabled to afford us through a voice
    Subdued and tentative. Yet there's a sense
That nothing here gives reason to rejoice

On this account since then the best defence
    Of poetry's still that which makes a chief
Virtue of its preferring to dispense

With all the props of resolute belief,
    While the most favoured apologia's one
That happily adopts the stock motif

Of poets anxious to ensure that none
    Of their more topical or risky bits
Come back to haunt them. So they choose to run

Some variant of Sidney's point: that it's
    The poet's gift and privilege to feign
(Meaning both 'wish' and 'make-believe') what fits

A vision far transcending such mundane
    Or factual truths as tally with the drive
To clip its wings by those whose dull refrain

Insists no healthy order can survive,
    In soul or body social, where ideas
Like this exert their word-spell to deprive

Truth's homeland of the critical frontiers
    Drawn up against encroachments from the realm
Of idle fantasists or vision-seers.

Not that such dreams were apt to overwhelm
    This poet-traveller who, once Jutland-bound,
Keeps facts, not fictions, firmly at the helm

And so ensures the Danish killing-ground
    Not figure as a welcome substitute
For grim truths nearer home and so compound

The wrong, but – on the contrary – refute
    All such mythologizing ploys to blur
The vital line between those truths of brute

Reality and fictions that incur
    A greater long-term cost. That's why he brought
So forcibly to mind how grievous were

The wrongs endured not only by those caught
    Directly up in it but by the more
Extended company of those who thought

That mythic analogues could help restore
    Some sense of shared humanity despite
All the hard evidence of myths that tore

Their world apart. Yet while his poem might
    Keep this point clear in view, still it's inclined
To angle or deflect the line of sight

So that our soft perspective's prone to find
    Those analogues a handy way to kid
Ourselves that violent actions of the kind

Here graphically portrayed are such as bid
    Us heed their rootedness deep in the soil
Of age-old ritual, and so keep the lid

On questions that might otherwise embroil
    Us in those local histories whose claim
To factual reconstruction tends to spoil

Their image given back within the frame
    Of some enchanted glass. Maybe the case
Is general, and poetry's the name

For just the sort of discourse that, by grace
    Of feigning, offers truths beyond the scope
Of history, so doesn't have to face

The standard tests for whether thought can cope
    With such myth-busting facts or words confront
Those stubborn details that the master-trope

Of peatbog-man is liable to shunt
    Aside and seek more myth-productive ways
In which to write things up. These spurn such blunt

Fact-digging implements as else might raise
    Spectres or mud-caked body-parts more apt
To fix dates and locations than liaise

Mytho-poetically between the strapped-
    Down hooded victims of primeval rites
And those whose deaths might yet be roughly mapped

By colour-code across the various sites
    Marked off in any atlas up-to-date
Enough with every zone-change that re-writes

The thanatourist guide to correlate
    With new facts on the ground. The point is not
So much that mythic parallels create

A self-protective tendency to blot
   Clean out of working memory what jars,
Like Yeats's 'certain men the English shot'

Or such things that a queasy conscience bars
   From its tribunal since they'd otherwise
Amass a detailed inventory that, *pars*

Pro toto, would most likely compromise
   Then topple that whole mythic house of cards
Whose façade bids us elevate our eyes

From mere contingencies. These it regards
   As no more than a means to keep our minds
Fixed stupidly on the fragmented shards

Of a symbolic truth that better minds
   Discern entire since no such details stand
Between themselves and a high truth that binds

The company of victims in a band
   Where differences of time like those of place,
Creed, politics, and all we understand

The better for a bit of detailed case-
   Historic grasp is airbrushed from the scene
And we're induced to view the human race

As unified deep down by acts that mean
   Its killing-sprees are what most typify
The species and annul the gaps between

Such diverse lives-and-times. Still we'd best try
   To get our heads round those since they're the stuff
We'll need to let our thoughts be guided by

If we're to stock our memories with enough
   Non-mythic truths of history to make
That grim scenario seem more like a snuff-

Movie-addicted view of things and break
    Its hold by simply getting us to see
How truths like this can jolt the mind awake

From lethal dreams like that. Let's all agree
    With what quiet dignity he kept his nerve
Through murderous times, maintained a rhetoric free

Of Yeatsian rant, wrote poems that deserve
    Our gratitude for coaxing darkest deeds
Unflinchingly to light, and didn't swerve

From memories such that anyone who reads
    And pictures them will realise what it took
To find the words, or what the poet needs

To bring those words effectively to book
    In verse-forms that communicate the shock
Of their engendering. Not his way to look

For facile consolations or to block
    Its impact by some well-approved technique
Of tasteful euphemism from the stock

Worked up by serviceable bards who seek
    The church's, chief's, or state's approving nod
For this or that convenient verbal tweak

Of proven use to keep the killer squad
    From their front door. Yet, these fine things apart,
We might wish to avoid the path he trod

In Jutland following the victim's cart
    And meditating how those deaths composed
A timeless ritual of the kind that art

Alone brought to remembrance and disclosed
    As that which (so the myths would have us think)
Stayed constant while all else metamorphosed.

Then violent death would constitute the link
    That quite eluded those more sanguine sorts
Of civic-minded thinker who might blink

At such regressive, atavistic thoughts,
    Yet whose great project for a world redeemed
From all in human nature that comports

With Tollund Man turned brutal as they dreamed
    And so (the myth conveys) more than sufficed
To show how dark the flipside of what seemed

Enlightenment's best chance. That message, spliced
    With chunks of Christian doctrine to enforce
The depth of our depravity should Christ

Not turn things round, then makes a handy source
    Of everything the myth-promoters need
To carry through their pitiless divorce

Between the shared humanity that we'd
    Much better cultivate if we're to get
Along at all and what their sullen creed

Enjoins. Thus it requires that we not let
    Mere loving-kindness, charity, appeals
To fellow-feeling, or some kindred set

Of clapped-out sentimentalist ideals
    Persuade us they're equipped to lift the curse
Of our condition by a dream that feels

Like absolution but then leaves us worse
    Prepared to face the horror-show that still
Defines our fallen state. You'll say: his verse

Provides the best short answer to such ill-
    Judged claims as I've made here, since any good
Or half-way sympathetic reader will

Be sure to recognise – or surely would,
  If not in the response-distorting grip
Of some deep prejudice – what's understood

Instinctively by him as partnership
  In the long tale of suffering he presents
Not from a victim's standpoint that would skip

The awkward bit and take the innocents'
  Uncomplicated view, but as perceived
By one who feels the pressure of events,

Home and abroad, with conscience unrelieved
  By any such too easy route to guilt-
Free retrospect. This leaves him less deceived,

You'll say, and never one to let things tilt
  So far one way as to lose sight of all
Those reciprocities around blood spilt

In ceremony, war, or drunken brawl
  That blur the fixed apportionment of roles
Like victim/executioner. These call

For poetry, like his, that both consoles
  With its long views and leaves us more aware
How frail they are, the boundary-controls

Set up in those short intervals of rare
  Peace and lucidity to keep safe stowed
Below our civil decks the extant share

Of violence laid in store by an old code
  Whose unrequited eye-for-eye may burst
The bulkheads and at any time explode

To sink the ship. My answer: true, 'the worst
  Are full of passionate intensity', and his
(Heaney's, not Yeats's) poetry rehearsed

Some ways to calm those bad intensities
    Through tempered speech-acts that held firm against
The Yeatsian lure and let us hear what is,

Quite audibly, conviction not ring-fenced
    By any prudent wish to hedge his bets
Nor count himself poetically dispensed

From calmer passions – sorrows, fears, regrets,
    But also hopes, assurances, and shades
Of optimism ranged against the threats

And terrors. Yet this answer still evades
    The question squarely posed by mythic scenes
Of violence coupled with a style that trades

On such poetic speech-acts as a means
    To keep the other types of act at bay
Whilst still in mind, like superfine machines

Set up with fits so accurate that they
    Must perfectly self-regulate and curb
Every least tendency to go astray

From the fixed norm in ways that might disturb
    Their equilibrium and so induce
A Tinguely-like disaster. Such superb

Control means zero tolerance for loose
    Assemblage, whether of precision parts
That make the mechanism fit for use

Or of the likewise hi-tech verbal arts
    That go into the making of a rhyme
Or rhythm that by just so much departs

From metrical convention or clock-time
    As perfectly to counter any hint
Of artlessness unless of the sublime

Since art-transforming sort. Say it's by dint
   Of such consummate mastery combined
With depth of insight that his words imprint

The sense of here encountering a mind
   Uniquely qualified to get beyond
That myth-engendered view of humankind

With which high priests and oracles respond
   Whenever we petition them to grant
Some sign how best to cultivate the bond

Of shared humanity or re-enchant
   Our bleak existence and the plea's returned
To sender with the same blood-curdling slant

That set the tumbrils rolling as they churned
   The Jutland soil. But there's another side
Worth noting where the sober lesson learned

By Yeats late on should also be applied
   In this case, not to ask if 'certain men'
The poet's words sent out to fight then died

At English hands, but whether the squat pen
   That Heaney dug with, as his people had
With spades in heavy earth and juice-dark fen,

Could all the same have done its share to add
   A muted voice-part to the strident choir,
Albeit stirring no such mad or bad

Primeval passions as might yet inspire
   More peat-bog deaths. Still it's a tricky call,
Like Yeats's wondering if the speech-act 'Fire!'

That felled those men should yet be deemed to fall
   Within the perlocutionary range
Of speech-acts like his own which, after all,

Were fashioned with no thought how times might change
    Or circumstance contrive that they promote
An *après-coup* with such power to estrange

Act from intent. So maybe those who quote
    The verses about Tollund Man to show
How well and ecumenically he wrote

About 'the troubles' in some long-ago
    Time-out-of-time should take time to reflect
That certain myths and speech-acts may bestow

The dubious blessing of a disconnect
    Between our present sense of what befits
A value-system premised on respect

For human life, or comfortably sits
    With our (let's say) more socially advanced
Morality, and what in us submits

So unresistingly to the entranced
    Condition of balletomanes who fling
Aside mere audience-custom as they're danced

Into some all-involving *Rite of Spring*
    Where nothing stands between such acts of raw
Onstage ferocity and everything

That ethics, empathy, and rule of law
    Once strove to keep offstage. No doubt this type
Of image-mongering's liable to draw

The charge that I'm exploiting it to hype
    The whole thing up and make the poet out
A rabble-rouser just to give my gripe

The same emotive resonance or clout
    That all those poet-pictured *mises-en-scènes*
Of ritual violence just might bring about.

Then there'd be room for refuge, yet again,
    In that vague border-zone between the class
Of speech-acts that have consequences when

Pronounced with such intent and those that pass
    For fictional or mythic and contrive
Thereby to spike the guns of all smartass

Or cloth-eared commentators who'd derive
    The Yeatsian lesson, though now hedged around
With no such queasy doubts. It's one that I've

Seen fit to venture here, and – to compound
    The lapse of tact or taste – further surmised
That this involves the sorts of speech-act found

In just the kinds of poem chiefly prized
    For holding back from words more closely geared
To action, or performatives devised

Precisely to ensure the reader's steered
    Well clear of any upshot that entails
The fateful passage, rightly to be feared,

From speech to act. For it's when language fails,
    Or wilfully declines, to specify
Just which of all its mythic-sounding tales

Is history, or how we're to apply
    Some mix of context-principles with strict
Sincerity-conditions and thereby

Tell true from false, that we're left derelict
    Of any half-way adequate technique
For knowing whether maybe we've been tricked

Into some realm of fictive doublespeak
    Where no such categories fit the bill
Since here the only pertinent critique

Of speech-acts, as of actions good or ill,
    Is one that chooses to interrogate
The relative degree of art or skill

Their fashioning required. At any rate
    That realm's no country for young men, or for
Those active types who'd quick as thought translate

Some watchword from the poet's ample store
    Into a truly consequential act
Whose outcome speech-act theorists might deplore

As lacking warrant since so poorly backed
    By those grandiloquent performatives
That find small room for simple truths of fact.

On this account poetic licence gives
    Full dispensation from the flat demand
Of anyone who thinks that freedom lives

In that small gap between the mythic and
    Those thought-procedures that at length allowed
Our slaughter-sated kind to understand

And so reject what once induced the crowd
    Of death-watch ritualists to undergo
Such atavism though themselves endowed,

Prospectively, with means of saying no
    To its malign bewitchment. Let's admit
There's a fine art to his maintaining so

Adroit an equipoise or perfect fit
    Between the rival claims of membership
In that albeit nowadays loose-knit

Tribal community and what the trip
    To Arhus told him of the need for some
Much larger view of things whereby to slip

All such parochial bonds. Yet should it come
    Down to the sort of reckoning here proposed
In speech-act terms then, as a rule of thumb,

Let's say that what I've seemed to diagnose
    As case-specific to an heir of Yeats,
So that each word was taken to disclose

Some turn of thought that subtly correlates
    The private with the public, should instead
Be viewed in light of those set-piece debates,

From Plato down, where the one party said
    (With Sidney) how the poet's word redeems
Our fallen world and turns to gold the lead

Of mortal life, while the other party steams
    With rage and says that lot will fuck your head
By filling it with their delirious dreams,

In which case we're most grievously misled
    By fictions, metaphors, or endless streams
Of sense-beguiling imagery since fed

A soul-corrupting diet of what seems
    But is not. So when asked where fancy's bred
The answers run to opposite extremes

Like Sidney *contra* Plato. I should tread
    Cautiously here since none of these stock themes,
From Plato's carpentered or painted bed

To poets' dirty work for bad regimes,
    Is of the sort you'd think aptest to shed
Much light on why this nobler poet's schemes

Of conflict-management should conjure dread
    Despite what every grateful reader deems
His strife-appeasing art. Still there's a thread

That runs through this as through the peatbog seams
　　And asks if Tollund Man's potato head
Evoked in verse might yet send killer teams

For fresh blood to requite the restless dead.

Notes

p. 209: 'Performatives'. Utterances, for example, promises, vows, adjurations, commissives and self-binding pronouncements of various kinds that actually do or perform something through language (bring about a change in the way things stand) rather than simply stating something. For relevant discussion see J. L. Austin, *Philosophical Papers* (Oxford: Oxford University Press, 1961) and *How to Do Things With Words* (Oxford: Clarendon Press, 1963); also Jacques Derrida, 'Signature Event Context', *Glyph*, Vol. I (Baltimore, MD: Johns Hopkins University Press, 1977), pp. 172–97, 'Limited Inc. a b c', *Glyph*, Vol. II (Baltimore, MD: Johns Hopkins University Press, 1977), pp. 162–254.

p. 209: Jean-Paul Sartre, *A Critique of Dialectical Reason*, Vol. 1, *Theory of Practical Ensembles*, trans. A. Sheridan-Smith (London: New Left Books, 1976) and Vol. 2, trans. Quintin Hoare (London: Verso, 2006).

p. 210: 'some illocutionary force'. In Austinian speech-act theory: the aspect of commitment or verbally binding intent that gives promises their promissory character, marriage vows their (presumed) intentional content, threats their minatory content and so forth. For Austin it is distinct from 'perlocutionary' force which has to do with the actual carrying-through to some intended action or upshot.

p. 214: 'of *Geist* and its *Geschichte*'. Allusion to Hegel's world-historical vision of humankind as moving slowly but surely towards a state of achieved intellectual, moral, political and cultural perfection.

p. 214: 'mimetic violence'. This passage refers to ideas about mimetic desire and its paradoxical, often destructive consequences advanced by René Girard in books like *Violence and the Sacred* and *To Double Business Bound*.

p. 216: 'those men the English shot'. See Yeats's poem 'The Man and the Echo'.

p. 217: 'our Yeatsian ephebe'. An ephebe is a disciple, pupil, apprentice or junior guild member as yet not fully qualified to assume the master's skills and prerogatives. The word has acquired a special literary currency through Harold Bloom's psychoanalytically inflected writings on the 'anxiety of influence' as a major force in the incentives and resistances surrounding poets' achievement of expressive maturity against the inherited weight of tradition. Its relevance to the Yeats/Heaney relationship is the main point here.

p. 219: 'crypto-Cratylist/Word-magic'. Reference to Plato's dialogue *Cratylus* and subsequent debates as to whether linguistic signs (spoken or written) have a natural or a purely arbitrary relation to whatever they signify. The Cratylist (naturalist) doctrine amounts to something like a generalization of onomatopoeia to instances far beyond its usual (mainly literary) usage. Other versions of it range from the mystical-divinatory to the strain of depth-hermeneutic or etymo-poetic brooding practised by the later Heidegger. Here it has to do with the performative power of poetry to summon not only the meanings latent in certain, perhaps atavistic modes of speech but the actions – the potentially violent outcomes – that may result.

p. 219: 'of strong precursors'. See note (above) on Bloom's 'anxiety of influence' thesis.

p. 220: 'emanation of bare life'. Cf. Giorgio Agamben's influential book *Homo Sacer* on 'bare life', victimage, bio-politics and the exercise of mythico-juridical power.

p. 222: 'Guyon in the Bower/Of Blisse'. Alludes to episode of frenzied and seemingly wanton destruction carried out by the virtuous protagonist in Edmund Spenser's epic poem *The Faerie Queene*.

p. 222: 'late-come coloniser's guilt/At Ireland's grief'. A connection made to persuasive effect by critics of Spenser influenced by New Historicism and Cultural Materialism.

p. 223: 'metempsychoses'. Migrations of the soul from one body to another, as in ancient-Greek Pythagorean doctrine. Also crops up in garbled form – 'met him pike hoses' and variants thereof – in Joyce's *Ulysses*.

p. 224: 'a will to suspend/The act itself'. This passage combines Hamlet's self-reproaches for his introvert character and lack of resolution with the idea put forward by some theorists that the literary (poetic or fictional) speech act differs from normal (everyday-practical) performatives on account of its having no action-conducive or perlocutionary force. However that distinction may itself appear less firm or distinct in light of Derrida's deconstructive treatment. (See especially his 'Signature Event Context'; first note above).

p. 226: 'The poet's gift and privilege to feign'. 'Feign' = both 'pretend' and 'wish or desire' ('I would fain know thee better'). This piece of pointed homophonic wordplay came to bear quite a weight of implicit argument in texts like Sir Philip Sidney's 'Apology for Poetry', where he says that its Puritan detractors are wrong since the poet 'affirms nothing' (and thus never lies) but 'feigns' many things that are both desirable and morally improving or inspiring. Compare Shakespeare's Touchstone in 'As You Like It': 'the truest poetry is the most feigning'.

p. 228: 'blunt/Fact-digging implements'. See Seamus Heaney's poem 'Digging', where he compares the 'squat pen' resting between his finger and thumb 'snug as a gun' with his father's spade scraping on the stony soil outside the room where he, the poet, is writing.

p. 228: 'the thanatourist map'. For those who wish to make their way from one to another place of special death-related interest.

p. 229: 'fragmented shards/Of a symbolic truth'. See notes to 'A Plain Man Looks at the Angel of History' (in this book) for a brief account of recent critical debates around this issue of symbol, allegory and the politics of historical narrative or representation.

p. 232: 'the worst/Are full of passionate intensity'. Yeats, 'The Second Coming'.

p. 233: 'a Tinguely-like disaster'. Refers to the work of artist Jean Tinguely, designer/maker of wonderfully ingenious self-destructive machines.

p. 236: 'smartass/Or cloth-eared commentators'. Paul de Man offered a deconstructive reading of the final line of Yeats's 'Among School Children' – 'How can we know the dancer from the dance?' – which advised us not to go along too readily with the 'obvious' interpretation of it as a rhetorical question intended to prompt the symbolist response: we can't! Rather we should ask ourselves whether there might not be an urgent need to take it at face value – as a question or anxious request for clearer thinking – and thereby resist such tempting symbolist modes of 'aesthetic ideology'. On the other hand, some detractors have accused de Man of merely having a defective ear for the Yeatsian verse music (or poetry in general).

p. 238: 'Plato's carpentered or painted bed'. Reference to Plato's *Republic* where he charges poetry with (among other things) persuading us to rest content with appearances of appearances. Thus the manufactured bed is a copy of the ideal bed that exists (*really* exists according to Platonist metaphysics) in the realm of pure essences, forms or ideas, while the artist/poet copies that in turn and fobs us off with a double deception.

13

Lost for words

This is basically an attempt to come to terms through verse with the threat of age-related mental disintegration which for some reason seems more prevalent nowadays, or at any rate higher on our communal list of terrors, than in times past. It is the only piece here with anything like the apotropaic function – that of warding off some perceived threat to selfhood, identity or psychic survival – that has figured (as so often in the darker passages of literary Romanticism) among poetry's most important if not widely celebrated gifts. No doubt my approaching such a topic via the two types of aphasia or language loss analysed by the structural linguist Roman Jakobson will also be thought a preconscious defence mechanism or means of holding the horrible thing at bay. Indeed the same purpose is very likely served on and off throughout these pieces by the rhyme schemes, metrical patterns, complex syntactic structures and a whole range of kindred formal devices. That role is most prominent here by reason of the poem's highly intractable – indeed near-intolerable – subject matter, as well as the risk that its tone might otherwise seem too flippant or (in Dr Johnson's critical idiom) too 'conceited' by half. At any rate there is no truth in the idea, handed down from a degenerate Romanticism to the less gifted adepts of recent 'confessional' poetry, that an

over-concern with formal matters is a sure sign of emotional
disengagement or something worse.

That nervous laugh's what gives the game away.
    It says: these folk are trying not to think
What stops them thinking, sends their words astray
    Mid-sentence, makes their past perspective shrink
To scarcely further back than yesterday,
    Then to just twenty seconds in a blink,
And last of all contrives that somehow they,
    Though stone-cold sober, seem the worse for drink.

No comfort – apt to drive them even crazier –
    If they've consulted Jakobson and found
That basically there's two types of aphasia.
    One's where a word goes missing and they're bound
To get along by sheer paronomasia
    Until the sentence works its way around
Through boss-shots, paraphrase, and ever mazier
    Word-detours guided less by sense than sound

Along the quick-shift metonymic chain
    To where some random quilting-point may slow
Its dizzying slide. Then there's the other bane
    Their genes concoct where the first thing to go,
Conversely, has to do with how the brain
    (Or mind – a quibble here) construes the flow
Of words, the syntax and the ordered train
    Of thought that language-users mostly know

How to make sense of by preconscious skill.
    Thus these Type-Two aphasics fail to sort
The thing out not for lack of words to fill
    The proper slots, or being pulled up short
By word-shaped holes where nothing fits the bill
    (Like the Type Ones), but because words cavort
With syntax while their meanings overspill
    The bounds of sense and sense then runs athwart

The space of reason. So they're right on cue,
      These Type-Two folk, so far as it's a case
Of riffling through their word-hoard with a view
      To picking just the item fit to grace
Their discourse with the one word that will do
      To get their gist across and hold in place
Those ties of sense and selfhood that accrue
      From verbal aptitude. Yet that home-base

Recedes from view once those words fail to hook
      Up as the gist requires and thus compose
The sense-bestowing outline that they took,
      Back then, as quite sufficient to disclose
How their life-stories might be brought to book
      In *Bildungsroman* style. When syntax goes
To pot, or when anomalies that shook
      Their self-esteem once in a while now pose

A constant self-annihilating threat
      To everything that kept their minds on track
From thought to thought, that's when the symptoms get
      Past hope that they might yet be guided back
To a sure path with language-bearings set
      By straightforward *vouloir-dire*. So it's their lack
Of those syntactic protocols which let
      Most speakers exercise the common knack

Of stringing words together that decrees
      Their utterance will stumble, fall apart,
Trail off confusedly, or somehow freeze
      Mid-phrase before their minds can make a start
On figuring how to process or reprise
      That scrambled language-mass that no fine art
Of cryptanalysis might somehow tease
      Into good sense at last. That's why the smart

Ear-witness won't be fooled when they pretend
      Amusement at some odd linguistic slip,

Some speech-event they cannot comprehend
    Or suchlike symptom of the loosening grip
On words and world they half-suspect will end
    As badly as can be if they just skip
A few years forward yet still half-hope will mend
    If they ignore this momentary blip

Or put it down (a subterfuge employed
    By savvy types) to some cause that required
The kind of depth-deciphering used by Freud
    To sort things out. This gives just the desired
Excuse to think those slips might be enjoyed,
    Not stoically endured, since what conspired
To trip their tongue was not the yawning void
    Of sense that opened up beneath their tired

Speech-faculties but a packed story-line
    With complications and x-rated bits
Affording ample room to redefine
    Their lapses in a way that nicely fits
With all the fond illusions that combine
    To keep them sane or save them from the pits
Of knowing this is terminal decline,
    A tale whose looming denouement admits

No happy outcome. This they recognise
    Deep down, those stunned aphasics, though they seek
To block the recognition or disguise
    Their knowledge by inventing some oblique
Protective strategy in hope it buys
    A bit of extra time, or some technique
Whereby the battered ego might devise
    A further means of shoring up its weak

And over-stretched defences. So each lapse
    From proper sense according to the rules
Laid down to suture all the rifts and gaps
    In language – just a lamp for lighting fools

The wordless way to dusty death, perhaps –
    Spells out *Spem dimittite!* since it schools
Them in dumbfounded knowledge that the traps
    Catching them word-bereft between the stools

Of disjoined sound and sense were set in place,
    Not by some outside agency intent
On crossing wires and scrambling every trace
    Of sense that might recapture what they meant,
But – a much tougher truth for them to face –
    By tangles they can't hope to circumvent
Since all hard-wired right there, within the space
    Of their own skulls. The further to augment

Their misery, this thought: that the twin poles
    Or speech-coordinates by which they'd steered
A steady course with mind at the controls
    Now slewed so far off-compass that they veered,
Unwitting jargonauts, toward the shoals
    Of pseudo-sense that from far off appeared
Like archipelagos, but where the roles
    Of sense and sound, like sea and sand, were bleared

By such chaotic undertows that none
    Of those fast-fading coastlines could secure
Their language from the process, once begun,
    Of quicksand dissolution into pure
Sinnlosigkeit. Enjoy the Joycean fun
    And word-games, we're advised, but let's be sure
We know the score when language comes undone
    And *zoon logikon* has to endure

The loss of everything that once conveyed
    Their meanings, projects, life-hopes, and (in brief)
That whole delusive striving to evade
    What a more taxing ethics of belief,
After such knowledge, now insists be weighed
    Against the blissful ignorance whose chief

Protection lay in readiness to trade
    Hard truths for some short measure of relief.

Whence the vain hope that something might persist
    Of them – a self or soul – and so survive,
If not to tell the tale, then to enlist
    The speechless *haeccitas* of man alive
And show the logophiles how much they've missed
    Through their determination to connive
At propping up the myth that we exist,
    Qua human, just till some ill chance deprive

Our sounds of sense. Then there's the other theme
    They've always harped on, those who took that line
From Aristotle down, which has us deem
    Speech the sure mark of all that we assign
Solely to players on the winning team
    Of homo sapiens bearing the divine
Soul-spark of reason or, lest this should seem
    Too pre-Darwinian, what they incline

To count coeval with the native wit
    That (so the update goes) language alone
Could frame, articulate, or aptly fit
    To reason's need. No wonder if they're prone,
The losers, to see what tale they can pit
    Against one that consigns them to a zone
Of barely living-on, or how a bit
    Of speech-devaluation might atone

For the long history of put-downs dealt
    By *logos* to the tongue-tied types who fell
Beneath the bar its standards-office felt
    Most apt so *zoon logikon* could tell
Apart those who legitimately dwelt
    Within state bounds and those condemned to dwell
Beyond the speech-patrolled protective belt
    That reassures the *logos* all goes well

With its choice citizens. So, if they choose,
    The afflicted may cite Foucault to convince
Themselves that merely tending to confuse
    The sense of things should scarcely vex them since,
If reason's voice is all they have to lose,
    It's no great loss however they may mince
Words, get the grammar wrong, or so bemuse
    Themselves and others that those words evince

Mere chaos come again. What this portends
    Can then appear no more than what's entailed
For anyone whose *cogito* depends
    On Descartes' thought-experiment that failed,
Or in whose book *res cogitans* transcends
    All such corporeal mishaps as derailed
The train of thought that vainly sought amends
    For body's frailty in a soul that trailed,

Truth is, no clouds of glory. So it seems
    Their last escape-route's landed them on just
The high redoubt that figured in their dreams
    As self's last refuge yet betrays their trust
By now revealing how the strongest beams
    In its construction sag at every gust
Of time's chill wind. This penetrates its seams
    And tells them there's no refuge so robust

That one rogue gene won't wreck their dearest schemes,
    One haywire synapse leave the brain nonplussed,
Brain strike a blow to mind no thought redeems,
    And thought's whole edifice be brought to dust.

Notes

p. 244: 'If they've consulted Jakobson'. See Roman Jakobson, 'Two Aspects of Language and Two Types of Aphasic Disturbances', in *On Language* (Cambridge, MA: Harvard University Press, 1995), pp. 115–33 and 'Linguistics and Poetics', in *Style in Language*, ed. Thomas A. Sebeok (Cambridge, MA: MIT Press, 1960), pp. 350–77.

p. 244: paronomasia. Rhetorical term that covers various kinds of puns, wordplay, multiplied metaphor or other such figural devices.

p. 244: 'metonymic chain'. Jakobson defined metaphor and metonymy as the two chief structural axes of language, that is, the twin poles or organizing principles which between them accounted for our powers of linguistic utterance and uptake. Metaphor he linked to the axis of selection, or the language user's ability to pick the right (context-appropriate) word from a paradigm of related words, that is, near-synonyms, antonyms, figural alternatives, etc. Metonymy he linked to the axis of combination, or the ability to put words together in a syntactically ordered and semantically intelligible sequence. The distinction applied, so he claimed, not only to everyday 'normal' language but also to the two kinds of aphasia and to different genres, styles and periods of literature and art according to the relative predominance of metaphor or metonymy.

p. 244: 'some random quilting-point'. Refers to psychoanalyst Jacques Lacan's Jakobson-influenced theory of the unconscious as 'structured like a language', and of metonymy as that which drives human meanings, thoughts and desires from one to another temporary *point de capiton*.

p. 246: 'to suture all the rifts and gaps'. Again, alludes to Lacan's structuralist approach to Freudian psychoanalysis, here deploying the medical metaphor of suture (the stitching of a wound) to convey how rare and fleeting are the moments of convergence between signifier and signified.

p. 247: '*Spem dimittite!*'. 'Abandon hope!'; Latin version of the Italian words that, in Dante's *Divine Comedy*, are inscribed over the entrance to Hell.

p. 247: *Sinnlosigkeit*. 'Senselessness', 'lack of intelligible meaning'.

p. 247: *zoon logikon*. Aristotle defined the human being as a 'rational animal', making reason (along with the capacity for communal or social-political existence) a species attribute.

p. 248: *haeccitas*. 'Thisness', specificity, unique essence.

p. 248: 'logophiles'. Those attached to the idea of reason and/or language as the defining attribute of the human animal.

p. 249: 'the afflicted may cite Foucault'. Michel Foucault is instanced here mainly with reference to those early works, like *Madness and Civilization*, where he takes a decidedly sceptical or cultural-relativist view of what counts at different times and in different places as human rationality.

p. 249: *res cogitans*. 'Thinking substance'; alludes to Descartes' dualist philosophy of mind and body as radically distinct (the body is defined as *res extensa*). His method of hyperbolic doubt is here described as an 'experiment that failed' since he failed to offer any plausible account of how those two substances might somehow link up or communicate. So dualism holds no comfort for those whose body-brains begin to let down their cognitive or intellectual powers.

p. 249: 'that trailed,/Truth is, no clouds of glory'. Reference to Wordsworth's 'Ode: Intimations of Immortality'.

14

Poetry as (a kind of) philosophy: For Richard Rorty

Another verse-essay, this time in second-person mode and addressed to Richard Rorty, the chief proponent of neo-pragmatism – or the very mixed bag of ideas going under that name – in the context of post-1980 Anglophone (chiefly US) debate. I should fill in some parts of the background picture for those who may otherwise be baffled on the one hand by various moderately 'technical' bits of discussion and on the other, especially towards the end, by a few somewhat personal or anecdotal passages. I met Rorty on several occasions, mostly at conferences or seminars in the United States and Britain. The occasion was usually a debate involving one or more of such diverse though related topics as relativism, truth, pragmatism, critique, postmodernism, deconstruction, philosophy in relation to/conflict with literary theory and the historical fortunes of the European enlightenment. He took a strongly pragmatist view which pretty much endorsed William James's laid-back characterization of truth (fiercely contested by Bertrand Russell) as what's by and large 'good in the way of belief', that is, what best serves to protect, preserve and promote the interests of human physical, moral and cultural flourishing. At the same time he took a highly positive – even quite exalted – view of the United States and its role as an ethically progressive force for good both in domestic social-political terms and as a matter of expanding global influence. His attachment to the American pragmatists, Dewey in particular, and their recasting of philosophy in the vernacular grain was very much a part of that outlook.

This all went along with a naturalized but non-reductive since language-oriented and culture-responsive epistemology; a rejection of Kantian or other 'foundationalist' approaches; a consequent suspicion of 'enlightenment' values like truth and critique; a scepticism towards most of what passed for reputable or valid academic philosophy in the analytic mainstream; a growing preference for its sundry 'continental' alternatives; a creative (or strong-revisionist) conception of interpretative practice across all disciplines or areas of thought; and a view of hermeneutics – along with cultural and literary criticism – as what philosophy ought to look like once rid of its delusory pretensions of intellectual grandeur. He had no time for Kant-derived transcendental or condition-of-possibility arguments, regarding them as relics of old-style 'armchair' philosophizing, although he did devote a good deal of time to explaining and defending his reasons for thinking so. In his later years Rorty tended to mix more with people in departments of English, comparative literature, cultural studies and ethnography rather than (at any rate analytically inclined) philosophy, a habit no doubt reinforced by his ex-colleagues' less than generous response to his perceived apostasy.

This makes it doubly ironic that I, with an early background in literary studies, and having hopped across the disciplines to philosophy via literary theory, should have ended up opposing his position on most of these points. Our disagreements get a versified repeat airing here, most prominently those having to do with truth, critique, relativism, transcendental arguments and (in a pointedly different sense of the term) the transcendental or visionary strain in US social, political and cultural thought. I take a much less rosy view of US politics and its various social and cultural expressions, although – to be fair – Rorty himself was increasingly prone to doubts on that score after the election of George W. Bush and the advent of his 'war on terror'. Still I try to keep the tone fairly relaxed, even chatty at times, so as not to let this rehearsal of old quarrels get in the way of my admiring and affectionate memories of him as a wonderfully generous host when I visited Virginia. He was also a genial though resolute opponent in debate, a patient and kindly interlocutor in print and a fine advertisement for those progressive values to which his home culture has so far not managed to live up.

Elsewhere I look back at our differing views about Heidegger and Derrida, the two 'continental' thinkers who – along with Hegel – were of greatest importance for Rorty's revisionist project, albeit on a suitably naturalized (or pragmatized) selective reading. As regards the vexed question of Heidegger's politics, he thought that you could perfectly well drive a wedge between man and work and thereby hang on to the claim that Heidegger was a major thinker and source of vital new ideas while accepting, since the evidence left little choice, that he was also an unreconstructed 'Schwarzwald redneck'. In Derrida's case, Rorty urged that we forget all the earnest philosophical stuff, especially the bits that people like me construed as 'negative transcendental' arguments or as couched in a 'conditions of impossibility' mode, and just enjoy those other, more 'literary' texts that gave free rein to his powers of metaphorical or fictive invention. I disagreed in both instances and hope that my reasons will be clear enough from the poem. Beyond that I think there is nothing that really needs explaining except perhaps the bit towards the end about 'Trotsky and the Wild Orchids'. This was the title of an unusually self-revealing essay where Rorty discusses – among other things – his father's left-wing union activism and the somewhat Kierkegaardian tension in his own life and work between the call of commitment and the desire for aesthetic pleasures untroubled by such queasy issues of conscience. Writing the poem and reliving some of those debates made me very aware of how remarkably good-humoured he remained despite my lining up, as it must have seemed, with every hostile bunch in town. Anyway I trust that this poem will be read as an unfeigned tribute despite the one or two waspish passages when it comes to those touchy matters of politics.

Hope you won't take it as a backhand kind
    Of compliment, or something even worse,
Like old-score settling, if I try to find
    Some way to talk our issues through in verse.
At best it might be something that combined
    Word-magic with your talent to rehearse
Dilemmas in philosophy of mind,
    Language, or logic and yet intersperse

The expert stuff with writing of the sort
    That takes a larger readership on board
And never sells them or its topic short.
    The reason was, your prose-style could afford
To mingle idioms, like modes of thought,
    Unworried as to how they might accord
With the strict protocols set up to thwart
    Such ventures into regions unexplored

By the rule-sticklers. Yet, it may be said,
    Why rhyme and metre? when you stuck to prose,
Albeit of a kind that's likely read
    More often by non-specialists than those
Whose academic caution bids them tread
    A style-path narrower than the one you chose
As the best route for anyone who'd head
    Off on a high-ground hike that might disclose

Perspectives on the intellectual scene
    Unglimpsed and unimagined from inside
The mind-world of philosophers who've been
    Trained on the low road and thereafter tried
To take short views. But that's not what you mean,
    Not rhyme and metre, when you set aside

The plain-prose indicators of routine
  Guild-membership or signs of bona-fide

Professional allegiance and advise
  Your colleagues in the academic game
That, everything considered, they'd be wise
  To give up warming over all the same
Old chestnuts in a slightly different guise,
  Or seeking out new idioms to frame
The fixed agenda of an enterprise
  Well past its prime. Then theirs would be the aim

Of coming up with such inventive tropes,
  Such metaphors or narratives, as might,
If not too late, redeem the lost life-hopes
  Of those who'd suffered the perennial blight
Brought on by being forced to learn the ropes
  As tenure-track required. So they should write
Not just, you said, the sort of prose that copes
  With getting the main points across in tight,

Well-structured form but prose that tried to do
  What poets (and some novelists) do best,
That is, discover senses to pursue
  Far out beyond the denotations stressed
By all the hard-nosed literalists. They'd eschew
  Such verbal licence since it fails the test
Of making sense or coming as true
  According to the strictest standards pressed

So hard on other language-games by just
  Those house-trained intellects who'd brought about
The *trahison des clercs* or breach of trust
  By which philosophers presume to flout
The rule that says all living language must
  Transform itself by always trying out
Fresh metaphors to live by. So the thrust
  Of how you wrote was mainly to cast doubt

On the old kinds of metaphor that held
    Philosophy in their Cartesian grip,
Or classic narratives whose upshot spelled
    The moral that each ephebe be a chip
Off the old block and strike a pose that quelled
    All notions of creative authorship
By a strict etiquette whose code compelled
    Unruly types to give their guide the slip

Each time they fancied penning the odd phrase
    Where some non-standard idiom revealed
Thoughts out of kilter with such proper ways
    Of monologic speech. What lay concealed,
You let us know, in such communiqués
    Between the lines from somewhere out left-field
Was everything suppressed by the malaise
    Of a style degree zero that appealed

Only to those in whom the wonder-struck
    Thaumazein where philosophy began
For Socrates has somehow come unstuck
    And left them, tenure-seekers to a man,
Resolved that prose of theirs should have no truck
    With poetry. They upheld Plato's ban
On metaphor, mimesis, and what luck
    Or inspiration offered to the clan

Of rhapsodes and enthusiasts so lost
    In their wild, word-intoxicated state
As to allow no reckoning of its cost
    To reason's soul or pause to estimate
The civic harms poetically glossed
    As due to gods or muses. Still you'd rate
This verse-epistle evidence of crossed
    Wires or cross-purposes since to equate

Your idea that philosophy should take
    A more poetic form with the idea

That rhyme and meter might between them make
    Some big improvement seems a case of clear
Misapprehension. What you thought would break
    The spirit-wasting rule of that austere
Style without style – and maybe help to shake
    The sense that went along with it of sheer

Necessity that certain things be done
    In certain ways as laid down by the code
For normal practices – mandated none
    Of those verse-features that might grace an ode
By Pindar, Keats & Co., but that you'd shun
    (I guess) if they turned up, as here, bestowed
On writing of a kind that shouldn't run
    To formal structures apt to overload

The powers of concentration rightly trained,
    By readers of a less indulgent bent,
On more substantive issues. Point sustained:
    You still found room for reasoned argument,
Not least while telling us what's to be gained
    By taking on the freedom to invent
New language-games beyond the sorts ordained
    By fealty to some one line of descent

Against all others. So we'd better think
    That when you told us poetry could save
Philosophy, or pull it from the brink
    Of a not undeserved nor early grave,
The price of having its choice public shrink
    To miniscule proportions, this meant they've
Gone wrong, the current lot, in ways that link
    Way back to many another short-lived wave

Of intellectual fashion. They should learn
    More from the poets about how to spin
Fresh-minted metaphors, or how to turn
    A life-enhancing phrase, but not begin

On any verse-led binge that bids us spurn
   All remnants of analysis and pin
Our best hopes on those language-games that yearn
   For something more upliftingly akin

To that which rhyme and meter put in place
   Of dullard reason. So let's not deny
The obvious: when you suggest we face
   Philosophy's low prospects with an eye
To poetry's high hopes, it's not the case
   That you're just asking us to versify
The same old topics. What you want's more space
   Between the words so language can supply

The poetry that comes of hearing all
   The intertextual echoes that resound
On cue to every signifier's call,
   Or sundry connotations that surround
Each letter, word and phrase when not in thrall
   To denotative sense but – as you found
With Derrida's best efforts to forestall
   The dead hand of the literal – unbound

From signified or referent. Thus freed,
   It takes the less thought-trodden path that winds
Along whichever language-route may lead
   The *Denker*, like the *Dichter*, past what binds
The intellect to some accustomed creed,
   Or idiolect to usage, for those minds
Professionally groomed to meet the need
   That intellect conform to just the kinds

Of usage certified to hold the line
   Against such vagrant thoughts. That's why you waged
Ironic war on readings that, like mine,
   Took Derrida as one who re-engaged
With topics that the old guard still define
   As squarely philosophical since staged

In just such terms as those that you'd consign
    To the scrap-heap of words that once assuaged

Our craving for god-substitutes but now
    Must join the pile along with other such
Time-honoured relics. These remind us how
    Hard we shall find it to escape the clutch
Of outworn images or disavow
    Pythagorean echoes that still touch
Some chord in us despite what we allow
    To be their hollow ring. The case was much

The same – your point again – throughout the whole
    Unquestionably rich and varied tale
Of Western metaphysics and the role
    Within it of those metaphors whose trail
Leads back to the idea of mind or soul
    As glassy essence. This would then entail
The message that philosophy's main goal
    Must be to see that clarity prevail,

Mind apprehend that essence, and soul come,
    By constant mirror-polishing, to catch
Its own reflection unimpaired by some
    Small imperfection or minutest scratch
That might obstruct its gaze. Your rule of thumb
    With metaphors like this was: mix and match
Them as a poet might till they succumb
    To ordinary usage, then dispatch

Them to whatever limbo's set apart
    For tropes, as Nietzsche said, that masquerade
As concepts. Whence the counterfeiter's art
    (Amongst philosophers a stock-in-trade)
Of un-remembering, as if by heart,
    Those pre-Socratic metaphors that made
Philosophy from Plato to Descartes
    And in our time a dismal dress-parade

Of tropes now blanched anaemic by the shift
   From sensuous to abstract. This made sure
Their advent as imagination's gift
   To thought was long forgotten and secure
From prying intellects that gave short shrift
   To white mythologies in quest of pure
Conceptual instruments by which to lift
   Themselves above the thought-distracting lure

Of sensuous imagery and so attain
   Transcendent truths. Thus far one might agree
And think you'd hit bang on a major strain
   Of chronic self-delusion that might be
Put out of its long post-Cartesian pain
   By the shrewd mix of gentle mockery
And counter-statement that you hoped would gain
   More converts than if tendered in a key

Of *odium scholasticum* that left
   The opposition dug in deeper while
Its case, however strong, appeared bereft
   Of basic courtesies that civil style
And decency should couple with the heft
   Of a good argument. The point that I'll
Raise once again since, despite all your deft
   Rejoinders, it's the one I have on file

Under 'unfinished business' is your use
   Of that word 'transcendental' to include
Not only fictive entities like *nous*,
   Soul, spirit, mind, and the whole abstract brood
They fathered mainly as a poor excuse
   To smuggle God back in, but things that you'd
Deem just as bad, like all claims to deduce,
   From certain basic principles construed

As *a priori* warranted or backed
   By reasonings in a transcendental form

Such truths as otherwise we should have lacked
    The means to justify. This was a norm,
You thought, that held up merely through the fact
    That dumping it would kick up such a storm
Amongst philosophers who'd made their pact
    To play along that sticking with the swarm

Seemed, on the face of it, a better bet
    Than opting out of their protective guild,
Unlearning all the codes and passwords set
    For members, cancelling thought-routines instilled
Through years of work, and striving to forget
    The job-security that came with skilled
Observance of the local etiquette.
    Such were the benefits if one fulfilled

Conditions on sound usage of such big
    Load-bearing terms as 'transcendental' which,
If downed in your way with a hefty swig
    Of irony, say you're about to ditch
The whole caboodle and help that lot twig
    How they'd been taken in. The only hitch
With this fine plan of yours was how to rig
    The grand exposure so as not to stitch

The thing up so completely that there's no
    Room left for anything remotely like
The discipline you practised years ago,
    One that – an observation apt to strike
Shrewd readers – still engaged you even though
    You came to treat its bi-millennial *Reich*
As more a kind of vaudeville road-show
    With some enticing bits put in to spike

The guns of those who'd say: let's just call time
    On the whole thing, cut funding where it hurts,
And block philosophy's attempt to mime
    The natural sciences. Your view converts

To a slight variant on that paradigm
    And (though you'd balk at this) distinctly flirts
With 'end-of-history' wonks who make a prime
    Intent of rubbishing what disconcerts

The currency of plain old commonsense
    (For which read 'ideology') and try
To rouse the populace in its defence
    By methods that more fittingly apply
In contexts where the arguments dispense
    With any show of reason. A far cry
From the plain pragmatism you condense,
    In Jamesian style, as wanting to get by

On a truth-notion that at last comes down
    To what's good as a matter of belief,
Or what works out as the best game in town
    With 'good' and 'best' defined (to keep it brief)
As tending by whatever means to crown
    Our efforts with success, or bring relief
At other times when fortune seems to frown
    On our endeavours. Or – for you a chief

Plus-point – it fits in with the pragmatist
    Desire to keep our truth-talk within reach
Of practicalities too soon dismissed
    By those, like Kant, who much prefer to preach
From the high moral ground and so enlist
    Some abstract universal rule for each
New case-in-hand which then becomes more grist
    To the deontic mill where every breach

Of its strict regulations either throws
    A case-shaped spanner in the works or churns
Out some case-crushing judgment to impose
    Its sovereign law. Agreed, your thinking earns
High marks in this department since it goes
    Some way toward showing what the Kantian learns,

If ever, then most often at the close
    Of a rule-governed moral life that turns

Out, with the unaccustomed gift of long-
    Range reckoning, to exhibit all the signs
Of having gone life-damagingly wrong
    Whenever force of circumstance confines
The range of choice to seizing either prong
    Of some dilemma. Instinct then inclines
To kindly acts and answers like a gong
    At nature's call, while reason undermines

All that, decrees that precept substitute
    For practice, and demands that instinct grant
Law's reason-based imperative to suit
    Mere inclination to its rule as Kant
Sadistically enjoined. Such absolute
    Conceptions of the moral good got scant
Respect from you since lying at the root
    Of all bad creeds whose technique is to plant

Abstraction in the place where those to whom
    Such thoughts appeal had better cultivate
Breadth of acquaintance as advised by Hume,
    Make reason slave to passion, and sedate
Through social intercourse the will to doom
    All absolutes but theirs to the same fate
Reserved for infidels by tribes with room
    For no gods but their own. At any rate

Your laidback style does nothing to promote
    Such sermonizing and reminds us, when
We're tempted by it, of how well you wrote
    About the need to stand back, now and then,
From our most cherished values and devote
    Some uptime to imagining again,
Like a good novelist, how to keep afloat
    In these high seas. The finest of them pen

Inventive variations on the way
    Your liberal ironist might come to view
The issue from all sides and not betray
    That purpose by a sneaky will to skew
The moral compass-points and so convey
    Home-truths as universal. Still, if you
Think back a bit, you'll know I've kept at bay
    A bunch of issues that ensured we two

Were seldom in accord beyond what I've
    Set out as motivation just enough
For my verse-aided efforts to contrive
    This late *rapprochement*. Where the seas got rough
On previous trips was when we took a dive
    Into that choppy 'transcendental' stuff
And you said that the best way to survive
    The maelstrom was to call Poseidon's bluff,

Go with the flow and take it all in stride,
    As pragmatists commend, by holding fast
To something large and light enough to ride
    The storm out – empty barrel, chunk of mast,
Your choice – since centrifuged out to the side
    And buoyed up high as all the rest streamed past,
Then corkscrewed down. Most likely I've applied
    This metaphor in ways that must be classed

Pedestrian or frankly bottom-grade
    For creativity when set against
The scale you drew up as a reader's aid
    For sorting texts conservatively fenced
Around with the exclusion-signs displayed
    By faithful exegetes, from texts that sensed
Quite other possibilities but strayed
    Only so far, and then texts that dispensed

With the whole rule-book. This served just to vex
    Free spirits – poets, critics, novelists,

Philosophers, all those who long to flex
    Creative muscles – since the book insists
They not relax the standard range of checks
    That help to straighten out the teasing twists
Of connotation that can so perplex
    Plain readers. It's the transcendentalist

Gene-sequence in your DNA, I'd guess,
    That evokes Blake and Wordsworth, maybe Keats,
With Shelley, Byron, and – by more or less
    Predestined westward passage – what completes
Their project in the visionary *sagesse*
    Of Emerson and Thoreau, then retreats
(If that's the word) to a downtown address
    In pragmatism's stroller-friendly streets.

That's the back-story that has most to tell
    About the two ways 'transcendental' went,
The Kantian way that cast its lingering spell
    On each new cohort in the regiment
Of armchair ruminants whom it befell
    Like Noah's curse, the other what you meant
By telling us they go together well,
    The canny pragmatist and those whose bent

Runs more to the imaginative heights
    Of a sublime whose transcendental modes
Would stretch the power of reason that unites
    Our faculties until the strain explodes
Their fragile links. Yet in its highest flights
    Of streamlined uplift still the mind bears loads
That keep it tending earthward since, by rights,
    Its journey's end is that of all the roads

You said converged on the one truth-shaped thing
    Worth seeking. This was how to keep the charm
Of fantasy alive, and maybe bring
    Its wish to pass, yet let it not do harm

As you thought every fine utopian fling
    So far had done, and thus helped to rearm
The thought-crusade of those who sought to swing
    Opinion round by sounding the alarm

And tarring liberals with McCarthy's brush.
    The trouble is, this fell in all too pat
With something very like that same old rush
    To judgement, and too comfortably sat
With what you took as freedom's cause: to push,
    If not all things American, then that
Transcendent form of them that, at first blush,
    Might seem a fine thing to be aiming at,

Yet loses something of its first appeal
    When thoughts of all that's happened in the name
Of those high sentiments begin to steal
    Upon us and suggest that we reframe
Our notions of how real world and ideal
    Should properly relate. Then what's to blame,
In large part, for the regular raw deal
    Inflicted on the losers in this game,

Misfits or rogue-states, is that very knack
    Of managing to mix the highest-toned
Professions of intent with a laid-back
    Or downright cynic outlook that condoned,
As fit for its fine purposes, a stack
    Of wrongs, home and abroad, that you disowned
Only in passing. It's that curious lack
    Of joined-up thought by which a double-zoned

Weltanschauung – the transcendental linked
    With a pragmatic view of things that veered,
At times, way off the moral path and winked
    At motes and beams alike – adroitly cleared
Its conscience, though the issues stood distinct,
    By a well-practised trick of thought that steered

A zigzag course from high to low and blinked
  At just the moments when its pilot feared

Too close a view of what might else have posed
  A real and present danger to its hard-
Won sense of certain moral truths disclosed
  Only to some choice few. The message jarred,
As you found out, not just on folk disposed
  By hopes long disappointed to regard
The holdout hopers from a viewpoint closed
  Against them, or on those too deeply scarred

By various gods that failed, but on a bunch
  Of new-left types and radicals. We shared
A lot of your beliefs but had this hunch,
  Quite early on, that we should be prepared
To work out why, when it came to the crunch
  Of prime allegiance openly declared,
You'd count the US-bashers out-to-lunch
  And start to say more plainly that we'd erred

In thinking its high beacon might be crazed
  Or lantern poorly serviced so that we
Could best do a repair-job on the glazed
  Top dome by calculating the degree
To which its beams were discrepantly phased
  With more progressive thought. Then we might see
Clean through the ideology that dazed
  Believers in that old 'land of the free'-

Type spirit-raising stuff cooked up to fool
  Us into swallowing the usual lies
Put out by those whose most effective tool
  For mind-manipulation in the guise
Of soul-perfection came straight from a school
  Where pragmatism reigned. Here the top prize
Went to the firmest sticker to that rule
  Which said: give them the transcendental highs

Once in a while and then there'd be no end
  To the stuff they'd put up with when required,
Or benefit of doubt they'd soon extend
  When principle and circumstance conspired
To make sure any principle would bend
  As circumstance decreed. No doubt you tired
Of having constantly to dodge and fend
  Off brickbats from the sorts of people fired

By social passions you'd have thought in tune,
  At least on all the basic points, with your
Idea of how our best selves might commune
  In a pragmatic way that knew the score
And saw small chance of any big change soon,
  Yet still had social hopes worth living for
Since neither prone nor yet auto-immune
  To disappointment. Message: don't ignore

The history of failures and the sad
  Track-record, most especially, of calls
For social transformation that went bad
  Or came to naught but rather seek what falls
Within the range of upgrades we can add
  Without the plane becoming one that stalls
Because its rate of climb's more than a tad
  Too rapid. Yet if their response still galls

You now, those types (like me) who started out
  Your champions in the literary camp
But later found increasing room for doubt,
  Then maybe it's because they saw the stamp
Of ideals turned ironically about
  And so deployed first shrewdly to revamp
Those social hopes, then as a way to scout
  Their proper limits and, if need be, cramp

Their militant or rebel-rousing style
  By timely inculcation of the taste

For solvent ironies that bid us smile
    With fond indulgence on that chronic waste
Of energies. All this, remember, while
    Us lefties, whether Brits or US-based,
Saw their beliefs chucked on the rubbish-pile
    By neocons who cynically embraced

High-minded and hard-headed in the clinch
    That an old pragmatist like William James
Could still keep more than decent at a pinch,
    And even turned right round against the aims
Of warhawk palaeocons – men every inch
    The dark precursors of the bunch whose names
I'll spare you now – since not a man to flinch
    At chronicling his nation's sins and shames

Along with its strong points. Let us be clear:
    There's nothing in the least *ad hominem*
About the issues I've been raising here,
    Or nothing that would please the likes of them,
Those analytic types who chose to sneer
    At your supposed apostasy, condemn
Your style as an affront to their austere
    Word-habits, and decline a more *ad rem*

Engagement with your work. Thus nod and wink
    Implied that you'd now given up the sort
Of real tough-minded stuff they wouldn't blink
    At and elected rather to hold court
In the soft company of such as think
    Philosophy's an intertextual sport
Or just one more excuse for spilling ink
    In literary ways that won't support

Examination of the rigorous kind
    That tells which arguments have hit the mark
For colleagues of an analytic mind.
    Thus it presents, or so they'd say, a stark

Memento of the world you left behind
   When, mid-career, you opted to embark
On a more wayward course and then fly blind
   Since the downside of that free-as-a-lark

Or giddy aerobatic stuff's to leave
   You looping wildly just when their technique
Of concept-parsing might have helped retrieve
   Terrestrial reference-points by which to seek
Familiar landmarks. Talk like that would peeve
   A saint at length, so you did well to tweak
Their verbal dress-codes now and then, or weave
   New styles around them, rather than critique

The enterprise head-on since then you'd just
   Be falling back on something like the ruse –
As you perceived it – that the Kantians trust
   As a good failsafe strategy to use,
Either when momentarily nonplussed
   Or else when there's some point too big to lose
So that the game-plan says: just go for bust
   With transcendental back-up and *j'accuse*

As stock refrain. No question: you emerge
   Much better placed on all the tick-box counts
Of moral decency than those who'd urge
   We read your work in readiness to pounce
On anything that might invite the scourge
   Applied so vigorously to denounce
Your every thought as teetering on the verge
   Of 'continental', or – what this amounts

To in their language-game – far out beyond
   The intellectual pale. Thus devotees
Of Kant are just as likely to respond
   That way as all those others prone to seize
Their every chance to reinforce the bond
   Of guild-endorsed philosophers and squeeze

Out all such dwellers in the demi-monde
　　Of disrepute. Thus hard-won expertise

Like theirs sells at a discount while the price
　　Of shares in Continentals Inc is chalked
Sky-high and sure to double in a trice
　　(They grumble) when some current fad gets talked
Up in a hybrid style that lets you splice
　　The chat with old philosophemes that stalked
Mind's corridors till Ockham's fine device
　　Henceforth ensured that all sound thinkers balked

At such scholastic garbage. Let's accept
　　That they were wrong, that you were far from sold
On all things continental, that you kept
　　Close ties within the analytic fold,
And – above all – that you were too adept
　　At finding subtler ways to break the mould
Than to wish their whole culture might be swept
　　Aside and so give them good cause to scold

Your Jacobin designs. Then there's the deep
　　And not just anecdotal link between
The various sides of you that often leap
　　Together off the page – the sense of keen
Yet gentle irony, the will to keep
　　All aspects of the intellectual scene
Somewhere in view, the scintillating sweep
　　Of *Ideengeschichte* that could glean

So much from a review of past ideas,
　　Like Hegel naturalized, and the belief
That we do best to hold a course that steers
　　As far as can be from the moral reef
Marked 'cruelty'. Let's add to them your two-cheers-
　　For-reason outlook that takes half a leaf
From Hume's congenial book, and then the fears
　　That thought too closely tied to the motif

Of sovereign Truth might readily be pressed
    Into official service by some Grand
Inquisitor whose idea of the test
    For truthfulness will certainly not stand
A moment's scrutiny against the best
    Of your unholy virtues. This I'd planned
To bring out all along, but then (you guessed!)
    The argument got somewhat out of hand

Or (more like) tended to revert to type
    And re-stage quarrels that are running still
In quarters where they've not absorbed the hype
    About how everyone's now had their fill
Of truth-talk and forgotten the old gripe
    That Socrates once aimed at those whose skill
In speaking well enabled them to pipe
    Such pleasing tunes that they subdued the will

To truth in their rapt auditors. It's more,
    For me, the snag that comes up every time
We want to find some intimate rapport,
    Some near-equivalent of perfect rhyme,
Between a thinker's predilection for
    The one thought-ladder that could help them climb
Above their own life-indurated store
    Of prejudices, and (the point that I'm

Now keen to make in case I've seemed to pick
    Too many bones) all those integral traits
Of mind and character – what made you tick,
    In short – which, present orthodoxy states,
May have their proper role in any thick
    Description or biography that rates
Them on their proven tendency to click
    With readers, but which protocol dictates

Should count for nothing more. The only place
    You really take a line on this is where

You talk about a different sort of case –
   Flat contrary to yours – and say that there
Can be no valid reason to embrace
   A creed that has us solemnly declare,
As touching on the amply-vouched disgrace,
   Political and moral, of one Herr

Professor Heidegger, the need to take
   Account of man and work viewed in the round
And therefore not permit ourselves to make
   Exceptions from the rule for such renowned
Philosophers, if only for the sake
   Of hanging on to some last common ground
Where intellect and ethics hope to stake
   Their claim of being each-to-other bound

In virtue's cause. You didn't go for that
   High-minded but, you thought, misguided brand
Of earnest moralising since the flat
   Refusal, among some, to understand
How great minds might just not know where it's at,
   Ethically speaking, or have morals and
Behaviour like those of an alley-cat,
   Was too apt to promote the sort of bland

Consensual thinking currently the most
   Depressing trademark of a discipline
That's raised conformity to a high boast
   And used group-feeling as its means to pin
A 'Steer well clear of this one!' sign or post
   A 'Keep off!' notice, then proceed to bin
The offending work. For readers over-dosed
   On warnings, you advised: give it a spin,

Give him a hearing, and allow (since it's
   Now pretty much beyond dispute) that there's
Another label that quite aptly fits
   The thinker in whose work the *logos* shares

Deep truths unplumbed by all the sharpest wits
    From Plato down, and that's the one he bears
In your phrase 'Schwarzwald redneck'. So the bits
    In Heidegger worth saving for the heirs

Of Western metaphysics can be cut
    And pasted so as to produce a script
Less vibrant with the call of Being but
    Much likelier to chime with those who've skipped
A lot of that historic stuff and shut
    The book on *Dasein*'s epic. What this stripped-
Down version also skimps is how the hut
    He famously hung out in, though equipped

With stove and other basics, put across
    The same old tale incessantly rehearsed
Throughout his lucubrations on the loss
    Of truth's authentic voice, as in the worst
Of those texts that the faithful try to gloss
    As aberrations but which readers versed
In his life-history won't be apt to toss
    So quickly out of court. Granted, my first

Intention here (remember?) was to press,
    Despite your offstage ironies, the need
That thinking hold its nerve and not regress
    To the idea that arguments succeed
By suasive force alone (since what's success,
    You might ask, if not getting folk agreed
To see things our way?) or that answering 'yes,
    That notion fits in very well indeed

With my belief-set' adds up to a good
    Or half-way adequate account of what
Most rightly is – or should be – understood
    When words like 'truth' or 'knowledge' fill a slot
That 'best belief' won't fill. I said it would
    Be better for philosophy (and not

Just so as to provide a livelihood
    Or timely academic booster-shot

For tired philosophers) if it hung on
    To the most basic item in the stock
Of brand-name goods you thought had long since gone
    The way of all such woefully adhoc
Contrivances or strategies to con
    The laggards into putting up a mock
Display of expertise whereby to don
    The robes of science. This means, *pace* Locke,

Still searching for some last *sine qua non*
    Of true philosophy, that is, the mode
Of transcendental reasoning that alone –
    Or so its adepts claim – affords a road
To *a priori* truths that can be known
    For sure and quite aside from knowledge owed
To mere sense-certainty. Although we've grown
    Suspicious of ideas like this that load

(As you'd say) such a deal of otiose
    Conceptual baggage on the heaven-hook
Left dangling from the days of grandiose
    High-flying metaphysics, still the book
May not be shut or epilogue be close
    In that long thought-adventure that it took
For *Geist* to bid a first brave adios
    To myth or criticism cock a snook

At custom-bound belief. I'd say that we've
    A middle course to steer that won't just tip
This way or that and resolutely cleave
    To 'honest Uncle Kant' or simply flip,
Like you, the other way, resolve to heave
    That stuff clean overboard, and thereby clip
Scientia's wings. That is, we'd best conceive
    Some way that reason can retain its grip

On our beliefs yet, so as not to yield
    Straight off to the assorted booby-traps
You laid down for it, come prepared to wield
    The kind of argument that fills the gaps
In any concept-system vacuum-sealed
    On *a priori* grounds against a lapse
Of knowledge with the sorts of truth revealed
    By opting to revise the mental maps

That drew such clear-cut demarcation lines
    Between the twin imperia of Hume's
'Matters of fact' and 'truths of reason'. Mine's
    Not the conclusion everyone assumes
Must follow if one takes the force of Quine's
    'Two Dogmas' as an argument that dooms
All such distinctions or that undermines
    Thought's last defence against the threat that looms

(Although of course you'd find the claim absurd)
    When the whole question as to what's a sound
Or reputable case fit to be heard
    And acted on, and what's with justice found
Deficient on that count, goes by the word
    Of those best placed to put the word around
Amongst those likewise placed. So it gets blurred,
    The precept most philosophers felt bound

To honour until recently, that truth
    May come apart from any of its near
(Or not-so-near) replacement terms for sooth-
    Saying generally, or – lest this appear
A choice of phrase offensive or uncouth –
    Those sundry substitutes for the idea
Of truth *sans phrase*. These the Sherlockian sleuth
    Would deem defective since designed to steer

Far wide of any thought that 'truth' defined
    As 'best belief', or even as what stands

At journey's end for those brave souls inclined
    To seek it, cannot all the same join hands
With truth in the objective sense assigned
    To word and concept by the strict demands
Of those whose compasses remain aligned
    With true magnetic North and point to lands

As yet unreachable by any routes
    Marked on our atlases. So there's the nub
Of all I've said: that this, like most disputes
    That periodically disturb the club
Of old philosophy's new-found recruits,
    Is one where both belligerents could rub
Along quite well if those false absolutes,
    Like truth and reason, that you'd have us scrub

From our vocabularies don't reside
    Above, beyond, or in a realm remote
From the mundane contingencies you tried
    To make us see were all that underwrote
The shape and meaning that events supplied
    To lives whose *genre* was the anecdote,
Not *grand récit*, and whose narrators vied
    One with another not just to promote

Their own-brand truths but more in hope to lend
    A new spin to the old *roman à fleuve*
Of braided story-lines. This then might bend
    The talk toward new topics that could serve
At last to knock away all those dead-end
    Delusion-props that helped supply the nerve
For spirit's age-old hankering to transcend
    Necessity's iron grip without the swerve

Of hooked Lucretian atoms whose slight nudge
    This way or that did nothing to assuage
Such all-too-human yearnings. Though you'd judge
    It merely a reversion to the stage

Of Kantian tutelage or a hopeless fudge,
    Still we need some thought-instrument to gauge
Just what philosophy can do to budge
    Our stubborn preconceptions or engage

Creatively yet critically with ways
    Of story-telling that may strike a chord
So sympathetic as to gain straight A's
    From everyone or get them all on board
And yet, by some unlooked-for turn of phrase
    Or stray plot-detail, show how they'd ignored
One crucial thing. That detail's what betrays
    How many of the reasons why it scored

So high in their joint estimation came
    Down chiefly to group-pressure plus a touch
Of wishful thinking and the need to frame
    A tale around all this that bears no such
Unwelcome implications as to shame
    Our better selves. No doubt we'll often clutch
At straws, or straw-polls, so as to disclaim
    All thought of leaning on the feeble crutch

Of self-reliance that the poor old *moi*
    Haïssable uses to fend off the gibes
Aimed at it by the crowd whose guiding star
    Is one whose kindly light gives back the tribe's
Fixed thought-routines. These may be such as are
    Reliably adjusted to the vibes
Of a whole culture and its thought-bazaar,
    Or else the sort the specialist imbibes

Once they're inducted (by all the techniques
    Of guild-recruitment you exposed to view
As an ex-member) into various cliques
    Or expert subdivisions like the crew
Of trained philosophers. Yet this bespeaks
    Another requisite that maybe you

Don't emphasise enough: that any tweaks
    To their consensus not go in for too

Much talk of how philosophy has run its course,
    Run out of steam, drained all its rivers dry,
And so forth, since that might seem to endorse
    A narrative denouement that would fly
Clean in the face of your big plan: to force,
    Or better yet persuade, that lot to try
Some way around the guild-approved divorce
    Between what lets the tenured types get by

With least risk and what lets those with a yen
    For certain riskier, more inventive 'kinds
Of writing' do their thing. Then they can pen
    Texts of the sort no rule of genre binds,
Or no such rule as served, time and again,
    To house-train undomesticated minds
And save them from their own devices when
    Some tell-tale touch of metaphor still finds

Their weakness out. That's how you seem to treat
    The two types as flat opposite, as if
Inventiveness were something so offbeat,
    So apt to run a syncopating riff
On thought's four-in-a-bar, that a complete
    Exclusion-rule (or else another tiff
Like Plato's with the rhapsode) must defeat
    All efforts to remove the lingering whiff

Of scandal that attaches to *topoi*
    Such as – think Nietzsche/Derrida – the role
Of figural devices they employ,
    Those concept-frontiersmen, whilst on patrol
To make sure nothing like the fate of Troy
    Befall philosophy should that old mole,
Horse-shaped or metaphoric, redeploy
    Within its city limits. What this whole

Verse-colloquy has tried to do is state
    The case (I hope not too perverse a slant
On things) that all your arguments relate
    Both ways, that is, to concepts that transplant
By metaphoric means or conjugate
    'Poetically' and metaphors that can't
Be subject to exchange at some low rate
    Determined by our willingness to grant

'Poetic licence'. Curious, then, that it's
    Avowedly your one great aim to coax
Us off all versions of the creed that splits
    Apart the unity our mind evokes
When not compelled to test its native wits
    Against a thought-predicament that pokes
Up only if the intellect permits
    Itself to perpetrate a crafty hoax

Of just that sort. I trust your genial shade
    Won't take it ill that I've seen fit to nag
Once more at issues you'd hoped to persuade
    Us we'd do best at this late stage to tag
'Cut-price old stock', or just allow to fade
    From view like those (as Hegel said) that lag
Behind the *Zeitgeist* in a dull parade
    Called by the Owl of Minerva to drag

Out their sad afterlives. Then there's the now
    Far off yet vivid memory of a walk
With you round Monticello and of how,
    Predictably enough perhaps, the talk
Turned toward Jefferson (no sacred cow
    For you but better than the tales they hawk
About him currently), his splendid vow
    Against all tyrants, and – where our paths fork,

Now as back then – your faith (that seems an apt
    Word here) that 'our America', though yet

To be achieved, was the sole nation mapped
    By dream-cartographers with compass set
For gorgeous palaces and towers cloud-capped,
    To me a baseless fabric though a threat
Should it materialise beyond such rapt
    Imagining, to you the unpaid debt

Thought owes to hope. Truth is, although I try
    To sort out man from work, or get a fix
On how far hopes like that may underlie
    (Let's not say 'undermine') the various tricks
Of your old trade you'd later re-apply
    To non-trade purposes, the effort sticks
Each time around at the same point where I
    Can't manage to disintricate the mix

Of reasons, motives, causes, temperament,
    And class. Then factor in the side-effects
Of US academe on one whose bent
    Ran counter, and what any eye detects,
In 'Trotsky and Wild Orchids', as intent
    To make amends as well as pay respects
To him, your father-activist, who'd spent
    His life (a self-reproach your piece deflects

But can't quite lay to rest) in ways that went
    To further emphasise the disconnects
So keenly felt in yours. Yet you present,
    As well, a case for writing that neglects
('On its own time') that duty to augment
    The public good and privately directs
Its energies to helping us invent
    New styles of self-description that the sects

May do with as they wish. But, since you've lent
    My verse a lot more time than it expects,
Best if I now let go (or 'circumvent' –
    Your favoured term) these issues one suspects

You never had much time for, and content
  My quibbling soul with all that interjects
To conjure up the Rorty text-event
  As kindliest of modern gustropholects.

Notes

pp. 253–84 : On some of the issues raised in this poem, see for instance Richard Rorty, *Philosophy and the Mirror of Nature* (Oxford: Blackwell, 1980), *Consequences of Pragmatism* (Brighton: Harvester 1982) and *Objectivity, Relativism, and Truth* (Cambridge: Cambridge University Press, 1991).

p. 257: *trahison des clercs*. 'Treachery of the scholars', 'betrayal of intellectual or academic responsibility'. Title of 1927 book by Julien Benda deploring the politically partisan character of much French thinking at the time, especially on the ultra-nationalist right, and calling for a return to the classical values of dispassionate, open-minded debate.

p. 258: *Thaumazein*. Wonder or amazement; authentic philosophy begins in such a state of mind, according to Socrates in Plato's *Theaetetus*.

p. 260: 'as you found/With Derrida's best efforts'. See Rorty, 'Philosophy as a Kind of Writing: An Essay on Jacques Derrida', in *Consequences of Pragmatism* (op. cit.), pp. 89–109 and 'Is Derrida a Transcendental Philosopher?', in *Essays on Heidegger and Others* (Cambridge: Cambridge University Press, 1991), pp. 119–28; also Norris, 'Philosophy as *Not* Just a "Kind of Writing": Derrida and the Claim of Reason', in *Re-Drawing the Lines: Analytic Philosophy, Deconstruction, and Literary Theory*, ed. R. W. Dasenbrock (Minneapolis: University of Minnesota Press, 1989), pp. 189–203 and Rorty, 'Two Versions of "Logocentrism": A Reply to Norris', ibid., pp. 204–16.

p. 261: 'the mind or soul/As glassy essence'. Rorty thinks of such metaphors as having held philosophers captive since Plato, and even more so since Descartes took them for veridical concepts and gave them a more pronounced epistemological spin.

p. 261: 'tropes, as Nietzsche said, that masquerade'. Refers to Nietzsche's essay 'Of Truth and Falsehood in an Ultra-Moral sense'.

p. 262: 'tropes now blanched anaemic'. A thesis not so much argued or propounded as examined from a range of angles in Jacques Derrida's extraordinary essay 'White Mythology: Metaphor in the Text of Philosophy'.

p. 262: 'reasonings in a transcendental form'. See especially Rorty, 'Is Derrida a Transcendental Philosopher?' (note above). Some of our main disagreements turned on different (e.g. Kantian, pre-Kantian and non-Kantian) senses of the term 'transcendental', although for him it came to signify something like philosophy's old-style claim to have methods, techniques, arguments or specialized subject areas that set it apart from the wider 'cultural conversation of mankind'.

p. 264: 'end-of-history' wonks'. The primary reference is to Francis Fukuyama's 1992 five-minute wonder *The End of History and the Last Man*, but this passage might apply to a whole range of roughly contemporaneous postmodernist, post-Marxist, 'post-ideological' and neo-pragmatist offerings.

p. 264: 'in Jamesian style'. William James, brother of the novelist Henry, was a founding figure of American pragmatism who famously held – much to Bertrand Russell's disgust – that truth came down to what's 'good in the way of belief'.

p. 265: 'to its rule as Kant/Sadistically enjoined.' The psychoanalyst Jacques Lacan was first to remark on this resemblance between, on the one hand, the Kantian moral law with its strictly enforced dictates and rigorous thwarting of natural inclination and, on the other, Sade's meticulously planned routines of eroticized pain and degradation.

p. 266: 'your liberal ironist'. Rorty recommended an attitude of 'liberal irony' – the large-minded readiness to see all around any given issue and not take our own opinions too seriously – as the last, best defence against the risks and temptations of over-zealous doctrinal attachment. This basically meant regarding some thinkers (the most interesting or inventive ones) as engaged in a project of 'private self-fashioning' which we might or might not choose to emulate, and regarding the others – the system builders – with qualified respect but a high degree of sceptical caution.

p. 267: 'a sublime whose transcendental modes'. This conjunction of sublime imagining with a down-to-earth pragmatist mode of thought goes deep into US philosophy, literature and cultural history. It is plainly visible in the Concord transcendentalists Thoreau and Emerson, finds striking expression in the poetry of Wallace Stevens and emerges again in a range of contemporary thinkers from Rorty and the later Hilary Putnam to Stanley Cavell and Cornell West. My poem raises certain doubts concerning the social-political implications of what West describes, in his book of that title, as pragmatism's role in the 'American evasion of philosophy'. Still it clearly has a claim to constitute the central and most distinctive tradition of American thought across philosophy and allied disciplines.

p. 268: 'a stack/Of wrongs, home and abroad'. Of course, it is absurd to suggest that Rorty, or indeed American pragmatism, should somehow be held to blame for these political (especially foreign-policy-related) US crimes and misdemeanours. Still I do think – to this extent concurring with Russell in his rejoinder to James – that the conjunction of starry-eyed idealism and deep-dyed cynicism is something that pragmatism is apt to facilitate through its lack (or programmatic refusal) of more striïngent philosophical, argumentative and self-critical resources.

p. 270: 'first shrewdly to revamp/Those social hopes'. For more on these topics from his pragmatist angle, see Rorty, *Philosophy and Social Hope* (Harmondsworth: Penguin, 1999).

p. 271: 'not a man to flinch/At chronicling his nation's sins and shames'. Principally the US/Philippine War of 1899, which William James opposed very strongly and vocally.

p. 273: 'philosophemes'. Minimal distinctive items or units of philosophical significance, by analogy with phonemes in phonetics, semes in semiotics and lexemes in lexicography, plus (more recently) memes in memetics and narremes in narrative poetics.

p. 273: 'Ockham's fine device'. Refers to Ockham's Razor, that is, the scholastic philosopher's first rule of intellectual hygiene which held that abstract entities were not to be multiplied beyond strict necessity.

p. 273: *Ideengeschichte*. 'History of ideas', 'intellectual history'.

p. 273: 'Hegel naturalised'. Rorty's idea that we could best read Hegel for his idea of philosophy as a (quasi-fictive or novelistic) narrative of favourite episodes from its own history while junking Hegel's deluded notions of Absolute Knowledge or some ultimate meta-narrative 'truth at the end of enquiry'. 'Naturalised', then, in the scaled-down (de-transcendentalized) sense of claiming no distinctly philosophical viewpoint atop all those shifting historical-cultural perspectives.

p. 274: 'the old gripe/That Socrates once aimed'. Refers to Socrates' reiterated attacks on the sophists, or the well-paid professional peddlers of what he saw as mere skills of artful speaking and persuasive rhetoric, as opposed to the genuine knowledge and wisdom afforded by philosophical reasoning.

p. 275: 'of one Herr/Professor Heidegger'. Rorty's attitude towards Heidegger's Nazism was typically easy-going, un-agonized and – in a word – pragmatic. We shouldn't be amazed, much less disillusioned or outraged, if great thinkers in this or that relatively specialized region of enquiry turn out to have been fallible (or downright contemptible) in other aspects of their lives. Heidegger was a great thinker, Rorty happily concedes, and also – quite compatibly with that – a 'Schwarzwald redneck'. Our disagreement about this, as on other matters, had to do mainly with his drawing such an impermeable line – where need arose – between intellectual-creative activities in the 'private' and 'public' spheres. This might work for really specialized thinkers like the logician Gottlob Frege (who also held some obnoxious political views) but not for one like Heidegger whose political convictions were deeply, even constitutively, tied to his entire philosophical project.

p. 276: 'on *Dasein*'s epic'. Heidegger used the word *Dasein* ('being-there') as a stand-in for others like 'subject', 'person', 'human being' or 'individual', since he considered them all tainted by the residues of humanism, metaphysics and the whole legacy of Western (post-Hellenic) thought.

p. 277: '(*pace* Locke)'. The seventeenth-century empiricist philosopher John Locke thought that philosophy should properly serve as a modest though useful 'under-labourer' to the physical sciences. This view has something in common with Rorty's neo-pragmatism, although he sees the arts and humanities, rather than the sciences, as fields where philosophy should nowadays be hanging its serviceable cap.

p. 280: 'poor old *moi/Haïssable*'. 'Le moi est haissable' ('the "I" is hateful'); an aphorism from Pascal's *Pensées*.

p. 281: 'think Nietzsche/Derrida'. Derrida follows and surpasses Nietzsche in his close attentiveness to the role – indeed the ubiquity – of metaphor and other figural devices in the texts of philosophy.

p. 283: 'Gorgeous palaces and towers cloud-capped'. Cf. Shakespeare, 'The Tempest', Act IV, Scene 1.

p. 283: Rorty, 'Trotsky and the Wild Orchids', in *Philosophy and Social Hope* (note above), pp. 3–22.

15

Mallarmé 2
('A cast of dice ...')

My dear Degas, poems are not made out of ideas.
They're made out of words.

The flesh is sad, alas, and I have read all the books.

The work of pure poetry implies the elocutionary
disappearance of the poet, who yields the
initiative to words.

Everything in the world exists in order to end up
as a book.

I, who am sterile and crepuscular...
STÉPHANE MALLARMÉ

It's still a toss-up (or so Mallarmé
    Would have us reckon) even though the dice,
Once cast, must surely come to rest this way

Or that and so relieve us in a trice
    Of any thought that randomness might play
Some role beyond that moment of precise

And punctual outcome. Yet the *coup de dés,*
   For him, entailed no such dehiscent slice
Through time's continuum since it *jamais*

N'abolira le hasard. If the price
   Of this was constellating the array
Of signifiers page-wide (a device

That neutered rhyme and rhythm) then he'd pay
   It happily since then we'd profit twice:
By liberating hazard from the sway

Of pitiless Ananke with her vice-
   Like grip, and breaking free of that *passé*
Verse-idiom whose methods to entice

A better class of reader now betray
   Their less than noble lineage. Suffice
It here for old-guard classicists to say

His revolution found no room for nice
   Prosodic points ('absente de tous bouquets',
These blooms) or fine-tuned strategies to splice

The even measure of a well-made line
   With such slight upsets to the steady beat
As might allow the odd alexandrine

To risk its dignity with some discreet
   Yet innovative shift to reassign
Stress-patterns over the adjacent feet

And tease the ear. No wonder they decline,
   Those prosodists, to contemplate retreat
From principles that let them thus combine

Verse-discipline with strategies that meet
　　The challenge of Ananke through a fine
And subtly-judged refusal to deplete

Too much of their good stock and so enshrine
　　Pound's 'make it new!' as just the cry to greet
Each *succès de scandale*. They intertwine,

These issues, with his master-plan to cheat
　　Necessity as if on some cloud nine
Where words no sooner land than, *tout de suite*,

They self-configure into sibylline
　　Star-patterns whose receding waves delete
All signals save from those white dwarves that shine

As witness to a universe whose heat-
　　Death's imaged in their intricate design.
By such means only might his words secrete

The chemistry of that *explosante-fixe*,
　　That finite though unbounded cosmos traced
By cancelling the metric troughs and peaks

Of old-style scansion so that their displaced
　　Vocalic energies, through verse-techniques
More exigent in kind, not go to waste

But reconfigure in a form that seeks
　　An end to all mere poetising based
On *voix humaine*. Here language never speaks

In modulated tones and accents graced
　　By rhyme and metre, or more subtly sneaks
Its *entre-nous* back in to meet the taste

Of readers unimpressed by such critiques
    Since refuge-seekers in that even-paced
And sonorous verse-music that now reeks,

To modernists, of all that once disgraced
    The poetry of those – from ancient Greeks
To Hugo and beyond – who interlaced

Art-speech and common parlance. By such tweaks
    To that eurhythmic partnership they braced
The vocal nerve to furbish up antiques

Of prosody instead of such mad haste
    To free the page of any sound that freaks
The Mallarméans or offends the chaste

Since ear-decoupled gaze of those intent
    On coupling eye and intellect. The main
Idea behind this epochal event

(For such he deemed it) in the verse-domain
    Was to display how words might represent
The throw of dice by which Ananke's bane

Might yet be lifted or perchance relent
    So far that all the outcomes still remain
In play as if time's arrow underwent

A freeze-frame on its flight to ascertain
    Some further outcome, or as if the bent
Of natural necessity might strain

Against itself. Then think to what extent
    Effects of rhyme or metre both constrain
And liberate, or how they supplement

The work of thought in ways we can't explain
    Except by retrodicting what we meant
To say from what we said. Even so, this train

Of reasoning's sure to throw us off the scent
    Since no sign-constellation can ordain
It in the poet's gift to circumvent

The fact that their best efforts to sustain
    That saving power might better yet be spent
Musing how chance events in rhyme's domain

Are thought's best guide to freedom's continent.

Afterword

This book has ended, just as it started, with a piece about
Mallarmé's symbolist poetics, although this time with an eye
not so much on his formal innovations in verse technique – his
response to the 'crisis' he perceived as afflicting the classical
tradition of French poetry – but more on the themes of chance
and necessity evoked most suggestively in *Un coup de dés*.
Seeing no future in anything like the traditional rhyme schemes
and metrical forms which had entered that presumptive state
of crisis Mallarmé set out to create poetry of visual, spatial
and (perhaps) ultimately mystic-numerical import that would
break with all such precedent. This would bring about the
conditions for an epochal advance in the currently stalled
unfolding of poetry's formal possibilities and expressive scope.
Moreover it would show by such means how certain kinds
of highly disciplined poetic creation – or certain modes of
highly wrought analogical thought – might demonstrate (as
promised in the poem's opening line) that 'a cast of dice will
never abolish chance'.

My verse-essay makes its point *contre* Mallarmé by sticking resolutely to iambic pentameter (the national-cultural equivalent of the French alexandrine so despaired of by Mallarmé) and adopting a rhyme scheme about as tight, 'classical' and (seemingly) restrictive as could well be conceived. However this is just my point: that if we want a perfect analogy for the paradox that Mallarmé obliquely propounds, that is, the idea of chance (and hence, he implies, of freedom or creative choice) as somehow re-emerging on the far side of necessity, then we could hardly do better than invoke the instances of poetic rhyme and metre. It is just such formal exigencies that may prompt the poet, even (or especially) when hard pressed, to all sorts of otherwise improbable discovery or invention. In which case, ironically enough, Mallarmé's theme in *Un coup de dés* might be said to find its most striking enactment or exemplification in just those features of the classical tradition whose obsolescence he so fervently proclaimed. At any rate, such has been my experience during five years' work in the interstices of poetry writing and poetics: that it is chiefly through those distinctive verse attributes – their capacity to dislodge or sidetrack thought from its habitual linguistic-conceptual grooves – that poetry differs from prose. Or rather, since sweeping claims in that regard are always open to objection by counter-example: it is one chief line of defence for verse-essays like mine that their various turns of argument are carried, invigorated, sharpened and sometimes sprung upon the rhyme-questing mind by the pressures and challenges of formal constraint.

'Mallarmé 2' can therefore be seen as a compendium of topics that have run through this whole sequence of poems and which, I now recognize, have much to do with my own (not merely) academic life history as a constant hopper across the disciplines of philosophy and literature. That I should eventually have turned to philosophizing or theorizing in verse as a way to reconcile that dualism, or at least achieve a workable *modus vivendi*, was always to this extent on the cards though still an odd twist when I think how remote the prospect would have seemed just ten years ago. All the same, my hope is that these poems will do something to revive the creative practice of, and receptive interest in, such basically discursive or argumentative poetic forms and genres. What they offer is the kind of counterbalancing effect that is often needed when a powerful new movement captures the high ground of literary-intellectual fashion. In this case the hegemonic tendency concerned is a movement principally and at times dogmatically premised on the superiority of symbol, image and analogical structure over anything pertaining to the exercise of rational or consecutive thought. Most likely the desire to resist it – or the conviction that it calls for resistance – goes back to the unusual conjunction in my work of a near-obsessive fascination with Empson's writing and, quite compatibly with that, an early exposure to the undeceiving rigours of deconstruction as directed very often against such showings of 'aesthetic ideology'. Whatever its motives, the idea of pursuing this project in the form of verse-essays is one that owes its originary impulse to the life-changing couple of weeks when I first, as an undergraduate, read *Seven Types of Ambiguity* along with Empson's poetry. Later reading in the texts of other poet-critics and critic-philosophers, among them the Jena Romantics and their latter-day (including deconstructionist) progeny, only helped to convince me all the more that this kind of intensely self-conscious, self-reflexive and self-critical discourse stood urgently in need of a large infusion of Empsonian rationalism.

Still there's no denying the powerful appeal of that German idealist line of descent for anyone who, like me, discovered the challenge and pleasures of literary theory at just the time when it took the second major turn towards philosophy that put 1980s Yale so closely in touch with Jena during the remarkable period 1790–1810. I'd be selling short both that blissful dawn and my own earlier self if I did a late Wordsworth, so to speak, and affected to look back on it now from a standpoint of wry disdain or (worse still) fond indulgence. On the other hand I should do myself no favours if I left off this Afterword at a point where all the Jena/Yale-style poetico-philosophical talk seemed to announce my verse-essays as in any way fulfilling such high speculative hopes. For the most part they are too much *about* those ideas – too reflective, self-conscious, 'sentimental' (in Schiller's sense of the term) as opposed to 'naïve' or spontaneous – for their language to actually achieve (or really attempt) what the Romantic poet-critics sometimes envisaged in theory. Besides, as we know from any number of deconstructive readings, there is plentiful evidence in their texts that its achievement may lie beyond reach of coherent verbal articulation. I take comfort from Schiller's own very marked ambivalence on the topic and his willingness to grant that the sentimental was now the poet's most fitting home territory since the unreflective was by then apt to seem just naïve in the other (pejorative) sense. Whether all this reflectiveness does enough to warrant the enterprise is of course for readers to decide.

Notes to poem and afterword

p. 290: *jamais/N'abolira pas le hasard*. 'Will never abolish chance'; line from Mallarmé's poem *Un coup de dés*.

p. 290: *pitiless Ananke*. Greek mythological goddess of fate, necessity, implacable destiny.

p. 290: *absente de tous bouquets*. Refers to Mallarmé's notion of an ideal flower 'absent from all bouquets'.

p. 291: For some relevant texts, see Stéphane Mallarmé, *Selected Poetry and Prose*, ed. Mary Ann Caws (New York: New Directions, 1982).

p. 293: 'that would break with all such precedent'. See for instance Alain Badiou, *The Number and the Siren: a decipherment of Mallarmé's* Coup de Dés, trans. Robin MacKay (Falmouth: Urbanomic, 2012).

p. 295: *the exercise of rational or consecutive thought.* The classic discussion is Frank Kermode's *Romantic Image* (London: Routledge & Kegan Paul, 1957).

p. 295: *such showings of 'Aesthetic Ideology'.* See for instance Paul de Man, *Aesthetic Ideology*, ed. Andrzej Warminski (Minneapolis: University of Minnesota Press, 1996).

p. 296: *sometimes envisaged in theory.* Friedrich Schiller, 'On Naïve and Sentimental Poetry', in *German Aesthetic and Literary Criticism*, ed. H. B. Nisbet (Cambridge: Cambridge University Press, 1985), pp. 177–232.

INDEX OF NAMES